D1300245

This is the first full-length study and assessment of the career of Frédéric Le Play (1806–1882), now recognised one of the founders of modern socio It gives an account of his pioneering of the methods of observational sociology and shows how his work was a particularly important contribution to the genesis and early evolution of some principal doctrines of sociological theory. The book's main theme consists of a detailed and impartial analysis of the most significant feature of Le Play's thought— the problem of the relationships between sociology and technology.

Le Play is a fascinating character by any standard. He began his working life as an engineer and later obtained some experience of practical management before abandoning his career in order to devote himself to social studies. He observed, with shrewdness and humanity, the bewildering changes which the new technologies of the nineteenth century were bringing to civilisation. He carried out extensive technical and social case studies in the metal and mining industry in almost every European country; the case studies, though neglected for many years, are full of valuable and absorbing information for students of social and economic history.

Dr Brooke traces the development of Le Play's thought from his origins as a technologist with a social conscience to his later attempts to apply advanced technical and scientific methods to social research. His numerous other interests and and his contributions in many fields other than sociology are also considered. Dr Brooke's careful evaluation of Le Play's entire career does not ignore his limitations and inconsistencies, while it also indicates the breadth and imagination of his thought and establishes his unique place in the history of sociology.

M. Z. Brooke, M.A., Ph.D., graduated in
History at the University of Cambridge
and was awarded bursaries by the
University of Manchester and the French
government to carry out research on
Frédéric Le Play, the subject of this book.
After completing his thesis on Le Play, he
was appointed Research Assistant, and
later Lecturer, at the University of
Manchester Institute of Science and
Technology. He conducts numerous
courses on management and business
organisation, either within the university
or for industrial bodies, and specialises in
Industrial Sociology and the Sociology of
Organisation.

1918/5743

Le Play: engineer and social scientist

Le Play in the Luxembourg Gardens, Paris (*see page* 1)

Le Play: engineer and social scientist

The life and work of Frédéric Le Play

Michael Z. Brooke, M.A., Ph.D.

Lecturer in Management Sciences at
the University of Manchester Institute of Science and Technology.

LONGMAN

Longman Group Limited
London

Associated companies, branches, and representatives
throughout the world

© Longman Group Ltd 1970

First published 1970

SBN 582 46519 2

Set in 11 on 12 pt Garamond

Printed in Great Britain by
Richard Clay (The Chaucer Press) Ltd
Bungay, Suffolk

Contents

Contents

Foreword

On the occasion of the 113th anniversary of its foundation by Frédéric Le Play on 1 August 1856, *La Société d'Economie et de Science Sociale* rejoices at the publication by Dr Michael Z. Brooke of a work devoted to this great scientist. Our Society considers, in fact, that Le Play should justly be recognised as the first person to have developed a scientific method for the observation of social facts, and to have personally applied this method for twenty-five years in almost every country of Europe. He was undoubtedly the inventor of a true social science whose object was to study human groups, and the phenomena they produce. The method used was that of observation, in case-study and analysis, applied personally by the sociologist to the society or group studied from samples of working-class families, because this type of family was the simplest, most permanent and most universal group in society at the time. Also, so as to leave nothing out, the family and its environment were studied with the help of a framework which included the annual budget and at least thirteen sections where everything about the life and organisation of the family and its external relationships were reviewed.

This method was not perfect, but it was capable of being improved and has been, greatly, by the immediate disciples of Le Play, especially Henri de Tourville (†1903). This latter took up the categories of social facts established by Le Play and his collaborators in their monographs and cast them in a new framework. This replaced the budgetary framework and was called the 'nomenclature of social facts' and applied to every type of group. Demolins and others focused attention on the idea of 'social repercussion' for research into causal relationships between facts. Thus sociology, which had been at first principally descriptive, was becoming explanatory. All this progress made way for a considerable development of the works of the Le Play School as can be seen by looking through *La Science Sociale* – 'this valuable scientific publication' as the great American sociologist who died recently, P. Sorokin, described it in his book *Contemporary Sociological Theories*. *La Science Sociale*, published between 1886 and 1903, consisted of 36 volumes each running to 500–600 pages, while a sister publication, *Le Mouvement Sociale*, ran to 300 pages a year. From 1904–1933 *La Science Sociale* produced 159 issues each of more than 100 pages, not to mention a number of works, some of which became famous, including those of Demolins. Le Play pioneered social science, and he clearly deserves credit for this.

Some commentators have not been very fair to Le Play in this respect. They have not distinguished between the exact scientific works, the monographs, and the essays in synthesis, or the booklets of popularisation and propaganda for social reforms. It should be noted that the 'Travels in Europe' on which Le Play based his investigations ceased after 1853. At the insistence of his friends and of Napoleon III, he devoted himself from then on to the publication of his monographs (*Les Ouvriers Européens, 1855*) and of works in the second category mentioned above. These included some very opportune criticisms of an industrial civilisation and some prophetic forecasts which have since been realised; but they also included some reformist views too clearly marked by an obsolete paternalism, or by an over-static conception of social life which did not take sufficient account of an evolution which was accelerating and was inescapable as a result of the pressure of technical progress and inventions. Le Play fully realised how premature was this campaign for reform into which he threw himself against his will, in order to please his friends. Dr Brooke quotes a letter to Count de Ribbe in which Le Play wrote that 'our science' was still in an imperfect state, that he had done 300 monographs but that there should be 'some thousands'. After 1870 he wrote also to the *Unions de la paix sociale* that social investigations must be multiplied in order to project beyond the family case-studies to the study of regions, provinces and whole countries. After Le Play's death, *La Réforme Sociale* and more still *La Science Sociale* with Henri de Tourville actively set out to do this.

Dr Brooke has devoted a prolonged and conscientious investigation with the object of doing full justice to Le Play. The idea for this was born in his mind nearly twenty years ago when he 'discovered' Le Play in a book by Professor Elton Mayo of Harvard University, entitled *The Social Problems of an Industrial Civilisation*. He confirmed, also, a strange fact: even in France there was no complete and objective biography of the great man. There were many books which treated certain aspects of his life and work, too often with the object of exploiting them for political, philosophical or religious ends. Now Dr Brooke has discovered that Le Play was an extremely complex personality and that to understand him properly, every side of the man must be studied. These include the mining engineer, the metallurgist, the technologist, but 'with a social conscience', the geologist, the prospector, the economist, the statistician, the director of vast industrial and mining enterprises, the leader of technical missions, the General Commissioner for the Universal Exhibition, the sociologist, the social reformer, the moralist, the believer, the public figure, the Councillor of State and the Senator.

This sums up the gap in the literature about Le Play that Dr Brooke has wished to fill by a truly exhaustive biography. We congratulate the author for having succeeded, as we think, to a very great extent. More than 80 years after the death of Le Play, this book enables one clearly to grasp the full value and the very contemporary interest of his work. This work casts a vivid light on the beginnings of the Industrial Revolution in Europe and on the changes that it brought about in half a century. It provides a valuable basis of comparison for our western countries and for our times. Finally, thanks to the important bibliography at the end of the book, those who are interested will be able to deepen still further their knowledge of Le Play. They will also be initiated into the progress of 'empirical' methods, and be able to use those methods to their own profit in their everyday lives, and so gain a better understanding of events and of people in the light of their own personal attempts at experimental sociology.

PHILIPPE PÉRIER

Former Ambassador of France
President of *La Société d'Economie et de Science Sociale*,
Member of the Council of the International Institute of Sociology,
Co-editor of the *International Review of Sociology*

Preface

Le Play is a fascinating character by any standard. He lived through most of the nineteenth century and observed, with shrewdness and humanity, the bewildering changes which new technologies were bringing to civilisation. He carried out his observations, both technical and social, in almost every European country. The following pages quote letters from places as far apart as Nizhnii-Tagil and Madrid, Glasgow and Venice; a map (facing page 1) shows that social case studies were compiled over an area almost as large. If his geographical range was wide, so were his interests. Their many-sidedness catches the imagination, above all his concern for a mutual relationship between technology and social science. This included the implications for technical developments of social policy, and the relevance of scientific method for social research.

I first came across Le Play by reading Elton Mayo, the passage is quoted below in Chapter 1. This introduction took place in 1950 in Sheffield where, by good fortune, the City Library has the six volumes of Le Play's major study of the Workers of Europe. For the next ten years I collected notes on Le Play in a desultory manner, until a prolonged illness gave me time to look at him more closely. This study brought out the breadth and imagination of his work. Naturally, too, it brought out his limitations and inconsistencies. Indeed it showed a far more interesting character than any preliminary reading had led one to expect. It is only to be hoped that some of the fascination has rubbed off onto the following pages.

After recovery, I followed Le Play's example and embarked on a new career. This was launched by a research grant from Manchester University for the full-time study of Le Play's role in the history of Industrial Relations, and furthered by a French Government Scholarship. Since then Le Play material has come in from many sources. Dr W. O. Henderson supervised the whole study, read the manuscript and made invaluable suggestions. Madame Germaine Le Play, widow of Le Play's grandson, accepted this inquisitive Englishman into her home and allowed him to spend much time looking at her family papers. Madame J. Marchal, a direct descendant of Le Play, compiled the family tree

*

(p. 141). Monsieur Philippe Périer has written the foreword. My colleague Dr Olga Narkiewicz read the proofs. Help which can rightly be described as indispensable was given by Rémi Gossez (secretary of La Société d'Histoire de la Révolution de 1848), Jean-Baptiste Duroselle (author of *Les Débuts du Catholicisme sociale en France*), Prince Paul of Yugoslavia (who kindly presented a copy of Le Play's report on Southern Russia), Dorothy Emmet (Emeritus Professor of the University of Manchester), Barry Ratcliffe (University of Manchester), David Bell (University of Glasgow), John Halliday (University of Warwick), Barry Hollingsworth (University of Manchester), Magnus Hedberg (The Swedish Council for Personnel Administration), Fritz Walch (Technical University of Karlsruhe). The following libraries were consulted – Paris: Le Bibliothèque nationale, Les Archives nationales, Le Bibliothèque de l'Institut de France, Le Bibliothèque de l'Ecole nationale supérieure des Mines, Le Bibliothèque de la Faculté de Droit; Schaffhausen: Eisenbibliothek; Manchester: The University Library, The City Library, The Rylands Library, The Library of the Cooperative Union; Keele: The University Library; London: The British Museum Library; Cambridge: The University Library; Liverpool: The University Library. Mrs M. F. Heywood typed the manuscript. Finally my family put up with the constant intrusion of Monsieur Le Play into our family affairs, and especially into our family holidays. My two older children, Jacqueline and Robert, have worked hard at sorting and arranging Le Play material and indexing this book.

I can only hope that all these people will not be too disappointed at the use I have made of all their help.

M.Z.B.

References to the Bibliography are by a number with a prefix in the case of works written or studied by Le Play (see p. 143). Writings about him are referenced by the author's name and date of publication. French names and phrases used in the text are defined in the index, and usually also explained in the notes.

I

The technologist
with a social conscience

Among the cherubs and goddesses in the Jardin du Luxembourg, in Paris, there stands a remarkably natural statue. The figure is of a little old man sitting in an uncomfortable position – his face intense, alert. The inscription says that this monument was erected to the memory of Pierre Guillaume Frédéric Le Play by his friends and disciples in 1906, the hundredth anniversary of his birth. To the right of the statue is the Ecole des Mines, to whose history the little man made no small contribution. The statue faces the Palais du Luxembourg where Le Play attended the famous Commission on the Workers, and where he later went as Senator of France. A few minutes' walk from there again is the Place St Sulpice where, in the later years of his life, he held an international salon. For the little man had 'done a Whittington'; he had come from a poor home in the provinces to be known as 'ce grand bourgeois' in Paris. He had come, one might add, by the unromantic route of passing exams. He passed these exams in the 1820s to become a qualified engineer, a member of the Corps des Mines. His various managerial appointments were made on the strength of education, not of birth or experience. He was what would nowadays be called a technologist. But the particular form of his training combined with his temperament to make him also a sociologist. The two disciplines interacted continually in his thought.

No straightforward biography of Le Play has ever been written. There are 165 titles listed in the Bibliography (pp. 156–63) under the heading 'Studies of Le Play and his work'; these fall mainly into two categories. The first is that of reminiscence or enlarged obituary; this category includes a selection of his letters edited by his son. The other books deal with some particular aspect of his work, and were often written for propaganda purposes – to use Le Play's work in support of some social, political or religious programme. Another selection of his letters, edited by de Ribbe, comes in this category. The only English biography of Le Play, by Mrs Herbertson, is slight and unreliable.[1]

Nevertheless there are plenty of books in the English language which bring out Le Play's importance. These include the writings of Zimmerman and Sorokin, but perhaps the most widely read book that mentions Le Play is Elton Mayo's study of industrial civilisation.[2] 'Vision of the seamier side of progress was not confined to artists,' writes Mayo; 'one might say of recent history that each successive decade had brought a competent observer to warn us of our failure to study man, to consider the effect upon him of all this progress.' Le Play was a professional engineer, trained in a pioneer school of technology. Mayo points out how he brought his trained mind to bear on the social effects of technical progress, and saw disaster. 'Indeed Le Play feels that the outstanding character of an industrial community is a condition of extensive social disorganisation in which effective communication between individuals and groups has failed.'

This was the vision of a successful man at the peak of his career. He stands out, in an atmosphere of brash self-confidence, as one who put many questionmarks beside the civilisation he was so effectively helping to create. His was not, as Mayo points out, the reaction of the poet and the artist to the ugliness of the Industrial Revolution. His reaction was that of the technologist with a social conscience. Technical decisions have human consequences, the delicate ties of personal relationships must be considered. This is what Le Play was saying to his contemporaries. Mayo thinks that the Anglo-Saxon world has underestimated Le Play. This may be true of the French as well, but not of Louis Baudin who, writing in 1947, optimistically listed Le Play along with Adam Smith, Karl Marx and Lord Keynes, as one of the four 'masters of economic theory'.[3] But then a fellow-countryman of Mayo's has written even more recently that 'sociology was launched in the nineteenth century with such sponsors as Durkheim, Le Play, Giddings, Small, Cooley and Lester Ward'.[4] These, among some less flattering estimates, point to his versatility neatly shown in a book of French mining history which has a chapter headed 'Frédéric Le Play was a Miner too!'[5]

The eighteenth century saw two developments which were to have special significance for Le Play. One was the beginning of higher technical education, and the other was the emergence of the social survey, the study of social systems. Higher technical education, carrying with it the formation of a corps of professional engineers, came to France from the German States. In 1785, for instance, was founded in Paris the Ecole royale supérieure des Mines for the study of mining, metallurgy and related subjects. This school was a foundation of the *ancien régime*, using German precedents. It may be said to represent a forward-looking project of Bourbon France in its death throes. In its early days the school was small and its hold on life tenuous. It had several changes of premises until 1815 when it moved to the site it occupies today. When the Ecole des Mines was founded, it can hardly have been foreseen how large a system of higher technical education was to grow up in France, separate from but parallel to the University – the *hautes écoles* with the Ecole des Mines as one. The most famous of these schools today is the Ecole Polytechnique, a foundation of the revolutionary government.[6] Set up during the Terror, the Polytechnique was part of a major reconstruction of higher education. The other *hautes écoles*, including the Ecole des Mines, were brought into a unified system. The Polytechnique was organised on military lines, and provided a general course leading to either the military or civil schools. Senior positions in the state services were to be reserved to successful pupils of these schools. Le Play was at both the Polytechnique and the Ecole des Mines, where he later became a professor.

The other development mentioned was that of the study of social systems. The history of social surveys is usually taken back to the seventeenth-century discussion of family budgets by Sir William Petty (*Political Arithmetic*, London 1690). By the end of the eighteenth century social studies, which attempted to give detailed accounts of how people lived, were becoming almost common in England. But the beginning of the nineteenth century saw an increase in these studies everywhere, connected with the growth of interest in statistics. Quételet was the great figure in this movement, although his most famous work (*La Physique sociale*) was not published until 1836, by which time statistical societies and statistical units were springing up all over Europe. Le Play himself founded the Statistical Commission for the Metal Industries, and his English friend, J. R. Porter, founded the Statistical Section of the Board of Trade. Both these foundations were in the early 1830s.

As the collection of social facts and statistics was increasingly practised at the beginning of the nineteenth century, so also was the study of society. Diderot, Voltaire, Rousseau, Montesquieu in France, Bentham and Paine in England, Herder and Fichte in Germany, and many others, had produced a climate of discussion of social issues. Apart from Montesquieu, the more immediate influences on the atmosphere in which Le Play grew up were Comte, Saint-Simon, Fourier, De Maîstre and De Bonald. This list includes men of violently opposed views, but all of them were much discussed in France at the time, and all were quoted by Le Play. Indeed, these names illustrate the variety of influences which appear in his thought. Auguste Comte (1798–1857) is credited with the first use of the word Sociology. His 'Positivism' provided a theory which underlay much of the thought of later social scientists. This outlook was at first one of the few clear links between the theorists of society and the collectors of social facts. If the mutual influence of empirical studies and theoretical constructions has become a major issue since, it was hardly an issue at all in the early nineteenth century. There was little contact between exponents of the two methods except through Comte. The influence of Saint-Simon and Fourier on Le Play is mentioned later. These two exponents of different forms of social reorganisation had many followers in the *hautes écoles,* and were much discussed there. De Maistre and De Bonald, on the other hand, were right-wing prophets of reaction, providing a philosophic defence of Church and Monarchy.

The two most obvious facts of life in 1800 were war and technical progress. The technical progress had already produced some seminal discoveries, notably in civil and mechanical engineering and metallurgy. Communications and trade were part stimulation and part consequence of these discoveries. So also were the various tools of commerce – banking, credit, insurance and so on. The war may have stimulated technical invention; it certainly interfered with trade. Outbreaks of peace were rare in the eighteenth century, and a period of considerable disturbance ended on 25 April 1792, when France declared war on the Austrian Empire. From then until 1815 war was general in Europe with brief intermissions. One of these was from 1802–3, after which the war was intensified. Among the methods of intensification were the naval blockade of the French ports by the British fleet and, later, Napoleon's 'Continental System' for stopping trade with Britain. These measures caused much unemployment and distress among the fishermen and other workers in the ports of northern France. The coastguards and the customs officers, on the other hand, found themselves overemployed dealing with illegal trade. One of these customs officers was Pierre Antoine Le Play, who lived in La Rivière-Saint-Sauveur near to the Normandy port of Honfleur. Here, on 11 April 1806, was born his son Pierre-Guillaume-Frédéric.

Frédéric Le Play's own son recorded over a hundred years later the opinion that his grandfather left home soon after his father's birth. Although he knew his grandmother well and was twenty years old when she died, he never heard any mention of his grandfather.[7] Frédéric Le Play frequently mentioned the distress among the fishermen among whom he was brought up. Since he left Honfleur at the age of five, and the war ended before he was ten, it would appear that his 'memory' must have been stimulated by the reminiscences of his friends and relations. At any rate, he often had occasion to say that noticing the impact of external forces and social change on this hitherto stable society in the Seine estuary was the first step in his education as a social scientist. Meanwhile in 1811 he went to live with relations in Paris. His uncle was obviously better off than his mother, for he held a salon in his flat to which came right-wing catholic royalists, albeit men with a social conscience, in the paternalist tradition of De Maître. The future sociologist thus spent some years among the intelligentsia of the counterrevolution. But he was still very young when his uncle died in the same year as Napoleon was defeated and the counterrevolution arrived. He then returned to La Rivière-Saint-Sauveur to live with his mother who intended that he should become a clock-maker.

In 1818, aged twelve, he went to the Collège du Havre, a student of the humanities. He left there in 1822 and was soon offered a post as assistant by a land-surveyor, who was impressed by his command of mathematics. This surveyor, a friend of his mother, proposed to take him into partnership in the future. Phrases like 'moments of decision' would have had little appeal to Le Play; and he would have had little use for Kierkegaard even if he had ever heard of him. Nevertheless, much later in life, he looked back on his career as formed by a series of dramatic, if not traumatic, events. The first of these was sometime in 1823 when he turned down this offer of a safe, reliable career in his favourite Normandy countryside, and aimed for Paris. Once the decision was taken, help came in the person of another friend of the family – Dan de la Vauterie – with whom he went to live in 1823.

De la Vauterie had been one of the first students at the Ecole Polytechnique, to which he now directed his pupil. An expert on land-drainage, he had been stationed in the Netherlands during the Napoleonic occupation, and afterwards came for a time to Honfleur where he met Le Play's family. At the time Le Play went to live with him, he was engineer-in-chief at St-Lô. Like so many others under whose influence Le Play came in the 1820s, de la Vauterie believed in combining technical with social subjects. He also believed in a strict curriculum. From 4.0 a.m. to 2.0 p.m. each day was spent on 'professional studies', while the evenings from 4.0 p.m. to 9.0 p.m. were given over to 'literary and social studies'. The routine was sometimes varied by a day spent in some social investigations. Thus the 'field studies' for which Le Play became famous were part of his education and began before he was twenty years old. The routine that de la Vauterie devised was, we have pointed out already, designed to combine technology with social science; he can hardly have guessed how thoroughly his pupil was to follow up this education.

After a year of this personal coaching, Le Play went to the Collège de France to acquire the formal qualifications which enabled him to enter the Ecole Polytechnique on 1 November 1825. Among his contemporaries were Gratry, Lamoricière, Michel Chevalier, le Comte Daru and Jean Reynaud.[8] Le Play was not happy at the Polytechnique and later described the atmosphere as 'suffocating'. The regime he found narrow and restrictive, and he disliked the militarism of the School. It should be said, however, that the intellectual atmosphere which he thus disparaged did not noticeably stifle Le Play or his contemporaries. The intellectual ferment that led up to the Revolution of 1848 was strong among polytechnicians of the 'promotions' of the 1820s, Le Play himself among them. Further, he flourished academically to the extent of passing out fourth in his year, and first among those who went on to the Ecole des Mines where he established new academic records.

He entered this latter School at the end of 1827 and immediately found himself in a more congenial atmosphere. Indeed, he was to spend most of the next thirty years there, and only to leave with much heart-searching on his appointment to the Conseil d'Etat. He started those thirty years with the highest technical qualifications (in 1830 the Principal of the Ecole des Mines was writing to the appropriate Minister that Le Play had gained more marks than any previous pupil, although he had completed in two years a course over which many had taken four),[9] and ended them a sociologist with an international reputation. Always a technologist with a social conscience, Le Play strove for greater technical expertise and rigour in social science. As will be seen later, he had to fight for the importance of empirical studies even in metallurgy. He carried on the same struggle in sociology. This struggle, together with his own work in the collection and classification of social data, assures his permanent place in the history of sociology.

Since, later, Le Play was himself to campaign for the teaching of management and social science at the Ecole des Mines, it would be an exaggeration to say that he was himself taught such. Nevertheless, as at the Polytechnique, the students were expected to develop some understanding of the society in which they practised their skills. One means of acquiring this understanding was by the student journeys which were a feature of the courses. Lectures were for half the year only, and for the other half (June to October) the students visited mining and metal-working installations at home and abroad. During their tours, the students wrote dissertations about the technical and social phenomena they saw. These dissertations are still preserved in the library of the School.

Le Play's tour was an achievement by any standards. In company with Jean Reynaud, he covered over 4,000 miles, mostly on foot. The route was a circuitous one through the Saar, over the Harz Mountains and across the Saxon Plain to Berlin, returning through the Low Countries. His diary of the journey[10] is entirely concerned with technical descriptions and drawings of the metal works and mines he visited. His letters, however, contain many other observations and he recorded later in his life that the abiding memory of this journey was of the connection between technical innovation and social change, and the subtle and reciprocal nature of this connection. He noted incompetence among management, mentioning for instance a foundry at Thionville where promotion seemed to be by piety rather than by ability. He noted, too, great distress among the workers in many districts. But he also reported some areas of satisfactory conditions and relationships, and these included a stable mining community in the Harz Mountains.

Perhaps the greatest influence of this journey on Le Play resulted from the company of Jean Reynaud. Reynaud was a radical Saint-Simonian at the time; later he became a mystical philosopher while still holding to his radical views. Le Play asserts that Reynaud never converted him to Saint-Simonian views, but says that they discussed endlessly the implications of what they saw. As a matter of fact Le Play never admitted much influence of Saint-Simonian ideas, although these were strong among his contemporaries. They provided a belief in the opportunities offered by technical innovation combined with sympathy for the workers. This outlook was prevalent among the 'polytechnicians' and fully shared by Le Play. Saint-Simonianism also provided a philosophy of life for those who found current catholic outlooks too reactionary. These outlooks could well have been acquired in the circumstances of the time without the influence of Saint-Simon;[11] Le Play did, on the other hand, acknowledge the influence of Fourier. The setting up of small, independent cooperative communities was congenial to him and Fourier's influence would seem to account for his sustained if intermittent interest in such experiments. It was the gaining of ability to interpret his observations that was critical to Le Play's development – the ability to 'understand'. Both Reynaud and Le Play agreed on the necessity of exploring further the social consequences of the new technologies. Through their conversations Le Play developed at least the rudiments of a theoretical system which made possible his social studies of later years.

After the journey Le Play returned to Paris in the spring of 1830 and was appointed to a post as assistant in the metallurgical laboratory of the Ecole des Mines. Some weeks later he was seriously injured in an explosion there. As a result of this he was in hospital when the revolution of July 1830 broke out. As he lay in bed, desperately ill, and heard the screams and the shooting outside, there came to him another of the determining 'impulses' of his life. Years later he described it thus:

Since 1789, ten regimes have governed France. Each of these has been set up and then overthrown by force. These unstable and uncertain conditions are without parallel. Thousands of statesmen and writers have searched fruitlessly for a remedy. Although a stranger to politics and literature, I have set out, under the burden of a great ordeal, to find again the secret of a government which would not have a blood-bath for its beginning and its end.

In 1830 a wound which held out little hope of healing kept me hanging between life and death. Eighteen months of physical and mental torture worked in my mind a change which a whole lifetime of good fortune could not have produced. At the sight of the bloodshed in the July Revolution, I dedicated my life to the re-establishment of social peace in my country. I have never forgotten this vow; and I am offering to the public studies begun half a century ago in the Saxon Plain and the mountains of Harz.

In order to rediscover the secrets of governments which provide for their people goodwill based on peace, I have applied to the observation of human societies rules analogous to those to which my mind has been trained for the study of minerals and plants. I have built up a scientific system; or in other words, I have created a method which has allowed me to understand personally all the underlying currents of peace and disharmony, prosperity and suffering which are present in contemporary societies in Europe. The present volume undertakes to describe and justify this method. I have decided, firstly, in the middle of social phenomena varying infinitely according to the nature of the environment, that the preliminary condition of goodwill is reduced to a fundamental truth inherent in the nature of man. Above all society is happy when each individual possesses his 'daily bread' and practises the 'moral law'. I have learnt accordingly, in studying four types of society comparatively, how a race can acquire, keep, lose and eventually rediscover these two essentials of manhood.[12]

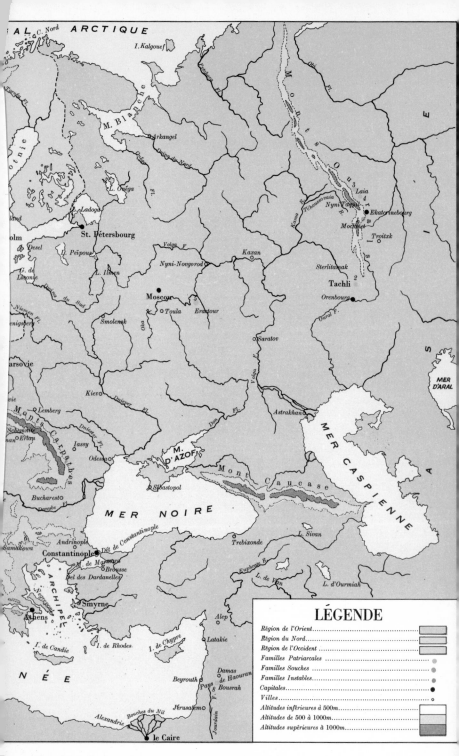

LÉGENDE

Région de l'Orient.....................................

Région du Nord.......................................

Région de l'Occident.................................

Familles Patriarcales..................................

Familles Souches......................................

Familles Instables.....................................

Capitales...

Villes...

Altitudes inférieures à 500m.........................

Altitudes de 500 à 1000m............................

Altitudes supérieures à 1000m......................

kers of Europe (Bibliography no. W42). The

s of that book. All the case studies of Le Play

is given where appropriate.

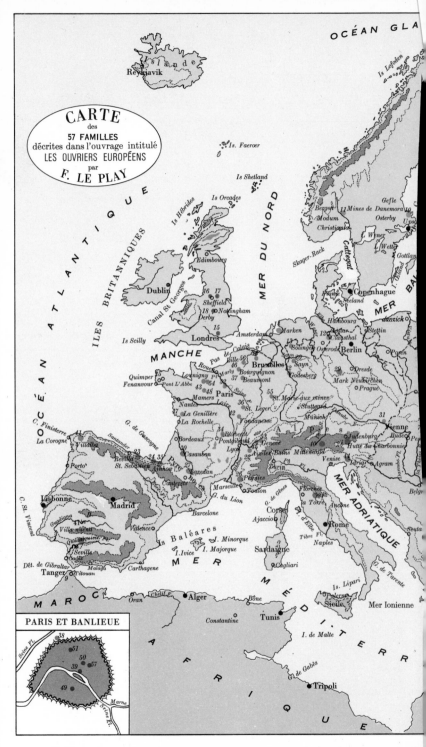

CARTE
des
57 FAMILLES
décrites dans l'ouvrage intitulé
LES OUVRIERS EUROPÉENS
par
F. LE PLAY

PARIS ET BANLIEUE

This map is an exact reproduction of the one Le Play used in *The Wo*
colouring and numbering are his, and the numbers refer to the sectio
and his circle are listed on pages 147-153, and the number on this ma

Once recovered, Le Play returned to his work at the Ecole des Mines, but left soon afterwards as a result of friction with the head of the laboratory. The record of his activities from then until he returned to the School in 1840 leaves one almost as breathless as the record of his great 'hike' around Europe. One appointment was to assist in the re-founding of the *Annales des Mines*. This periodical, founded as the *Journal des Mines* in the previous century, had ceased publication in 1833. The following year it restarted in an enlarged form and for the publication of major papers on technical developments. Le Play was appointed as an assistant editor; later he joined the editorial board and served on it for many years. The studies that he himself wrote for the *Annales des Mines*, some of them major works which were reprinted as books, are listed in the Bibliography.

Earlier the same year, 1834, the Statistical Commission for the Metal Industry had been founded with Le Play as its first secretary. He built up this pioneer statistical unit in its early years, remaining a member until 1848. In the summer of 1834 he undertook the first of a long series of foreign tours on which he collected information for the French Government. Some of these journeys served other official purposes as well; all were partly spent collecting social facts, such as the conditions of life of the industrial workers in the area visited, which formed the basis of his later case studies. The 1834 journey was to Spain, and on it he collected the material for his first book, *Observations sur l'histoire naturelle et sur la richesse minérale de l'Espagne* (Bibliography, W19). This book contained geological and much other data; it also contained an account of the early stages of industrialisation of that country, including the establishment of a School of Mines at Madrid. This Le Play described as primitive and ill-equipped, but at least it existed. He told how the workers at the mercury mines and processing plants in the north died young from the poisonous effects of the processes, another insight into the human consequences of industrialisation. The end of his stay in Spain reads like a passage from Voltaire's *Candide*. He was taken seriously ill, and ascribed his survival to the fact that he still had enough strength physically to prevent the surgeons from bleeding him. Then, on the way home, he took command of the ship in a violent storm with the crew drunk and the captain mad. In spite of these Panglossian adventures, his report was ready for publication before the end of the year.

In 1835 he was in Belgium, making a study of the iron industry there. It appears that his report greatly impressed the Minister of Commerce, who asked him to go to England the following year. His remit was to discover the reason for the reported English superiority in the iron and steel industries, and to find answers to three questions. First, to what was the progress of these industries to be attributed? Second, what was the present state of these industries? And third, what had been the results of the changing habits of consumption in recent years? Some of the major issues he brought out – such as the significance of the use of Swedish ore, which could not be used in France because of import duties – in this and other reports are discussed in the next chapter. Meanwhile the tour of 1836 took him to most parts of the British Isles, but especially to the Midlands, Shropshire, Staffordshire, Derbyshire and South Yorkshire. He visited innumerable iron and steel plants and mines. On the problems of research into English industrial methods, he wrote:

> The true English manufacturer is among all men the least disposed to speak of his affairs to a stranger. He is also the least inclined to understand how anyone can undertake researches like mine with a scientific object and a generalised interest. As soon as he notices the least knowledgeability in the questions of the visitor, he at once assumes that this stranger is a speculator who is using him for some interest opposed to his; with very rare exceptions, the most influential letter of recommendation to the manufacturer is only a means of getting a rapid walk round the works, some vague information which is almost always false or incomplete, and too often a formidable meal which takes up half the day and in which one can only overcome usefully the English reserve if one is lucky enough to be able to master accurate statistics after the tenth glass of port.

This was in a letter to the Ministry of Public Works written from Liverpool after his tour of Staffordshire. He added that fortunately the workmen were well-informed, and a tip would usually loosen their tongues. Later in his life he would entertain meetings with reminiscences of conversations with English workmen in their 'pubs'.

In 1837 he was visiting the Donets Valley in South Russia. This journey, the subject of a voluminous report (W26) was undertaken at the request of a Russian landowner, Anatolii Demidov. But Le Play was also there as a representative of his country and was sending home reports to the appropriate ministry. In one letter he complacently writes: 'You would be surprised, Director-General, how internal questions gain sometimes by being studied from outside.' Demidov organised a major and comprehensive survey of areas of the Crimea and the Donets Valley. Most of the survey engineers were French, and Le Play was put in charge of the Donets section.

'Monsieur Anatole', as he is always called in Le Play's letters, was one of the 'characters' of the century. Four generations earlier, Peter the Great had granted a forgeman, Nikita Demidovitch, a mineral concession in the Urals together with a derelict state ironworks. Nikita, in many ways a typical figure of the industrial revolution in any country, prospered to such an extent that his great-great-grandson received vast possessions. In spite of subdivision in his grandfather's time, Anatolii inherited a mining and metal-working complex in the Urals which in the mid-nineteenth century employed 45,000 serfs. He lived in Paris and was married to Mathilde Bonaparte, who left him after four years with hair-raising accounts of his brutality. He had estates in Italy, which carried the title of Prince, and founded a silk industry near Florence. He also had extensive and largely undeveloped possessions in the Donets Valley, and it was these he asked Le Play to survey. Of a visit to Le Play at his headquarters in Lugansk, Demidov wrote:

> I found myself now, at last, in the midst of this other section of my companions in fatigue, who, less fortunate than their comrades of the Crimea, were working in dull regions, and in a burning climate . . . a minute geological investigation of the soil had been carried out in the basin of the Don and on the banks of the Donets; not a single valley of any importance, not a single ravine had escaped the indefatigable researches of our enthusiastic engineers.[13]

In this work Le Play clearly gained experience which taxed his administrative as well as his technical ability. He also noticed the significance of different styles of management. So impressed was Demidov at Le Play's competence and his ability to build up a high morale among those under him, that he later took him into partnership.

The first assignment in Russia took him two years, and soon after its completion Le Play returned to the Ecole des Mines as Professor of Metallurgy. From 1840 to 1856 he delivered his course each winter, a course which reorientated the teaching of the subject. The contents of his lectures are discussed elsewhere in this study, but above all he emphasised the experimental approach. His lectures were constantly amended as a result of his journeys during the spring and summer. Indeed, a new motive now appears for these journeys. Each spring the Principal of the Ecole des Mines wrote to the appropriate minister that it was important for his teaching that the Professor of Metallurgy should travel abroad, and asked the government to pay his expenses. Almost every year this was agreed, and he collected social case study material as well as technical information on his travels.

In 1840, too, he was married to Augustine Fouache. For four years he had been writing affectionate letters to her on his travels, and these continued for another twenty-five years until the journeys ceased. The letters always suggest a happy and intimate relationship. However, none of his wife's replies have survived to show what she thought of these constant and prolonged absences, except that his letters often contain passages to the effect that he will come home as quickly as possible to suggest what her replies may have said. He does not discuss his work or his researches with his wife, although he gives shrewd and interesting accounts of the places he visits and the people he meets. Nevertheless, these letters, as all of his writings, are a fascinating source of social history. For instance, in 1845 he describes how he took Prince Demidov and Prince Napoleon[14] down a coal-mine at Aix-la-Chapelle. The latter evidently did not take to wriggling along an eighteen-inch seam. A few years later, again, Le Play was writing to his wife:

> Yesterday evening we made a most original excursion into the East End of London, near the St Catherine Docks, and in Whitechapel, St Giles and Shoreditch.
>
> These districts are inhabited by the most dangerous population of crooks, thieves and murderers and women to match. We were accompanied by four representatives of the police who got us into all the pubs and the lodging-houses where they can get a bed for six sous. We were glad to be accompanied for the company was not very reassuring. The faces of the people awoken from their sleep, in the lodging-houses where a dozen beds were occupied by twenty people of all ages and both sexes, were truly curious to see, and here it was lucky that the authority of the police was respected. We began this excursion at 9.0 and finished it at 2.0 in the morning.

During this particular visit to England, Le Play arranged for his wife to join him for a week. The itinerary he planned for her included visiting a forge in Staffordshire, a lead-mine in Derbyshire and a hill near Dudley from which (he alleges) you could see the greatest concentration of smoke in Europe. Once again it seems a pity that his wife's reply is not extant. One other family matter: after their first child, a daughter, died in infancy, their only son was born on 28 June 1842.

In 1841 Le Play was visiting metal-works in various parts of France, and then in the following year he was back in England again. Material collected on this visit was used in his social studies, and his later study of English life – *La Constitution d'Angleterre* (W38); but the main purpose of his visit was to write another long article on the steel industry and a book on the copper industry of Wales.[15] In 1844 followed his second visit to Russia, which produced his biggest commission yet in the Ural Mountains on the borders of Europe and Asia. Here Prince Demidov owned a huge complex of mines and metal-works, producing a range of base and precious metals, whose centre was Nizhnii-Tagil. Le Play spent some months here – on 'the boundary of the inhabited world' as he wrote to his wife – and produced a major report which covered both management and manufacturing methods.[16] Demidov then invited Le Play to take over the management of the works and the mines and to implement his proposals. For the next ten years Le Play managed the undertakings from Paris, living for part of the time in a flat over Demidov's office there. By 1853, however, he was growing increasingly exasperated with his partner, as his letters to his wife show, and resigned after a final visit to Nizhnii-Tagil in that year. But this experience of large-scale organisation influenced him greatly. Immediate signs of this were shown in his lectures. He had always emphasised the importance of managerial as well as technical skills, but now this emphasis was strengthened considerably. In 1845 he was in Scandinavia, writing more about the iron industry there, and in the following year he was in Austria. This visit was at his own expense, for a financial crisis had hit France and the minister regretted (in a letter dated 14 May 1846) that he had no available funds. Le Play's expenses were eventually repaid; but financial crisis was in the air and led, in February 1848, to another Revolution.

Like many of his academic contemporaries, although unlike his friend Michel Chevalier, Le Play welcomed the Revolution. He threw himself into assisting various projects of the Provisional Government, especially the 'Luxembourg' Commission for the Workers, and the Commission on Higher Education. The latter established a School of Administration of which Le Play was an active governor. The Luxembourg Commission, for its part, was a piece of conciliation machinery for industry of a type which has become familiar since, but was original then. There were employers, workers and independent members. Le Play was in this last group. Both these shortlived but important projects are discussed in the next chapter. Meanwhile Le Play was enthusiastic about this particular revolution, a fact which he played down in his conservative old age. His enthusiasm stands out in a correspondence he had with the English economist J. R. Porter, mentioned earlier as founder of a statistical unit.[17] Porter wrote in trenchant criticism of the Provisional Government, and especially of state control over industry. He regrets that 'eighteen centuries of Christianity' have not 'humanised' people more. On 31 March Le Play aggressively replied:

> If not republican feelings but at least feelings of plain Christian charity existed today among the governments of Britain and Russia to the same extent that they do among the people of France, I would have no fear about the future of humanity.
>
> The fears that you express regarding the promise of full employment made by the Provisional Government are just and shared by many people here. But again you exaggerate the trouble. An English mind appears unable to grasp the nobility of what we call socialist ideas. I know, my dear friend, what a conviction inspires you; with what religious faith, indeed, you hold to the economic doctrines of the English school. I will not try then to show you what appears to me practicable in the ideas being worked out here with such fervour; but, since you have asked for my opinion, I can only truthfully say that in my view good will come out of principles which to you seem to be leading our society to disaster.

Some of Le Play's words distinguishing this Revolution from previous ones read sadly in the light of subsequent events. But he shows some prescience in questioning the long-term future for free trade in England, and in forecasting the ultimate decline of the mining industry. Subsequent letters contain strong words from each about the warlike intentions of the other's country, although Porter does also say that the large size of the British army is due to noblemen seeking jobs for their younger sons. Then some time in April[18] Le Play wrote:

> You raise some fundamental questions which I had previously thought too big to discuss by post; but I am very truly a socialist, while accepting most of the economic principles which in my eyes are true and clear as daylight and which belong to socialism as much as to English political economy. I believe that no definitive organisation of society has been reached (*conclu*) by this English political economy; and that in particular delicate questions such as wages, competition, international exchange are not sufficiently resolved by the principle of leaving the greatest possible freedom to private interests. I believe that these questions can be settled

in a way suitable for humanity only by means of a certain organisation of work, of industry, and of exchange.

He then goes on to disclaim any allegiance to any socialist theories, explaining that his views are purely pragmatic. After saying that the abolition of poverty is a practical possibility, this letter concludes:

> I must say flatly that by reading to some other Europeans the account of some observations that I made in 1842 in London, Manchester and Leeds, I have aroused such incredulity that an enlightened inhabitant of Eastern Europe could not conceive that the suffering and degradation of humanity could reach such a point.

To this Porter replied portentously:

> I regret to see that you, and I fear many of your educated countrymen, are not sufficiently impressed with respect for those scientific principles which govern the wellbeing of every society, and which can never be violated with impunity by any government . . .

In a later letter he goes on to say:

> Your definition would cause you to be rejected from among the recognised disciples of that (socialist) sect, while it has disabused me of the impression that adopting the socialist theories you had therefore bid adieu to common sense.

In the same way Porter calls himself a Christian, but as he believes in brotherly love and not dogma he is not accepted by the Christian Churches. The correspondence ended because Le Play was going to England to stay with Porter, and so they could continue the discussion personally; but in his last letter Le Play puts his finger on the contrast between his views and the optimism of the English, when he says that industrial development has in fact led to worse conditions of life for most people.

As the situation in France deteriorated, Le Play became disillusioned. The Republican Government, he wrote to Jean Reynaud, is no improvement on the Monarchy because nothing has changed. Necessary social reforms are delayed because in all the agencies the talkers outweigh the doers. This disillusionment was another critical moment in Le Play's life. Indeed, it formed a dividing point in his life to such an extent that one writer imagined there were two Le Plays.[19] The failure of the Revolution, which started his move to the right politically, also helped to persuade him to give priority to social studies. Further persuasion came from those who met him on the Luxembourg Commission. He had spoken at one of the sessions of this Commission about his studies of the miners in the Harz Mountains,[20] and this so impressed the other members that they urged him to publish his work. He himself later regarded this as the time when he decided to turn from technical to sociological writings. Other friends besides the members of the Luxembourg Commission were urging this change upon him, including Thiers. However, he did not take such a decision immediately as he later alleged, for he still adhered to his favourite project of those years – the writing of his own *De Re Metallica*,[21] a mid-nineteenth-century encyclopedia of mineralogy and metal-work. He did not abandon this project in 1848, for two years later he was still writing that he needed time to get on with it. But eventually he did give up his technical work altogether, and his first book of social case studies was published in 1855.

With the coming to power of Louis Napoleon, Le Play was drawn gradually more and more into public life. He had been introduced to the Bonaparte family in 1845 when Demidov introduced him to the future Emperor's cousin. At that time he wrote to his wife: 'Our dinners are very gay, Prince Napoleon is young in age (23), and younger still in outlook. He is a very ardent republican and that produces some very entertaining discussions with Monsieur Anatole.'

Once again like many of his friends, this time including Michel Chevalier but not Jean Reynaud, Le Play supported Louis Napoleon as a ruler likely to create more favourable conditions than had existed for technological progress. In this he was often disappointed, but with Prince Napoleon and others he formed a loose-knit group who were sometimes known as the social conscience of the Emperor. Le Play collaborated with Prince Napoleon on several projects; he also knew the Emperor personally. For apart from the meetings of the Conseil d'Etat he had at least three private conversations with him. On each of these he thought he had converted the Emperor to his point of view, only to be told afterwards that the government had turned down his proposals. One subject discussed between them was a plan for forcing employers to provide some social security arrangements for their work-people. Another subject was freedom of inheritance. Le Play's sustained and often solitary campaign for testamentary freedom is discussed in another chapter. But on this subject also, he seems to think that the Emperor agreed with him, but was prevented from acting by his ministers. In fact to two crowned heads of Europe did Le Play forecast revolution – the Emperor of France and the Tsar of Russia. But the forecast was on opposite grounds. In France social reform was needed to restore the damaged links in a highly disturbed society. The state must intervene to enforce responsibility on the masters, otherwise the workers would revolt. In Russia, on the other hand, he saw (before the event in 1861) the danger of a too precipitate emancipation of the serfs which would leave them exposed to economic forces previously unknown to them.

Another matter discussed further below is the great part of Le Play's life taken up with the International Exhibitions which were such a feature of the nineteenth century. An official of the Paris Exhibition of 1849 and the London Exhibition of 1851, Le Play was appointed to the Imperial Commission for the Paris Exhibition of 1855. This Exhibition was dogged by troubles, and some days after it was due to open but before it had actually done so, the Commissioner was peremptorily dismissed by Prince Napoleon and Le Play was placed in charge of the organisation. In 1862 he was French Commissioner in London, and he was the unquestioned choice for control of the Paris Exhibition of 1867. In this his imagination and ingenuity were given full play, and his ideas are illustrated by many of the features of this Exhibition.

Another sequel to his handling of the 1855 Exhibition was Le Play's appointment to the Conseil d'Etat. This appointment brought him officially into the apparatus of government. It *was* an appointment, he always refused to stand for an elective assembly. He had refused in 1855, and previously in 1838 and 1843. He was to do so again in 1870, when he resigned from the senate on its becoming elective. In fact, the Conseil d'Etat, with forty members nominated by the Emperor, was a major part of the legislative apparatus. The elected chamber, the *corps législatif*, had limited powers but was able to reject measures which the Conseil d'Etat proposed. Since it was a full-time post this appointment involved Le Play's resignation from the Ecole des Mines, which took effect at the end of the session of 1855–6. For the next ten years he was employed in a series of official investigations: one of these was into the state of industrial relations in the various Departments of France, another was into the Bakery Industry in Paris, and there were many more. During this period, too, he published several further volumes of case studies,[22] and in 1864 a major work on social theory named *La Réforme sociale*.

By now the revolutionary of 1848 had become very conservative indeed. He had taken up Montesquieu's view about different types of government. Democracy was suited to the city state, but the larger unit required a less diffuse form of government. Since industrial society was by nature a mass society, some form of autocracy was inevitable. But the ruler must earn the right to govern. There was no sense of divine or any other right to rule in Le Play's thought. Although he constantly expressed his personal dislike of revolution, he as constantly said that irresponsible rulers would be overthrown. And as the 1860s wore on he began to predict another revolution. Towards the close of the Second Empire, Le Play had his last meeting with the Emperor, dining with him *en famille* at St Cloud. After dinner they discussed the whole industrial situation. Some years later Le Play commented:

> Held back by his extreme good nature and even by a benevolent
> timidness, the Emperor could not bring himself to exercise any
> constraint on his ministers. He asked me to condense *La Réforme
> sociale* into a small book. I offered him this two months later
> entitled *L'Organisation du Travail*. His Majesty approved in 1870
> the summary that I gave him, and invited me to present it to two
> members of the government. Then, after he had learnt that I had
> met at their hands the indifference and prejudice which had
> paralysed the efforts of 1858 and 1865 the Emperor finally gave up
> hope of accomplishing reform in his lifetime. . . .

Instead he plunged into his last military adventure which brought disaster to the Empire and a fresh blood-bath to Paris. In spite of his friendship for the Emperor, Le Play had constantly prophesied that lack of a social policy and predilection for military adventure would produce another revolution. After his prophecy had come true and the Third Republic had been established his reputation was at its peak. But he refused to play any more part in politics. As he saw it the main political debate was now between republicanism and monarchy, and this debate did not interest him. He regarded such constitutional 'niceties' as secondary to economic considerations. The important question was the development of a social policy whatever the form of government.

Les Ouvriers Européens, his first book of social studies, had won for Le Play in 1855 a prize awarded for work of special significance in the field of statistics known as 'le prix Monthyon'. The citation mentions his conscientious collection of facts and figures. It also mentions a feature of Le Play's activity which became even more obvious later – his ability to collect and inspire able collaborators. A few months later a group of these collaborators formed a society to further empirical social studies. The first meeting of this society was in the summer of 1856 with the Emperor and Prince Napoleon as patrons. The elderly social investigator and writer Dr Villermé was in the chair. The society was called La Société internationale des Etudes pratiques d'Economie sociale.[23] The farreaching work and influence of this society is analysed in a later chapter. A similar society was founded in London two years later, and in the following years societies developed in many parts of the world.

La Société d'Economie sociale was primarily a research body – stimulating social investigation. After 1870 Le Play became convinced of the need of some form of social action to humanise society regardless of the political system. To this end he founded a series of local *unions de la paix sociale*. These were autonomous bodies with a coordinating office in Paris and propagated the principles Le Play claimed to have deduced from his researches. Founded under the impulse of the traumatic experiences of 1870 and 1871, the 'programmes' of these 'unions' did not do justice to the fascinating and impressive collection of material from which they were supposed to have been deduced. As has been said of other people, Le Play's 'mature' judgment on his life's work does not add to his stature. Indeed one of his closest friends and disciples, Edmond Demolins, says that this attempt to draw practical conclusions from his researches was premature and set back the progress of sociology by many years.[24] Ten years later, Le Play did his last piece of promotion, a fortnightly review to be devoted to both the development of research and action. Like one of his books this was called *La Réforme sociale*, and Edmond Demolins was its first editor. The future professor of social studies and exponent of a kind of geographical determinism was a worthy successor to his master. The first issue, published on 15 January 1881, contained an introductory message and an article by Le Play himself. It also contained a trenchant attack on Moltke's glorification of war by Le Play's son. At this time Le Play was in semi-retirement due to a long illness; he died fifteen months later.

On 23 April 1882 a special meeting of *La Société d'Economie sociale* was held with his cousin, Adolphe Focillon, in the chair. The Chairman said that this meeting was a special conference planned by Le Play to celebrate his return to health. The papers were to be read by experts from different countries on workers' housing (by Emile Cheysson), profit-sharing (by Sedley Taylor), security of employment (by Jules Michel), the movement for social reform in Belgium (by Victor Brants) and others. Some days earlier some of them had met at Le Play's famous Monday evening salon. An obituary writer has described 'ce grand salon de la place Saint-Sulpice' where you could find a member of the English House of Lords was answering a question from a student at the Ecole des Mines, or a French bishop talking to a Turkish diplomat. 'They were talking five languages at once.' On this particular occasion there was a discussion about the forthcoming conference. The evening ended early, because Le Play's doctor had prescribed that his patient should retire at 9.0. As he said goodnight, he reminded them that they would meet again the following Monday. They did, as Focillon added, at his funeral; and the special meeting was his memorial.

There is much disagreement about Le Play's exact position on political, social and religious issues; and many people have claimed his support for their views. Earlier influences have already been mentioned. Later the backbone of La Société d'Economie sociale was made up of right-wing Catholic liberals like Cochin and Montalembert, although there were many with quite different sympathies, like Henri Ameline and Charles Robert. Albert Le Play sat for a short time in the senate, after his father's death, as a liberal republican. Le Play's position was a highly individual one. His strong belief in private property did not prevent him from advocating government intervention where necessary. For instance, he says in *La Réforme sociale* that there seems to be no private enterprise capable of administering either the forests or the mines in France and that therefore the state or provincial government should take over. He counters this apparent swing to the left by some savage comments on French trade unions, in which nevertheless he took some interest. His religious as well as his political position is hard to fix. Himself a nominal Catholic for most of his life, he persuasively advocated religious belief in his writings, and his work was welcomed by some of the clergy. Here was one eminent technologist who believed in God and (one might add) read St Thomas Aquinas. But usually he expressed himself in language more Comtian than biblical; indeed his interpretation of the Decalogue, to which he often referred, bore more resemblance to what was needed for the reform of French society in the nineteenth century than to the ancient Jewish law or the modern Catholic social teaching. He was a close friend of Père Hyacinthe and other opponents of papal infallibility, although by 1870 he was advising them to submit to their employer. The most important contribution of his theology to his views on society was his strong belief in original sin. On this ground he condemned Rousseau and his followers. Consistently with his general outlook he warned against optimistic solutions for social problems which did not do justice to real human needs. In spite of the suspicions of many of the orthodox, and his own strong dislike of clericalism, Le Play was decorated by Pope Leo XIII.

His versatility was typical of a nineteenth-century character. As a technologist, he was interested in many branches of science to the extent of being consulted on such matters as mineral resources and foundry practice. As a sociologist he developed a method of study and classification which produced his series of monographs; he also developed some powerful and original methods of classification, and some useful concepts for assessing social health. As an administrator he successfully managed some very large projects. As an educator he had wide influence on a generation of engineers. He also held philosophical and theological views which command attention. We shall compare his political position in the second half of his life with that of the Tories in England who made up the Tory-radical alliance to fight for factory legislation. His sympathy with the workers' efforts at self-help led him to encourage the cooperative movement, in which several of his school played a part. Moreover, in keeping with his general attitude, he took an ambivalent view of the trade unions. He gave the French unions some practical help, while he constantly denounced their irresponsibility. This irresponsibility, as he realised, was not surprising in view of their legal disabilities. Indeed, the position of the unions in the Second Empire was curious. Some of the regulations against them were relaxed, but it could be dangerous to call a meeting. Nevertheless Le Play was able to hold official conversations with the unions in connection with the 1867 Exhibition. With the English unions, on the other hand, Le Play showed much more sympathy. They had displayed organising ability and statesmanship. They maintained contact with the employers and avoided irresponsible strikes. One of his friends said that England had more responsible workmen and more irresponsible employers than any other country.[25]

One famous pen-portrait of Le Play is contained in two essays by Sainte-Beuve.[26] Considering their differences in temperament and outlook Sainte-Beuve writes sympathetically. Indeed, he expresses unlimited admiration for Le Play's insights and methods; he makes fun of him sometimes as he does of all his subjects. He does this, however, in such a sympathetic manner that the reader almost thinks him a disciple. He ridicules Le Play's emphasis on thrift, for instance, in noting that he has not done a monograph on a 'Literary Worker'. When he comes to correct this omission, Sainte-Beuve says, Le Play will find that this

type of worker never does any saving; his public will not let him. In his
second essay he compares Le Play to the counterrevolutionary writers,
the Catholic 'theocratic school' of legitimists. He writes of Bonald and
de Maître, both of whom Le Play had read. He writes of their suspicion
of change, of their irrational praise of the old regime, of their support
for the purest reaction. But, he goes on to say, there were worse; and
he brings out of obscurity a Monsieur Rubichon, a man of the old
regime to such an extent that he could hardly bring himself to visit
France after the restoration for fear of breathing air which had been
contaminated by revolutionaries. Beside these people, Sainte-Beuve
says, Le Play is a man of modern society 'par excellence'. He uses a
phrase that has often been quoted out of context when he calls Le Play
'a Bonald rejuvenated, progressive and scientific'. He may have been
'un Bonald' in some senses, but he did not seek to restore an outworn
order of society. What he did desire was to relieve the worst features of
hasty industrialisation through a study of social solidarity in the past.
He knew very well the changes that were coming over every sphere of
human activity. He was conscious of the part he himself was playing in
bringing about these changes. This consciousness impelled him to try
to mitigate their effect on the 'suffering classes', his own phrase.

Le Play's own sense of humour and hyperbole were often distorted
by over-solemn disciples. One minor example of this is the story of
Monsieur Delor, the Mayor of Vigen where Le Play's country house
was. This gentleman organised a campaign for a railway and a station
for his township. Le Play refused his support: 'Have no doubt', he told
Delor, 'of the disorganisation the construction of a railway will bring!
. . . It is, in my opinion, one of the most powerful means of social
destruction.' There is no difficulty in finding contrary quotations from
one who spent much of his life developing new metals for railway lines;
but these latter did not circulate among his followers as did sayings such
as this one. Indeed, a few years after Le Play's death Delor was solemnly
writing how prophetic his statement had proved. The coming of the
railway had indeed brought strange customs to Vigen – extremist
politics, *un gaspillage de temps*, unheard of wages, workers with no settled
occupation and – finally to trouble a worthy mayor – strikes. But the
harassed mayor had been brought up in the Le Play tradition. He was
horrified at the strike; but he investigated conscientiously the causes,
and found right on both sides.[27]

The confusion about where Le Play stood on many points was well-
illustrated in the obituary notices after his death. These ranged from
fulsome flattery of his 'progressive' activities on the one hand, to sour

comments on his alleged efforts to bring back the 'feudal system' to modern France on the other. But a shrewd, if biased, comment was made by one of his most unlikely friends. Charles Limousin, one of the founders of the first International, wrote on the day after his funeral[28] that the Place Saint-Sulpice had just witnessed a gathering of the most reactionary elements of France. They had been attending the last rites of one who had given them a theoretical system they had not the wit to devise for themselves. But he was not one of them. He did not defend the ruling classes; on the contrary: 'He reproached them for being and having been without feeling, and for having failed in all their duties towards the people. . . .'

Some years later, on the centenary of Le Play's birth, an anonymous writer gave another estimate: 'The poet that was Corneille and the thinker [*savant*] that was Le Play represent moreover the same ideal. Both, in their different works, exalted the same virtues, the same duties, the same morals. Both were, as Sainte-Beuve said of the latter, "restorers of the statue of Respect".'[29] The paradox that was Le Play, one is tempted to add of the reactionary-revolutionary, positivist-Catholic. And the key to this paradox was his hatred of bloodshed, his longing for social peace. This longing led the versatile technologist along many strange paths, beginning with the strenuous journey of 1829 which ended his career as a student.

2

The engineer

1829 The metal industry and technical education

'If the impossible could happen and the present could set an example to the past, Louis XIV would visit the factories established by Colbert and George III would deign to give deserved praise and recompense to Arkwright and James Watt.' Thus a writer in 1856 pointed to the early development of the factory system and its present prestige. The same writer tells how, when he was a student, many years earlier, one possessed a knife with a wooden handle and a shapeless blade which twisted on use. When he later became an artillery officer, he suggests, his views on the iron industry became even less favourable. But things were beginning to change. By 1812 iron and steel production in France had increased by two-fifths in a quarter of a century, and the industry employed 111,371 workers.[1] But the proportion of labour cost to material cost had not altered much in that period; there had been little technical development. The age when mechanical aids were to cut the proportion of labour costs was just beginning when Le Play entered the Ecole Polytechnique. His training was meant to equip him for the promotion both of more devices to replace manual labour and of the acceptance of these devices by the labour force. The other main industry in which Le Play was interested was also developing fast, but from small beginnings. The use of coal in France was almost unknown in the eighteenth century and only reached half a million tons in 1818. The figure had risen to nearly one and a half million in 1829, three-quarters of this mined in France. In that year Le Play was finishing his studies and beginning an association with iron and coal industries which were rapidly developing, and in which mechanical aids were becoming important.

Iron and textiles between them made up half of France's industrial wealth at the time. Indeed, the relationship between the two industries was itself significant, for the 1820s saw the substitution of iron for wood in the manufacture of textile machinery. As in most other countries, the rise of textiles was the first mark of industrial progress. Here again mechanisation was in its infancy in 1830, but was rapidly increasing. One woollen firm in the Ardennes (Tranchart), for example, had only 12,000 spindles in 1821, but had increased this to 30,000 by 1830. Many examples of this sort of progress could be quoted. The collection of large numbers of workers in one mill was another phenomenon that was becoming common in 1830. By that date the problem of management was changing from personal supervision of small numbers of workers to the delegation of authority to subordinate supervisors, often employed as subcontractors. The workers had tended to blame the new machinery for their problems and hence to advocate machine-breaking. Managers, on the other hand, tended to blame the delegation for damaging their relationships with the workers. Hence the enlightened entrepreneur was apt to look back to a more personal relationship between the manager and the workpeople. This was the atmosphere that Le Play absorbed.

A number of other developments made the 1820s an important period in the rise of French industry, notably progress in the machine tool industry, minerals other than iron, and in the connected chemical industry. Indeed, Le Play's first published article was an analysis of a substance associated with hornblende in the quarries of St Yrieix.[2] This article was accepted by the *Annales des Mines* while Le Play was still a student. In 1832 he wrote a short article on tourmaline which was considered a classic study; and in the same year he showed his interest in the wider economic aspects of industrial development by publishing an article on the export and import of minerals and mineral products. Figures showed that the gross annual value of 'other mineral products' at the beginning of the century was increasing in about the same proportions as the products of the iron industry. The increase was not caused by the discovery of new or precious metals, but by the development of fresh uses for existing resources: as ancillary to the iron industry, in the growth of other metal industries, in the increase of the pottery and glass industries, and in the chemical and salt industries. This last should not be exaggerated as the total number of workers in the chemical industry was about 3,200 in 1812, and only 5,610 in 1850. Nevertheless the growth of these smaller industries shows all the signs of the establishment of a new industrial society. Printing was also growing and becoming organised in large factories. It is hardly necessary to point out that Le Play entered industry right on the eve of the railway age. Indeed, in the mid-1830s he was offered a job on the Ohio Railroad by his friend, Michel Chevalier, who was living in America at that time. His later work in Russia was much concerned with the manufacture of rails for the first lines in that country. Before Le Play

B

reached middle age, railway networks were developing all over Europe.

Apart from Paris itself, French industry was grouped in small areas around mineral resources or in traditional centres of the textile industry, such as Lyons. One of the former, also in central France, was the great coal and iron centre of Le Creusot. In 1829 the Le Creusot company (at that time under English management) had been in financial difficulties for many years, and in 1836 it went bankrupt. It was then bought by the Schneider brothers, bringing into French industry a name that was to become famous. Their work also features in the Le Play story, and points to two other problems in which he was interested. One was the problem of human relations in a small self-contained and well-established industrial region like Le Creusot. The other problem was the opposite one of setting up industry in a completely new region, where industry had never existed before. In a way this was a typically nineteenth-century problem *in Europe*. The first industries had grown slowly and later industries grew round established centres. But the coming of the railways saw the explosive growth of industries in new areas, with the rapid recruitment of workers who had to live away from their families until new towns were built. Just at the time when a non-military discipline was finally being settled on, new industrial centres were growing up which had many of the features of army camps.

Le Play finished his studies, as has been seen, at a time of expansion – the after-effects of the impetus of the Napoleonic Empire. Odette Viennet[3] has described this surging industrial development, with its expansive self-confidence. She describes how the 'manipulators of money' boosted new industrial enterprises. She speaks of the wandering Englishmen, the enquiring landowners and the patriotic officials who helped forward the movement. But she also tells of the rising 'bourgeois dynasties' who were to form the first managerial class. The great industrial fortunes had still to be made; in this age temperament was as important as capital. The men who built up the new industrial concerns were hard fighters who had to use opportunities against every form of difficulty and opposition. Never secure, struggling to mould forces they little understood, they were unpromising material to found a tradition of good relations between masters and men. Many of them were born between 1760 and 1770, and in the 1820s they were being replaced. To use the language of Weber, when Le Play came on the scene the charismatic characters were passing away, and the process of routinisation was already setting in.

The founding of a system of higher technical education in France has been mentioned in Chapter 1. By 1830 this system was producing at least sufficient engineers to make a considerable mark on French industry. The men from the *hautes écoles* went into government service, either military or civil. But private industry was affected in at least four ways. Firstly, there came into existence an expert inspectorate with at least some powers to regulate industry; for instance, unsafe mines could be closed. Secondly, there grew up a corps of professional engineers. These had been educated in underlying technical theory, and had at least some orientation if not education towards management. Thirdly, the results of research came out of the *hautes écoles*. Fourthly, the engineers sometimes moved in to private firms and brought their expertise with them. The value of this became so clear to the private sector that in 1829 a group of industrialists founded a privately sponsored institution. This was the Ecole des Arts et Manufactures. In 1856 it was integrated into the state system, but continued to produce qualified engineers for private firms.

A university education for engineers was provided free of charge at the Ecole Normale. Here the syllabus was less specialised, but included more academic teaching. Contemporary critics were apt to say that the *normale* course was remote from life, and did not bring the students into contact with the people they were going to manage, as did the *polytechnique* course. Other institutions for technical education were coming into existence in the first half of the century. An interesting one was the Ecole des Mineurs à Saint-Etienne. This was founded by decree in 1816, and was for training professional engineers. Entrants could be between the ages of fifteen and twenty-five, and the examination was less comprehensive than that for the *polytechnique*, but included an oral test. Some places were reserved at this school for mineworkers, and hence the establishment of this school was an early example of planned promotion from the shop-floor. If you were under twenty-five and could pass the entrance examination, you could come straight from a coal-face to this college. There was also a junior mining technical college, which took boys from the ages of twelve to fifteen. The emphasis here was on practice, since the boys spent eight hours a day down the mine; but they also studied for four hours a day. The course had some absurdities such as learning suitable songs to sing 'on going down the mines, and in their work'. Le Play constantly returned to the theme of technical education later in life. In *La Réforme sociale*,[4] for instance, he advocated the setting up of a miniature system of *hautes écoles* in each Province. These schools were to provide a corps of trained management for public and private enterprise. They were to be based on what Le Play regarded as the German model, and would inject new life into regional affairs. This regional system of higher technological education was one of the farsighted proposals that Le Play made.

1829   Industrial relations

The phrase 'industrial relations' is taken here to include every form of contact between those who give instructions and those who carry them out. Those who give the orders may 'own' the factory, and the workers, too, if they are slaves; or they may themselves be employees at different levels. They may represent an international concern, a state or a committee. The number of employees may be one, or 100,000. The orders may be given in such a way that it means dismissal to refuse or even to hesitate; on the other hand they may be open to discussion by the employee. It is characteristic of industrial employment that measurement becomes all-important – the measurement of hours of work, the measurement of the amount of production, the measurement of remuneration. Apart from these measurements, the method of giving and receiving instructions and the conditions of life for the employee are the main subjects which concern a study of industrial relations, in the days before there were elaborate 'procedures for avoiding disputes' to consider. Writers like Lewis Mumford have shown that these characteristics of an industrial society have a long history.[5] During the nineteenth century, industrial employment gradually became the normal form of employment in Europe. It is not always realised how slow this process was. In 1851 England had the highest proportion of industrial workers of any country in Europe, but still agriculture claimed half the labour force. Twenty years later in France 51·5 per cent of the population worked on the land. But by the end of the century, both agriculture and the professions were beginning to acquire 'industrial' characteristics. So in the twentieth century, accurate measurement and a bureaucratic structure became normal for all employment. The main characteristics of industrial relations in the nineteenth century are set out in the following analysis, beginning with the five main types of employment policy. These types cannot be rigidly distinguished, and a company can move almost imperceptibly from one to another, but they provide a frame of reference with which to understand Le Play's preoccupations.

1 Traditional (*paternalisme*)

Many traditional forms of employment policy still existed at the beginning of the nineteenth century, which had become obsolete by the end. The principal one was the master–serf relationship which existed in the Austro-Hungarian Empire, Russia and Asia Minor. This disappeared from the legal systems of Europe in 1861. Le Play called this type of relationship *paternalisme*; but in modern English usage the word 'paternalism' is properly applied to the second type. There were other traditional employment systems in existence, like the 'guilds' which still existed in parts of the French building trade and some German coal-mines. The word Le Play uses for guild is *corporation*. This word is used to cover several similar traditional organisations. In English the word 'guild' is usually reserved to organisations of employers and employed. The nineteenth-century *corporation* was usually for employees only. The *corporations* are characterised by strict rules about entry, prospects of promotion and a highly personal relationship between the master and the apprentice or the journeyman. Although the traditional types of relationship were becoming obsolete in the first half of the nineteenth century, the memory of them affected the attitudes of employers and employed. For instance, some employers took it for granted that their role still resembled that of a Guild Master. Thus one might speak of his wife running a hostel for their young employees. Free workers, similarly, were apt to expect from their employers the fringe benefits of an earlier system, and at the same time to react against these if they limited their freedom. Constant use of the phrase 'Industrial Revolution' has tended to obscure the continuity of employment methods and outlooks through the early stages of technical innovation. In the 1820s, when Le Play began to study industrial relations, traditional attitudes and behaviour patterns were still very strong, and influenced his thought in many ways.

2 Paternalistic (*patronage*)

Le Play uses the word *patronage* to describe this type, which is a normal development in the early stages of industrialisation in a free economy; it survives into the later stages under certain conditions and with marked limitations. The paternalistic employer strives to bring into a free society such features of the earlier employment system as permanent employment and concern for the workers' general wellbeing. Power is not shared and is exercised autocratically, although not always freakishly. The employer will normally speak about his 'responsibility' for his workpeople. The workpeople, on the other hand, may accept or may strongly resent this exercise of 'responsibility'. The paternalistic employer sets out to provide more than just employment; additional facilities or amenities may include housing, recreation and education. There may be pension schemes and sick benefits and some care may be taken over comfort at work. Typically the paternalistic employer does not consult his workpeople about these amenities. He provides what he thinks is best for them, although he may take some steps towards workmen's representation on committees for specific projects. A later development is the skilful employer who manages to retain control while establishing a democratic structure. For the purposes of this study, the firm moves into another ('consultative') classification as soon as serious efforts are made to hold discussions with the workers.

A feature of the paternalistic system is that the employer is 'hard to replace'. So much depends on the man at the top that his successor has to make some definable gesture on assuming control. This gesture may be 'I will continue my predecessor's policy', and this is likely to be the case where the predecessor was also his parent. On the other hand, the gesture may be one of change: 'For all our sakes, unfortunately, changing conditions must be taken into account in considering our policy for the future.' Such a statement may herald a change to the 'hire and fire' type; or some such phrase as 'I believe in leaving workmen to run their own affairs' may be the prelude to the introduction of some consultation. Economic conditions and pressures from outside, but also the character of the new management, will help to decide this. The fact that this change may be the easiest way of overcoming the problem of succession in a paternalistic set-up makes this type unstable and liable to further change once there is a free and mobile labour force.

Individual proprietors and companies of any size or type could be paternalistic. Certain factors made this more likely. Prosperous economic conditions with competition for labour encouraged paternalism. Similarly newly developing industrial areas demanded training and amenities before a labour force could be recruited. In few countries in the nineteenth century was the state a large employer of labour apart from the armed forces and such civil servants as existed; but where the state did employ labour then it was liable to be a paternalistic employer. This was largely because, in the prevalent mood, the paternalistic employer was the 'good', the 'responsible', employer. The state was expected to 'look after' its employees, but not to initiate experiments which might embarrass private firms. In view of the problem of distinguishing between Le Play's use of the word *paternalisme* and 'paternalism' in modern English, the word *patronage* will be used throughout this study in Le Play's sense of this second type of industrial relations.

3 'Hire and fire'

In its extreme form this system means that the employer provides equipment, materials and a place of employment; he hires an employee for just so long as he has use for him and no longer. In fact the system is generally moderated by some form of understanding, which might or might not be enforceable at law, about terms of employment. Thus the engagement could be on a time basis, requiring a certain length of notice – an hour, a day, a week or occasionally longer; or it could be on a piece basis, when employment would normally be guaranteed up to the completion of a certain task. In this case, payment would also be fixed according to the length of time that a normal worker took to perform this task. Usually employment would continue as long as work was available, but sudden dismissal remained a constant possibility. Some employers would make efforts to keep their more skilled workers during a period of slump. But the threat of unemployment was constantly with the worker. The 'hire and fire' system usually developed in established industrial areas, where paternalism broke down with a change of personnel at the top. Difficult economic conditions could also lead to firms changing to the 'hire and fire' type. In the early nineteenth century, England was considered the home of 'hire and fire' conditions of employment. Later in the century, America was regarded as the most ruthless exponent of this method.

Whether the 'hire and fire' method was the cause or merely a symptom of the struggle between masters and men is not the concern of this study. In its more ruthless forms it was attacked by some who supported the capitalist system, as did the Le Play school, on the grounds that it brought that system into disrepute. On the other hand 'hire and fire' was supported by the classical economists, who gave to this method a theoretical rationale. The paternalistic system was rigid; it mitigated the immediate effects of industrialisation, but was often insufficiently adaptable to the pace of technical development. The 'hire and fire' system could mean the greatest misery for the worker and his family; it could also mean a greater share in prosperity. Besides, the worker often preferred the greater freedom that he was given. He felt more his own master. One of the paradoxes of the 'hire and fire' system was that the economic difficulties which helped to bring it into existence also exaggerated its drawbacks. When the employers were struggling for their existence, then piece rates could be very low, tenure of employment very uncertain – and the whole uncertainty and intense competition led to practices which produced a demand for state regulation. The autocratic employer could be an individual proprietor, a company of any size or a government or public agency. In its more extreme forms the employer was likely to be an individual strongly imbued with a sense of 'I do what I like with my own.' The larger the company the more likely was the autocracy to be mitigated in some way. Le Play called this type of industrial relations 'temporary engagements with free labour'.

4 The consultative

A twentieth-century analysis on these lines would have to assume some consultation and classify a company on its bias towards paternalism, 'hire and fire' or consultation. In a nineteenth-century study any move towards formal consultation with workpeople may be regarded as a change of type – provided there was some formality and some permanence about this – for even the most autocratic employer could walk round his workshops discussing future plans with some of the workmen. This informal consultation, an interesting study in itself, is not relevant here. Le Play does clearly see that some new system is emerging from both the paternalistic and the 'hire and fire' methods. Much of the industrial history of the nineteenth century has been written round the struggles for recognition of the trade unions. Before this struggle was won, any system of consultation was embryonic. Once individual unions began to gain recognition the first joint consultation procedures developed.

5 Producers' cooperatives

Among the areas of traditional relationships, groups of commuted serfs developed producers' cooperatives for agriculture and light industry; but among the areas of 'free' labour the numbers of producers' cooperatives were limited in 1829. Later in the century these became more common. In firms where the proprietor made some profit-sharing arrangement with his employees may well be seen the first beginnings of a system of joint consultation mentioned above. They still retained the relationship of employer and employed. Associations which were really complete copartnerships, such as the revolutionary government in France in 1848 tried to establish, were sometimes shortlived in manufacturing industry; they easily developed into partnerships or one-man businesses. Schemes of cooperative production often grew up in prosperous years when profits were easily made. When economic conditions changed it could be difficult for a committee to cut its own wages. Cooperative producers' associations grew up in many countries, sometimes developing out of a company which sold its shares to its employees. More usually, however, they were started by groups of workmen who pooled their savings and sometimes had financial help from sympathisers outside. One problem of the industrial societies was that they were not sufficiently different in their industrial relations from other types. Looking at them from the point of view of day to day relationships, they merely divorced management from ownership at an earlier stage in their development than private firms. Many firms sold shares to their employees. They may be regarded as consultative unless the workers held a majority of shares and with this holding an effective voice in management. For this is what makes the cooperatives a separate type; the ultimate decisions (at least) were taken by the same people as carried them out.

Employers can also be divided into five groups. The first type is the individual employer. He may be a large proprietor with many thousands of serfs, or he may be a small businessman with one employee. The work-place was closely connected with the employer-proprietor and described in possessive terms (e.g. 'Mr Watson's coal-pits'); and his character often determined for good or ill the views of the workers about their employment.

The second type of employer was in fact himself an employee. In the early nineteenth century, the system of subcontracting was the normal method of employment in many industries. This method, known in France as *marchandage*, consisted in the employer subletting a certain amount of work (in the textile industry it would be a certain length of cloth, in the mining industry an area of coal) to an experienced work-man for an agreed price. The workman would then virtually employ those of his fellow-workmen who assisted him, and would pay them out of the money the employer paid him. With a knowledge of the results of the system and the intense bitterness it caused it is easy to say that it was doomed from the start. But this assumption leaves some questions unanswered. For the system gave independence and status to the master-workman; it also gave a clear line of promotion for the other
*

workmen. It would seem, on the face of it, to have met some clearly felt needs. Indeed, the promotion system that still exists in the steel industry is often given as a reason for the stability of that industry. Of course, it was abused, but so was every system of payment. Why then, did it fail? Perhaps the main reason was because there was always too little to share. It was not necessarily that the masters treated their workmen more generously when they paid them direct, but that when life was a bread-and-butter struggle the sharing of crumbs caused a fight. It is an interesting speculation that had there been more to share, subcontracting (modified by technical necessities) might have prevailed. Team earnings in the coal and steel industries today have developed from the earlier subcontracting systems. The third type of employer was a joint stock company. The fourth was a cooperative society; the Rochdale Pioneers had not yet launched their famous venture, but in 1829 there were many experiments in cooperation. And the fifth type of employer, operating in a limited number of activities, was the state.

Employee organisations, on the other hand, can be classified into three groups. The first is that of the travelling organisations, such as the brotherhoods of journeymen (*Compagnonnages de Devoir*, they were called in France). These still existed in the middle of the century. The second were the trade unions; a limited number had a substantial history by 1829. The third group was that of the friendly societies. Sometimes these would be cover-organisations for trade unions, but many friendly societies and sick-clubs and suchlike existed just for their declared purpose. Le Play mentioned these often as the one means of thrift used by significant numbers of workmen. When he mentioned them, he often distinguished between those which were just thrift clubs, and those which served other objectives as well.

Finally, there were five main determinants of change working on the systems of industrial relations. State legislation was the first. This was contrary to the climate of opinion at the time, but some existed. There were also rights and customs which might be enforceable at law. Then there was the development of corps of professional engineers, which have already been mentioned since Le Play belonged to one of them. The third determinant was individual decision. In the days when proprietorship could be a personal matter, individual whims and hunches were very important. This is not to underestimate the limitations on individual preferences imposed by the fourth determinant, namely economic conditions and the state of technical knowledge. Finally, the fifth on the list was trade union activity.

Any development of consultation or copartnership met problems arising from the lack of skill, experience or education of the workers. These problems easily led to disillusionment, especially since attitudes on both sides often did not encourage experiment. But the existence of these problems does mean that symptoms of change towards greater consultation can be sought in subtle ways. For instance, adult education could be a paternalistic gesture to broaden the workers' minds; it could also be aimed to shape the workers' outlooks; but it could be a first step to some shared responsibility. Similarly, elective committees could be regarded as training grounds for greater participation by the workers. Hopes were being inspired, hopes which did not include tolerating an inferior status indefinitely. Just how inferior this was is brought out in a collection of texts published by the Société d'Histoire contemporaine in 1921. In the introduction to volume 2, the editors point out that under the Restoration the legislative chambers and the administrative machine were for use by the bourgeois only. Thus a mass of documents relate to production from the management point of view, but there is nothing in the official archives about conditions of work and wages and so on. Similarly, employers' organisations flourish, while workers' organisations are constantly suppressed with the arrests of their members. Indeed, the most accessible evidence for the existence of these organisations are the accounts of these arrests.

Official joint consultation for industry had not progressed far in 1830. But there was one institution for which France was famous and which is often taken to mark the beginning of a conciliation machinery – the *Conseils de Prud'hommes*.[6] These *conseils* were based on the principle, not carried far in practice, that a man should be judged by his equals; hence panels of industrialists were set up to judge industrial problems. The first was established at Lyons in 1806; this was followed by *conseils* at Rouen and Nimes in 1807. By the end of 1813 there were twenty-seven *conseils*, sixty-four by 1840. At first only employers sat on them; workers' representatives were added later, but in 1830 they still had a majority of employers. One function of the *conseils* was to provide a court of appeal for the worker against dismissal. In this they were unique to France, and their importance was increased by the fact that they were not just legal tribunals; they could mediate between master and man. To describe them as important is not to overlook their limitations; but they enshrined at least the principle that a man should have some rights in the matter of dismissal. Workers' reports, later in the century, spoke favourably of their work while demanding reform of their constitution. These *conseils* were not conciliation machinery in the sense that such would deal with wages and hours of work. They dealt with problems of individual workers rather than with groups of workers. They were not set up to mediate an industrial dispute – they could not have been since combinations of workpeople or employers were illegal. Nevertheless, they did make decisions which had far-reaching effects.

One example of the working of the *conseils* is provided by a discussion the *conseil* of Amiens had after the introduction of spinning mules.[7] They considered that the operator on the machine should be a man, and over a certain height, as otherwise he was liable to injure himself. The local manufacturers agreed with this, but said they were not altogether to blame if boys were employed as the parents were so anxious to find them employment. They looked forward to technical improvements to minimise the abuses. Other matters dealt with at this time included a workers' claim for his tools which an employer was holding against repayment of debt, a claim about non-execution of an apprenticeship agreement, a claim for non-payment of wages (by a curious freak of the law, such a claim could be settled on the employer's word alone; in this case the *conseil* mediated an agreement), a claim concerning piece rates instead of a day wage.

The use made of the *conseils* by the workers shows that they had some confidence in them; especially is this so with the independent 'sub-contractors'. Moreover, before 1830 workers were already trying to use the *conseils* to settle wider issues. For instance, in 1826, in a small textile manufacturing town,[8] word reached the workpeople that the employers were planning a cut in wages. They appealed to the *Conseil de Prud'hommes* to stop this, but the *conseil* replied that the matter was outside their jurisdiction. The matter was discussed between the local Prefect and the Minister in Paris. Neither seems to have been concerned about the illegal association of employers to reduce wages – the Prefect was only concerned about possible disturbances among the workpeople. The Minister, on the other hand, thought the employers could be relied on to keep order. He was anxious that the *Conseil de Prud'hommes* should not exceed its duties; he did not think it practicable to meet the Prefect's request for more troops, although he later passed the message on to the Minister for War. For all its limitations, there is no doubt that an embryo conciliation system existed in 1830. Some traditions on this matter were being built up or preserved, traditions which Le Play later tried to revive.

One scene of industrial trouble at this time was Lyons,[9] centre of the silk industry. Much attention has been concentrated on Lyons because there was undoubtedly some organisation behind the workers, possibly the Devoir Mutuel. The riots had a background familiar in much industrial agitation – a background of declining trade and of technical innovation. The first serious riots were in November 1831, when the workers were actually in command of the city for a short time. Among the events leading up to the outbreak was an attempt at conciliation by the Prefect. But for its disastrous sequel, this action might have gone down to history as a pioneer example of official mediation in a wage claim. Monsieur Dumolart, the newly appointed Prefect, was a man of progressive views who had refused office during the Restoration. The silk-workers, who had suffered much from the slump in 1830, demanded a system of payment by results to improve their earnings. To further their cause they addressed a petition to the Mayor of the city and the Prefect of the Department. There followed meetings between delegates of the workers and the employers. As a result of these meetings, an agreement was announced. A new wage structure had apparently been established on the mediation of the Prefect. Immediately a group of employers denounced the agreement in a letter to the press. They alleged that the acceptance of the agreement had been forced upon the employers by the Prefect, and that in any case their delegation had been unrepresentative. They ended by quoting the Prefect's own words that the authorities cannot regulate relations between manufacturer and worker, and hence the agreement had no legal force. A contemporary account points out that the government did not support the Prefect who was soon replaced and blames the Ministry for not giving clearer instructions to its subordinates. The next occasion when there was an official attempt to mediate in French industry was in 1848, and Le Play himself was involved. After further disturbances in Lyons, in 1834, the law against trade unions was tightened.

Regulations for the safety of workpeople did exist before 1829. For instance, quarry safety was the subject of a law of 1810 and a decree of 1813. In one of Le Play's monographs the provisions of these measures are set out. They included regulations insisting that the workings must be open to the sky unless they were in strata which would give a safe roof; they also provided standards for boring and tunnelling. The work had to be supervised by mining engineers. These were to check the actual siting of the workings, to make sure that the concessionaires kept within their boundaries, and to watch that the safety regulations were applied. This dual function had its problems, but was aimed at ensuring a regular inspection of the workings.

In 1829 the industrial workers had little proletarian consciousness, and what there was produced wide social aims rather than concentration on immediate issues. Hence there was little impulse from the workers' side towards consultation. To many of them, industry only provided a temporary occupation, and some expected to be masters themselves in time. If the workers were more amenable than their English opposite numbers, they were also more lacking in skill and experience. Far sighted commentators, like Le Play's onetime fellow-student, Michel Chevalier,[10] remarked on the need for more training and more consistent employment to overcome this lack. Trade unions were illegal, made so by a law of 1791 which forbade combination in restraint of trade. As in England, where the Combination Laws were modified in 1824 and 1825, the law applied to masters as well as to men. As in England, also, the law only had serious effects on the men; indeed, after it was passed in 1791, the proposer (Le Chapelier) moved a resolution to exempt Chambers of Trade, saying that it had been suggested to him that they might be held illegal under the measure. Against the workers, the law was often invoked. For instance, even the incomplete figures published by the Department of Justice show that, between 1825 and 1835, there were on average fifty prosecutions a year for illegal combinations to promote strikes.

The new type of workers' organisation took two forms – the friendly societies and the *sociétés des résistances*. The former were often organised by trades and in 1823 there were 132 of them. They performed some of the functions of a trade union; they certainly provided a method for members of a trade to meet in a way that the law generally did not interfere with. The *sociétés des résistances* were secret societies which existed for avowedly trade union purposes. They organised some common action in regard to employers, and arranged strikes and other forms of industrial action. Later in the century it was argued by some of Le Play's circle that their very illegality made strikes more likely – had they been allowed to discuss their problems openly, they would have been able to find a peaceful solution more often. The most famous of these secret societies was the Devoir Mutuel, founded in 1823 and allegedly the organisation behind the Lyons riots in the 1830s. Later the copper smelters and the printers in Paris developed such organisations.

One much resented feature of working life was the *livret*.[11] This was the identity card which the French worker had to carry, and on which his employers entered his record of work. The *livret* was introduced in 1803 to replace the traditional links between master and employee which had been broken in the name of 'Freedom of work'. These were issued to apprentices, and carried exact details of his training and qualifications. One object of the *livret* was for the master to enter any advances he might have made to the worker. If the latter changed his employer before he had repaid the loan, then this could be deducted by the subsequent employer. Originally, the *livret* had certain advantages. To the worker it provided visible evidence of his status; it could also be used to obtain credit. To the employer it provided information about a worker's skill. The disadvantages were foremost when there was war between employers and workers. The *livret* was a useful way of identifying a leader among the workers and ensuring that he did not get employment. It was administered by the police, and became a weapon in police espionage. The disadvantages as well as the advantages were evidently mitigated by the fact that the *livret* was easy to lose. Long after 1830 the law still made the carrying of *livrets* compulsory.

A survey of the types of worker in 1830 shows, as with the types of employer, a variety which included some classes left over from a pre-industrial age. For instance, the *compagnon*[12] was the freshly qualified craftsman, who originally lived with the master-craftsman for whom he worked. By 1830, the *compagnonnages* had split into several rival groups, but still numbered many members. They had some of the characteristics of trade unions, for they represented members in difficulties and sometimes called a stoppage over a grievance; but they did not directly evolve into trade unions. They did give their members experience of organisation and leadership, which was valuable as the unions developed. The *compagnonnages* were colourful organisations, with their own secret signs and passwords. Members had to be unmarried, and left when they got married or became master-craftsmen. *The compagnons* did their own *tour de France*, staying at hostels recommended by the organisation. In each place where they stayed they earned their keep, or if that was not possible their fellow-members paid for them to travel on to another place. The strength of the *compagnonnages* in 1821 is illustrated by the report of the Prefect of the Gironde. A conference in his department was attended by eighty representatives of twenty-three different societies. They had come together, they said, to compose the differences between their societies which frequently led to bloodshed. They did not succeed in their object, but they did succeed in attracting the attention of the police who closely questioned some of them. *Compagnonnages* still existed among the building workers in 1856, when Le Play wrote about them in one of his monographs.

Apprenticeship in 1830 was governed by the revolutionary legislation which had swept away most of the regulations, and with them the safeguards, for young people. It was not for another twenty years that state regulation of apprenticeship was resumed. However, some of the old structure had survived, and articles of apprenticeship were still drawn up even if they could not be legally enforced, although some safeguards remained. If the condition of apprentices had deteriorated, the position of other child labour was far worse. As in England, contemporary accounts are full of pathetic stories of the sufferings of the children.

As with the apprentice, so with the adult worker. The old order was breaking up and new defences had not been constructed. The worker was drifting to the towns, to long hours of work in unhealthy conditions. Families were separated. Le Play later described an industrial suburb of Paris with the women far outnumbered by the men, who had moved in to find work without bringing their families.

1829–1856 The lectures and the technical writings

In 1829, as we have seen, Le Play's first article was published. From 1840 to 1856 he was a professor at the Ecole des Mines. Between these years he was first and foremost a technologist. He influenced a generation of engineers, just as later he built up a school of social scientists. Among his pupils were men like Eugene Schneider who attempted to put his ideas into practice at Le Creusot. Another famous pupil was Pierre Martin who, together with his father, developed a new method of steel-making. The father, Emile, was an older man than Le Play but an admirer of his work, and he sent his son to study under him.[13]

Le Play's technical writings, published in *Les Annales des Mines*, show his concern that the technologist should not overlook the human factor. His interests included the social and psychological influences of work organisation. For him as much as for the Marxist the worker was fashioned in the image of his craft. He tried to disentangle the relationships between work, society, family life and the outlook of the individual. His technical works illustrate his attitude to employees as well as to materials and equipment. They also provide much information on industrial practices at the time. His first long article was on the movement of the principal minerals between France and foreign countries during the previous twelve years, and especially during 1829, 1830 and 1831. His visit to Spain was the subject of another long article and the book mentioned earlier. In an unpublished report on the mineral resources of Normandy and Brittany, he wrote that the local civil engineers did not appreciate the importance of good administration.

In 1838 he wrote[14] a short obituary of a young colleague in the Royal Corps of Mines – a Monsieur Malinvaud. Malinvaud died at the age of thirty-one from injuries received in a mining accident; in his short life he had, in Le Play's words, 'showed strength of character, much rarer than knowledge or talent, when he insisted on the intervention of the law to close two illegal mine workings'. In so doing, Le Play added, he prevented two certain disasters. In Le Play's view the humane man with the courage to stand against the current of economic greed was as much the hero of the Industrial Revolution as the inventor. This obituary also showed that in early nineteenth century France the law was used, if only occasionally, to safeguard the workers.

Between 1836 and 1848 Le Play paid three visits to South Wales[15] to investigate the copper industry. He described a well-established smelting industry drawing ore from many parts of the United Kingdom, and now from overseas as well. The smelting firms, who did not usually mine the ore themselves, bought their supplies in the open market and were very selective in what they bought. For the sale of manufactured copper, the smelting companies had a formula:

$$S \text{ (standard price)} = \frac{M \text{ (price of raw material)} + F \text{ (expense)}}{T \text{ (amount of copper in ore)}}$$

This enabled long-term contracts to be negotiated, and incidentally provided some stability of employment for the workers. He referred in this, as in other such studies, to the high standard of craftsmanship of the operative smelter, and the low standard of competence of the professional metallurgist. Here was clearly one of the key facts in industrial relations at the time, and one that disturbed Le Play. For he was one of the first to make explicit the view that the authority of the manager should be based on skill and competence and not on other sanctions or privileges. The remedy was again one to which he often returned, and which formed the basis of his sociology as well – the future progress of metallurgy depended on much closer observation of facts; the future progress of management depended on education. These would only be attained if the whole status of metallurgical study was increased. He referred to the efforts of Swedenborg who had toured metal works all over Europe to try to increase the prestige of the study of metal. In spite of this, Le Play maintained, old prejudices survived, prejudices going back to the Roman view that the study of metal was not only unbecoming but actually impious.[16] To counter contemporary mythology, Le Play found it necessary to point out to his readers that metallurgical progress arose from the study of metals and not from the exploitation of the workers.[17]

After attacking the lack of managerial competence, Le Play said that an important part of that competence was knowledge of how to promote cooperation on the part of the workers. He condemned those who reorganised work methods on the basis of theories not sufficiently tested in the workshop, and then blamed the workers for their failure. It was often a sign of incompetence to blame one's failure on 'the lack of skill, ill-will and – blessed phrase – love of routine of the workers'. Part of the art of metallurgy was to study the workers' own traditional methods to discover just what they were doing to the metal. Le Play described some very subtle effects produced by the skill of the workers, and not discovered in the laboratory. Indeed, he said that the conflict between theory and practice had arisen from the unskilful application of theories. The first line of research was to listen to the successful practitioner. Thus he developed in his metallurgical studies another principle he was later to apply in sociology. Le Play gave many examples of how the intuitive skill of the worker had produced results not at the time discoverable by theoretical research. For instance, he quoted the heating of the calcining ovens, which each had to be treated individually because they fulfilled slightly different functions. He said that the amount of air admitted to the furnaces during calcination seemed to him incompatible with existing metallurgical principles. He considered that more oxygen was needed to oxidise the metal and facilitate the burning. But he gained clear evidence that the furnace in which the workers had limited the air intake most produced the best and most economical results. He even found that a new type of furnace had been introduced which gave a greatly increased supply of air, but unknown to the management the workers had adapted it to function in the old way, further evidence that the practice was superior to the theory of the time. A priori, he said, labouring the point, these methods would have been condemned. In investigating the cost of calcining a ton of raw copper, he showed that labour charges amounted to over half. This suggested a low level of mechanisation, but a high level of fuel economy.

The book on the Welsh copper industry came out in 1848. A few years earlier, in 1843, Le Play had published his study of the Steel Industry of South Yorkshire. The steelworker, he judged, was in an even more independent position than the copper worker. He wrote of the difficulties of getting information from steel-masters who were very unwilling to release the results of their experience; but it was doubtful if they had much to release anyway: 'for they only direct commercial affairs, and leave the technical direction to the ordinary workers. These last are the real metallurgists of Yorkshire . . .' Here Le Play came up against another familiar difficulty, that of communication. For the workmen did not use words which lent themselves to metallurgical analysis – such words as 'body', 'health', 'strength', 'hardness' were not readily translated into formulae; but they had a precise meaning to the workmen, and upon this fact depended the quality of Sheffield steel. In spite of Sheffield's pre-eminence in the steel industry, the worker himself was very much at the mercy of the state of trade. For instance, in August 1842, when Le Play was in Sheffield, half the furnaces of Yorkshire were closed down. In his sociological studies later, Le Play refers to the lack of concern among English manufacturers about finding permanent employment for their workpeople.

In 1846 he published another book on the steel industry. This was part of a public controversy Le Play was having with another mining engineer, J. François, on the subject of import duty.[18] Le Play argued not only that this tax was unwise, but that its original imposition a century earlier had had disastrous results on the development of the steel industry. For the English had proved that Scandinavian ores were needed. François denied this and advocated the official view. This, as he thought, inept interference in trade reinforced Le Play's opposition to government action. When he later wrote a report on the bakery industry of Paris, he again advocated the removal of restrictions.[19] On other occasions, such as his report on the Donets valley, he advocated protection to enable new resources to be developed. Against the liberals, he was always a strong opponent of doctrinaire *laissez-faire*, as were most of his circle. The best sanction in industry or commerce was the sense of responsibility of the employer or merchant. But if he did not act responsibly, then the government had a positive role to play. Men's lives could not be left at the mercy of economic forces. If the 'law' of supply and demand produced unjust results, then the 'law' must be corrected.

Le Play's technical works present a picture of a mind at work on the connection between engineering progress and human and social skills. Indeed, in 1846, while visiting some mines in Hungary, he was prompted to write to the Minister of Public Works in Paris proposing that the state should found some experimental mines – for developing new techniques both in mining and in management. Sound management needed to be technically competent; it also needed to understand that technology existed to serve human beings. Le Play, the great enemy of reasoning *a priori*, nevertheless believed that moral considerations should dominate others. One of his friendly critics pointed out that Le Play was guided by more assumptions than he was prepared to admit.[20] He believed, for instance, that the purpose of social studies was to promote social peace and to strengthen family life. Thus his theory of industrial relations not only assumed that the moral criterion had priority over the technical or the economic, but also that the establishment of harmony was an overriding object in itself. This theory, of course, left no room for 'intelligent' or 'creative' conflict, although these concepts were not unknown to him, as is shown by his comments on industrial relations in Sheffield, described later in this chapter. He saw great dangers in the rapid weaning of industry in so many parts of the world. Human greed, national power politics, technocratic arrogance, were all being put before human need and human wellbeing. And this was being said by an engineer, a manager in the developing industry itself. Le Play was not a philanthropist condemning industry from outside; he was not ignorant of the real problems of management or the grim facts of economics. He did not romanticise the worker or vilify the employer. He looked at the facts through humane eyes, and found himself disturbed – this disturbance was implicit in works mainly notable for chemical formulae, commercial price lists and technical drawings; it was to become explicit in works filled with family budgets and the data of a suffering social order. *Les classes souffrantes* was a phrase he constantly used. Technical inventiveness was proving the enemy of social wellbeing; that was the problem Le Play set himself to solve.

He expressed his views most distinctively in his lectures to his students at the Ecole des Mines. For sixteen years, from 1840 to 1856, he conducted a two-year course of forty lectures on metallurgy.[21] In his first lecture each year, he emphasised that the students were to be much more than engineers. Concerned with their future status, Le Play stressed that if the engineers were ever to achieve a proper prestige in society, they must acquire social skills as well as technical ones. They must understand economics, for their art had to be turned to a profit. If they did not face up to this, they would continue to take second place in an industry run by merchants. But more important even than economics was the study of men and of society. Le Play constantly urged his students to investigate social facts in the same spirit as they investigated metals; he also urged that this was the most intricate and important part of their studies. Technical progress could become a blessing instead of a curse if the promoters of that progress understood the human and social consequences of their activities; this understanding would involve the social sciences in general as well as specific studies in the art of management; the future development of the social sciences would be by means of empirical studies. 'Disdaining books, documents and reports,' wrote one of his disciples, perhaps overlooking what a prolific producer of books, documents and reports he was writing about, 'Le Play dived into and observed the world of living people.'[22]

Industrial relations came into his lectures incidentally, and in 1848 a course of general studies, entitled 'Industrial Law', was introduced at the Ecole des Mines. This was the course that was taken by Jean Reynaud until 1851. However, it was not until two years after Le Play's death that the school established a separate Chair of Social Studies. For the first twenty-two years of its existence this Chair was occupied by Le Play's friend and disciple, Emile Cheysson. Meanwhile, Le Play told his students that they had a great opportunity for studying social facts on the tours that were a compulsory part of their course; and he stressed his own willingness to discuss such matters with any of them personally. In one lecture he pointed out that much academic study of metallurgy was useless since it overlooked the role of the worker in the metal works: 'It is very common to see metal works entirely left in the control of the workers; while I do not know a single example of a factory set up by professional metallurgists without the cooperation of workers already experienced from a long apprenticeship' (lectures of 1842). He also spoke, in a later lecture, of the misunderstandings that arose between the engineer and the worker. These, he said flatly to his students, were not usually the fault of the workers. The workers in the metal and mining industries had, too, a special stake in an industry often situated in infertile areas with little alternative employment. A student solely dedicated to technical studies could not hope to cope with the human factor properly.

In his lectures he first began to distinguish the different types of industrial relations mentioned above. He contrasted starkly what he called in his earlier lectures the Russian and the English systems of employment. In Russia the worker must stay where he is born, and work for the owner of the soil. There was no possibility of any bargaining between the owner and his workers about wages. The employer had a labour force which could not leave him; but on the other hand he could not leave them. He had to support them whether there was work or not, and he had to support them in old age and sickness. He had to organise health services, churches, schools, the care of foundlings and the maintenance of order; and he had to pay the doctors, clergy, teachers, police and others needed by these institutions. Furthermore, serf labour was not as productive as free labour. Le Play's calculation was that one free man did the same amount of work as about two and a half serfs. In his study of the mineral wealth of the Donets valley he discovered that Welsh coal from Swansea was sold more cheaply in the Black Sea port of Odessa than Russian coal mined in the Donets valley. This partly reflected the cost of overland transport, but largely showed the uneconomic nature of serf labour. This suggested to Le Play the significance of different methods of management.[23] If in Europe technical considerations were apt to be secondary to economic ones, in the Russian system administrative considerations came first. For the population had to be supported whatever the amount of work available.

The 'Russian' system applied in a great part of the world outside Europe; it 'does assure the physical wellbeing of the population, but to the detriment of their human dignity'; typically Le Play deleted the last phrase from his lecture and substituted the more factual 'by means which civilisation has long since rejected' – such corrections to his notes reveal much of his processes of thought. On the other extreme, he said, was the 'illusory independence' of the English worker who suffered from the pressures of industrialisation in their most extreme form. There were problems for the employer in this system which was supposed to rest on the 'so-called laws of supply and demand' (Le Play never referred to the 'laws' of the classical economists without prefacing them by 'so-called'). When times were good, the employer's problem was one of shortage of labour. When times were bad his problem was one of conscience; he could not pay a living wage. At all times, he was involved in an atmosphere of distrust and conflict. But if, said Le Play with heavy sarcasm, the employers had their problems, these were nothing to those of the workers. 'Unquestionably, the saddest scene in the world today is the destitution into which thousands of workers' families are plunged in England when a commercial crisis suddenly produces a shut-down in the factories.'[24]

After 1848 Le Play stressed even more emphatically to his students their need to understand the human factor. The 'English' system of very short-term engagements, he now said, applied to most of France and other parts of Europe as well. But there was another system, which applied notably in the Harz mountains, which he called *patronage*. This system, he claimed, left the worker completely free to move at will but ensured him some continuity of employment if he stayed. The employer gained a more stable labour force, and showed some sense of responsibility for the workers' general wellbeing. The problems to which this gave rise Le Play did not discuss in his lectures. What he did was to list a few objectives to guide a conscientious employer. One of these was that the worker should not be entirely dependent on the factory. The employer should help him to obtain and cultivate a smallholding as well. This suggestion, an attempt to provide some security for the worker, obviously assumed an early stage in industrialisation. Another means of providing the same service was a factory savings bank supported by the firm. This also Le Play advocated, and it became an important theme later in his life. Another principle was that the employer should not employ women and children under factory conditions. This might mean that he ought to provide some domestic industry for those who had to work. Le Play considered that it was the responsibility of the employer to find work for all members of the community which depended on his factory. Other provisions included free schools and medical and dispensing services. Finally, without actually speaking of a minimum wage, Le Play demanded some consideration on the employers' part for the basic requirements of the workers' family.

While Le Play spoke about three types of industrial relations, he did recognise that a fourth was emerging; in his lectures he only hinted at this. Even in England, he said, it was only in the textile industry where the worker was entirely at the mercy of the employer with regard to employment and wages. In other industries, and he quoted especially the Sheffield steel industry, some form of agreement between employers and workers had mitigated the system. Thus he noted the beginning of consultation, which had arisen through the power of workers in industries where their individual skill was important.

Two other matters Le Play put before his students: the importance of the selection of workers, the right man in the right job, and the importance of management as an art in itself. He put his finger on another drawback in the English system of industrial relations when he noted: 'In Great Britain, where great importance is attached to avoiding the expense of employing managers, and where the workers are usually more skilful than on the Continent, the master-moulder who works with his own hands is often the only intermediary between the proprietor and the shop floor.' This 'master-moulder', it should be said, was paid about three shillings a day, a little more in a large factory; he certainly had no training in the 'art of management'. In spite of such strictures on English industrial relations, Le Play was a great admirer of English institutions in general on the grounds that they combined freedom with peace. He was a very great admirer of English technical inventiveness, even if this did arise from rule of thumb methods.

However concerned he may have been with the welfare of the workers he taught his students that in planning a factory, fixed capital must be reduced to the absolute minimum. There was no idea in his lectures, as there was in his later thinking, of making the factory a better place to work in by better buildings. Also he assumed that low wages were a permanent necessity, even if he did advocate continuity of employment. One of the difficult tasks of the engineer, he said, was to maintain discipline and morale with wages that must always be low.

A problem mentioned in many of Le Play's technical writings is that of immigrant workers. The immigrants he had in mind came from a different part of the same country, they did not belong to another race or nation. Nevertheless, their problems resembled those of the international immigrants of a later age. Skilled jobs were usually closed to them, as apprenticeships were reserved for the sons of established workmen. At the same time, the lowest status occupations were filled almost entirely by immigrants. They were alleged to live at a lower standard than the locals, and to depress the areas into which they moved. The immigrants Le Play met were of two types. There were those who moved regularly each year, like the Italian miners who went to work on the land during the summer, or the Russian peasants who became dock-workers when the ice thawed. These were described in Le Play's social studies. More interesting were the permanent immigrants, such as those described in his report on the cutlery industry.[25] In similar terms he described how immigrants from other parts of their respective countries filled the unskilled jobs in both Sheffield and Solingen. Into this report he wrote his philosophy of industrial relations: 'Since we do not lose sight of the fact that the supreme end of civilisation is to extend the intellectual and moral inheritance of humanity at the same time as the manufacturing activity and the material wealth . . .' He did not find in the cutlery industry that mechanisation had done so much damage to the 'intellectual and moral inheritance of humanity' as in some industries. But he did say that the days of the independent worker were numbered as were those of the workman who built up his own business. These things continued to be possible long after Le Play noted that they were becoming obsolete; and in these matters, as in others, observers a century later were making statements similar to those of Le Play – and making them as if they were original.

In the case of Solingen, he wrote of the hold of tradition which had moderated the effects of mechanisation. But rapid mechanisation was beginning to produce changes. The Sheffield worker he found to be just as hard-working, but less docile. He described the endemic conflict between masters and men, but in this particular study he wrote more optimistically than elsewhere. After suggesting that the unions of Sheffield were almost as widely known as its products and that these unions had struck some blows at the social constitution of their country, he went on to say: 'They have resolved in agreement with the employers . . . the principal difficulties involved in the fixing of wages. He went on further to suggest that the spirit of conciliation among the upper classes, and the sense of responsibility and moderation of the union leaders had produced some happy results out of the strife. Le Play also made the point that the strength of the unions was a guarantee to the more conscientious employers against being undercut by less scrupulous rivals. Thus unions could be an advantage to the employer even in a system of *patronage*. Later in his life, he partly contradicted this in saying that the good sense of a responsible employer was a better guarantee for the workers than their own organisation. But he attempted to justify this statement by saying that it applied to French workers, and of their organising abilities he had begun to despair.

Two other factors he detected in industrial relations in Sheffield. One was the system of promotion. This system meant that the men attending a furnace, a hammer or a rolling mill were grouped in teams. A newcomer joined the team in the bottom position and worked his way up by a system of strict seniority. The team were paid by the ton of metal produced or processed, and the earnings were credited to each member of the team at a different rate according to his position. The other factor he mentioned was the character of the Sheffield employer. Le Play's impressions of English employers[26] were mainly of ostentation and extravagance. But the manufacturers of Sheffield, he wrote, lived more simply, espoused a puritanical religion, and were often teetotallers. Further, they gave their sons a thorough grounding in the business. These are some excerpts from lectures which, we have noted already, influenced a generation of engineers, and turned many of them towards social studies. Paternalistic some of the advice may sound; it was more humane than most of his contemporaries were giving.

1848 The Commission for the workers and the School of Administration

Eighteen forty-eight has gone down to history as the year of revolutions in Europe. The French Revolution of that year has provided much scope for speculation. The leaders have often been condemned for incompetence because they did in fact fail; but many interesting experiments were attempted in the early months of 1848, and the most cursory reading of the contemporary documents leaves an impression of what might have been. Not the least interesting of the experiments was La Commission du Gouvernement pour les Travailleurs, usually known as the Luxembourg Commission. Mention has already been made of the *Conseils de Prud'hommes* which dealt with personal disputes; the Luxembourg Commission was to be a permanent court in Paris for labour issues, and was to be made up of three elements – employers' delegates, workers' delegates and independent experts.

The Commission held its first meeting in the Luxembourg Palace on 1 March 1848. To this meeting came 200 workers, to be addressed by Louis Blanc. His idea[27] was evidently to promote discussion on the workers' problems, but he found his audience disposed to pass immediate resolutions. By the end of the meeting, two resolutions had been passed – the one to end *marchandage* (the system of subcontracting) and the other to limit the hours of work. The following day Louis Blanc summoned a meeting of the employers. They agreed to the workers' demands, which were then passed into law, and listed their problems in return. After this remarkable early success the Commission gained great prestige, and the 'independent' members were coopted to undertake an academic study of problems facing the Commission.[28]

Not only was the Luxembourg Commission the first piece of conciliation machinery of a type that has now become familiar, it proposed the first legal limitation of hours for adult male workers. After the initial proposals for industrial legislation the Commission's work took three main forms – studying current economic conditions, mediating industrial disputes, founding *associations*. It also set up an information office for workers. The studies covered many of the problems of the workers at the time, and included housing and the question of employment for prisoners. The most notable dispute involved the bakers of Paris. 'Paris was not aware,' says the official report, 'that on the morning of the 29th March, the inhabitants rose without any prospect of bread.'[29] The Commission brought together representatives of the master-bakers and their workmen as a result of which a wage-scale was drawn up and a strike avoided. Even allowing for an atmosphere in which groups of workpeople readily declared a dispute in order to see what the Commission could do for them, this shortlived body was involved in a wide range of industrial problems.

The *associations* founded by the Commission were, in fact, producers' cooperatives, a subject in which Le Play remained interested long after he was disillusioned with most of the ideas of the revolutionary movement. Initially these *associations* were promoted as a contribution to the need to get economic activities going and to find work. The one of which Louis Blanc was most proud, and which indeed was most successful, was the Association of Tailors. An old prison for debtors, at Clichy, was put at their disposal. Writing ten years later,[30] Louis Blanc said that about 2,000 unemployed tailors joined the Association: and 'I procured for them from the City of Paris an order for a hundred thousand military frocks.' Such initial contracts ensured plenty of work for the time being, and the Association soon made enough profit to repay the loans from the master-tailors that had enabled them to start. After the big contracts had been completed, the tailors' cooperative was wound up and restarted on a smaller scale, becoming one of the more permanent results of the Commission. Among other *associations* which survived the Commission's collapse were the saddlers' and the cabinet-makers'. At the Paris Exhibition of Industry of 1849 the file-cutters won a silver medal: the cabinet-makers exhibited at the London International Exhibition of 1851.

Le Play sat on two other Commissions established by the Provisional Government, both of which met under the Chairmanship of Jean Reynaud. One was set up on 12 May to investigate the problems of the coal industry.[31] The other Commission established another of the precedents set by the Provisional Government – a School of Administration. This Commission was called the High Commission on Scientific and Literary Studies,[32] and was set up soon after the new government came to power. The Commission reported on such subjects as the health of students and the expansion of primary education, but their main work was concerned with the setting up of the Ecole d'Administration. Le Play was one of the instigators of this project, which was fostered by Jean Reynaud and himself. The idea of a School of Administration was not a new one. Indeed, some scheme for teaching this subject was set up by Napoleon. After the Restoration there was an unsuccessful effort to set up a new School.[33] The one established in 1848 was for teaching administrative science to future civil servants rather than industrialists, but his enthusiasm for the project showed Le Play's strong belief that administration was a teachable subject; the part he played in the establishment and in the failure of this School showed both the strength and the weakness of his own proficiency at this 'subject'. As an obituary writer was to say many years later: 'These promoters of ideas, these great men of action, do not do their work without offending many interests, without upsetting many people.'[34]

Among the interests offended and the people upset on this particular occasion were the Collège de France and Michel Chevalier. The part that Le Play filled in this story is not clear, nor indeed is much of the story itself. But two facts are: the new School was to be organised on lines less institutional than the Ecole Polytechnique and yet with more corporate life than the University, and was to have the maximum prestige that could be given to it. The organisation was much in accordance with Le Play's ideas. He had often expressed the view that life at the Polytechnique was too narrow and restricted, but he valued some corporate life for students. In order to meet the organisational requirements and the desire for prestige, the students were to have their own building but to attend courses at the Collège de France. This link was the beginning of the School's troubles. That the authorities at the Collège never accepted this arrangement is shown by later appeals from the School to the Ministry to make them cooperate. A government decree[35] had suppressed three chairs at the Collège de France and established eleven new ones. Among the chairs suppressed was that of Political Economy held by Michel Chevalier. It has usually been suggested that the suppression of this chair (which he held for forty years apart from this brief interruption) was a political move against Chevalier because of his criticisms of certain members of the government. But there is some unexplained mystery here for the move was proposed by a commission of academics, dominated by Reynaud and Le Play, both lifelong friends of Chevalier; and in any case the change was logical because the course in Political Economy was divided between several of the new chairs. The Commission may well have thought that Chevalier's course was too narrow to allow of the rapid development in the social sciences for which they were hoping – they suggested as much when they proposed the range of subjects to be covered in future.[36] As a result of the controversy that followed Chevalier's dismissal, the government put out a statement which pointed out that he was fully occupied with his duties in the Corps des Mines.

Twelve appointments were eventually made, engineering being added to the original list. Many of the new professorships were filled by members of the Provisional Government – Jean Reynaud himself (French and Comparative Political Law), Lamartine (International Law), Ledru-Rollin (History of Administration), Garnier-Pagès (Economics and Statistics) and others. These appointments were the subject of acid comment in the press at home and abroad;[37] but the explanation would seem to be that they were intended to bring prestige to the School, and not for the benefit of the new Professors. For none of these was to be paid, and most of them never gave any lectures. 'The new Chairs . . . are entirely honorary', said the decree that announced the appointments. Six months later the old Chairs were re-established and the holders of the new ones were tactfully asked to resign. Some of them refused, preferring to wait and see what happened; some of them agreed; Poncelet (Chair of Engineering) left the matter with the Minister of Education but expressed great regret at the possible collapse of the whole project. Lamartine resigned, saying he had always regarded the appointment as purely honorary; one of them, Bineau (Chair of 'Economics and Statistics of Mining and Manufacture'), expressed the haste and confusion with which the idea had been put into practice when he wrote: 'I was appointed to this Chair without being consulted, I have not filled it for as much as a single day, and it does not exist any more; my resignation should be in the circumstances completely superfluous.'[38]

However much important personalities and interests may have been alienated by the arrangements, the prestige certainly got across to the general public. On 7 July Le Play was writing to the Minister of Public Works (after apparently failing to make contact with the Minister of Education) that they had a waiting list of 1,500 applicants. The reason for this popularity was probably the fact that successful students were guaranteed a place in the administrative services. The School was to have an annual intake of 150, and it was estimated that there were 294 suitable vacancies a year. So the guarantee would appear to have been sound.

Le Play was writing on behalf of the College Council and the Principal, who was ill. He continued to press urgently for top level decisions on a number of matters affecting the School; but times had changed. The Provisional Government had been replaced, and all its schemes were suspect even when there was any money to pay for them. On 27 July the Principal[39] wrote a bitter letter to the Minister. He clearly thought that too much attention had been paid to prestige and too little to premises. He had to have some money urgently to pay the domestic if not the teaching staff. He pointed to the many difficulties, but assumed that it would be utterly irresponsible to allow the project to collapse. His successor was writing six months later that, even after the admission of the second batch of students, they still had no heating system and no furniture in the lecture rooms. Meanwhile, in an undated report written some time during the autumn, Le Play expressed satisfaction at the calibre of the students, but desperation at the financial position. In this report he reluctantly envisaged the possibility that the School's existence might turn out to be only temporary. He asked, for instance, what would happen to students who were now too old to enter another school. In the New Year the Principal was expressing thanks to the Minister for a hint that all was not yet lost 'for our poor students and our candidates'. But in fact all was lost for the School which closed towards the end of 1849, after special arrangements had been made to transfer the students elsewhere.

This brief account of the School does less than justice to Le Play's part in the project. Throughout the hectic and frustrating months of the School's existence he was the most active member of the Council, writing several reports and innumerable private letters. If he had doomed himself to frustration by producing a scheme that was too grandiose and offended too many interests he can hardly be blamed for not foreseeing that the government would fail to find the money for their own creation. The plans for the School embodied his view that administration was a teachable subject and that the administrator needed a broad grasp of the social sciences. Selection of students was to be by competitive examination designed to test intelligence rather than knowledge. This examination was open to everyone and the School charged no fees. It would appear that in spite of all the problems and uncertainties a strong measure of corporate life was established, for many years later a group of old students still met annually. In 1866 one of them presented a petition to the government of the time for the refounding of the School. This curious postscript to the School's story shows that its indefatigable author was still in touch with 221 out of the 258 students who had once attended the courses.

1844–1853 The partnership with Demidov

Le Play's first experience as a manager was in the years 1837–39, when he supervised a survey of the Donets basin in South Russia. For this he was employed by Anatolii Demidov. Reputedly one of the richest men in the world, Demidov was a colourful character who came into contemporary history at many points; some of his career has been described in Chapter 1. His main wealth came from the Urals, but in the mid-1830s he agreed with the Tsar to furnish a large expedition to make a comprehensive survey of southern Russia – the Crimea and the Donets Valley.[40] This survey was to cover every aspect of the background and resources of the area. The expedition was mainly French, although it included some Russians. Many skills were represented, among them engineering, geology and natural science. The organisation was in two sections of which Le Play was in charge of one. His was evidently the most difficult assignment. The Crimea was comparatively fertile and civilised and had a reasonable climate. The Donets valley and the adjacent steppes were bleak, undeveloped and with some of the widest variations of temperature known anywhere. These ranged from 43 °C in the shade in summer to −28 °C in winter. Every detail, relevant or irrelevant, was catalogued – not even a species of plant escaped the vigilance of Le Play's organisation. But the results were discouraging.

Le Play made his headquarters at Lugansk, and here there was a government armaments factory to supply the Black Sea arsenals. Apart from this the main industry of the Donets valley was coal, where thirty-three seams were being exploited out of a total of ninety-four. The total output of the coal workings in 1839 was about 14,300 tons. Le Play calculated that it should be possible in the foreseeable future to multiply this by twenty up to about 320,000 tons. But this huge increase would only bring production for the area up to the level of one colliery in France, and in any case would be pointless if markets could not be found. Some of the coal was already being sold in the Black Sea ports, but here it met competition from English and French coal brought entirely by sea. The most obvious use for local coal was in the iron industry, especially as the forests which supplied charcoal had largely disappeared. But the condition of the iron industry was rudimentary. Le Play discovered fifty-one separate deposits of ore, but very few of them were being exploited. Then there was the difficulty of transport. The best coal measures and the best ore deposits were 200 miles apart and both were too far from the sea. In this matter Lugansk, the one industrial centre in the valley, was particularly badly placed. Because of water transport, the Ural and the Siberian factories were more economic. Le Play said that labour charges (including payment in kind) were so low in Siberia as to compensate for half the cost of the extra distance. He did suggest that conditions made the private development of the mineral resources difficult, and that the quickest way to industrialise would be by government initiative. He suggested that if the government factory at Lugansk used local materials this would itself stimulate industry and provide regular employment; but on balance he foresaw that a large-scale development of the area was still well in the future. In spite of this unpromising report Demidov was immensely impressed with Le Play's capacity, and especially with the high morale among his team of foreign technologists and local assistants.

In 1844 Le Play was once more working for Demidov, this time in the already industrialised Ural mountains. Here Demidov had 45,000 employees (mostly serfs) working in iron, silver, gold and platinum mines and processing works. In the eighteenth century the area had exported much of its iron to Britain, but by 1844 most of it was consumed inside Russia. After many months of investigation, Le Play produced his report and was then asked to implement it. Until 1853 he was manager of all the Demidov industrial undertakings in the Urals. Most of the time he did not live in Russia, but managed the mines and works from an office in Paris, returning to the Urals for a final tour of inspection in 1853.

The labour in the Ural mountains was still governed by 'feudal' regulations. That the relationship between master and serf could be very brutal is attested by many visitors. Le Play pointed out that the position of a serf in industry was not necessarily worse than that of a freeman. This comparison was on purely physical grounds, and was not intended as a defence of serfdom. The serf suffered many disabilities, and in any case the system was uneconomic for the masters – the serf had no incentive to conscientious work or training; the serf was expensive because of the fringe benefits involved; and the very institution of serfdom, carrying with it a labour force attached to the soil and that had to be supported whether there was work or not, produced a rigidity that was not conducive to industrial development. But the fringe benefits, or subventions as Le Play called them, and the responsibility of the master for the serf at least mitigated the physical hardships of industrial life. Le Play described how the rise of industry had affected the position of the serfs; with increasing wages and more status they had lost some of the disadvantages of serfdom. At the same time they had become westernised without acquiring all the disadvantages of the West.

The factories had a rural setting, and the worker normally worked in the factory or mine for four weeks out of five. There were two main classes of worker. The transport and other external work of the factory was normally done by semi-independent subcontractors; these formed the elite of the labour force, and were often able to buy themselves out of the obligations of serfdom. The other workers, usually much poorer, were those who worked inside the factories and mines. This system applied to heavy industry which was mostly run by the landowners or their agents and serf-workers. There was also and alongside this a typically Russian system of small industries, communally owned. These made textiles and consumer goods of all sorts. The village communities which ran these small industries paid money to the landlord, as a substitute for service, in the system known as 'obrok'. Le Play wrote of the change from the 'obrok' communities which were agricultural and had industrial sidelines to those which were industrial with agricultural sidelines. He told how many observers thought that this was the form industrialisation would take in Russia. They thought that the small industrial community was specially suited to the Russian genius. In spite of his enthusiasm for local traditions and initiatives, Le Play disagreed with this. These industrial communities, he thought, were too small to develop major industries, and besides they were held together by patriarchal ties. These ties were powerful but too rigid; they gave too much authority to the views of old age to be suitable for a dynamic and innovating industrial enterprise. In Russia, as in the West, Le Play implied, the future of heavy industry lay with large factories with professional management.

Le Play's first report on the Demidov estates in the Urals has, as explained in Chapter 1, disappeared. His second report, on the situation in the years 1851–52, after he had put some reorganisation into effect, still exists and is listed in the Bibliography as W33. This report shows his mastery of administrative detail in a complex situation. It also shows his personal conscientiousness. For the report contains four hundred pages of closely packed figures, including production and labour statistics and costs. These are sometimes calculated to 0·0001 of a working day and a similar proportion of a rouble. The entire report is in Le Play's own handwriting, and contains many thousands of observations and notes which illuminate the human, social and technical situations which lie behind the statistics. The report describes six of the local industries in turn: forestry, iron, steel, copper, gold and platinum. The figures show that the average cost of the worker is 0·658 roubles per day, where the horse costs 0·866 roubles. The silver rouble at that time was worth about 4s 6d. The free worker in an ironworks was paid 1·2 roubles; but the average was reduced by the serfs and the women and children. These figures include free meals and other fringe benefits; they were far higher than the foresters who cost 0·297 per worker and 0·417 per horse. In one of the iron mines, the extraction of 100 pounds of ore cost 1·41 roubles, made up of: direct labour, 0·73, indirect labour, 0·17, horses, 0·26, materials, 0·25.

The costings were clearly an improvement on the situation in 1844 when Le Play took over, although the earlier figures are lost. For in

c

spite of the problems of working with serf labour and overcoming traditional prejudices, Le Play evidently achieved a major reorganisation of the Ural enterprises. Working with Danilov, Demidov's steward, he achieved a considerable increase in production in ten years. In 1853, however, he resigned. Demidov was evidently sorry to lose him, and Le Play has left on record no reason for his decision. He hinted that he was having personal problems with Demidov, although from other hints he left the reason may also have been connected with the labour position. The emancipation of the serfs was clearly about to take place; and Le Play might well have been unwilling to continue to work with a system he was condemning in his current course of lectures. But the evidence for this is only hinted at in his letters. The other hint is that he was finding increasing difficulty in getting decisions out of Demidov.[41] Nevertheless, in under ten years he had achieved a major reorganisation of the Demidov metal complex, and made a contribution to the development of the Russian railway network. He had also proved that even in a serf economy, great improvements in management techniques were possible. Incidentally, the reorganised metal works were to win many awards at the International Exhibitions of the following twenty years.

Thus we have tried to demonstrate the significance of Le Play's first career – as engineer, educator, pioneer exponent of systematic methods in management and industrial relations. This career ended with his fiftieth birthday in 1856. His second career, combining the public figure with the social scientist, had already begun eight years before in 1848. In the first career, Le Play became especially interested in the relationship between technical and social change; but his interests were still mainly technical. In his second career he divested himself entirely of his activities as an engineer, but used his training in the natural sciences to study society.

3

The public figure

The Commissioner-General

The years immediately after 1848 were the busiest in Le Play's life. Had
he died in 1856, at the age of fifty, he would be no less well known
today, perhaps better known. During those years he continued his
course at the Ecole des Mines, he continued his regular tours abroad,
and until 1853 he continued to direct the Demidov enterprises as well.
During those years also he began to publish his social studies and to
develop his social theories. He became a government commissioner for
many causes, and he began his career as Exhibitioner-in-Chief for
nineteenth-century civilisation. By the middle of the century national
exhibitions of industry, commerce and culture already had a considerable history. These exhibitions were planned as shop windows by the
various nations which held them. In 1849, for instance, Paris had her
eleventh such. (Twelfth, if the Exhibition of 1797 is included. This never
actually opened, and the exhibits mysteriously disappeared. Hence 1798
is usually counted as the first.) There were seven stages in running these
exhibitions. First came the setting up of the organisation and recruitment of staff. Next, the buildings to house the exhibition had to be
designed and erected; some of these were temporary, but others were
to be permanent. In themselves they were intended to represent
contemporary architecture or technology, and many cities still have
public buildings which were originally erected as part of an exhibition.
The third stage was the collection of the exhibits: this included measures
to encourage exhibitors, and arrangements for the transport and care
of exhibits; when the exhibitions became international elaborate
arrangements had to be made for waiving tariffs without producing
wholesale smuggling. Fourthly, the making of awards for each class of
exhibit had to be organised, and this included the setting up of international panels of judges.

The major task of the administration of the exhibition as a whole
involved the scheduling of all the various operations, including the
opening and closing ceremonies. After the exhibition was over voluminous reports had to be compiled. The seventh and final stage was the

dismantling of the exhibition and the gradual rundown and final dissolution of the organisation.

The present writer has no information at all about the organising of the latest of the series of international exhibitions – 'Montreal: Expo. 67'; but it can be assumed that the administration differed notably from 'Paris 1867'. While many of the motives may have been similar in each case, at the former Exhibition a regime as well as a culture was on show, and the regime meant the Emperor Louis Napoleon. Notoriously delegation always has its problems, but a large element of personal control was inevitable in exhibitions such as Paris 1867, for its successes were the successes of Louis Napoleon, its failures his failures. There was a sense in which Le Play as Commissioner-General was a viceroy, and much consultation was inevitable. Le Play may have been temperamentally unsuited to delegating sufficiently, but again the system meant that he was bound to keep a close watch on a mass of detail under all seven of the headings outlined above.

At the Paris Exhibition of 1849 Le Play had taken a small part in the organisation and, as a member of the Jury, drafted the report on the steel section. In London in 1851 he was a member of the French Commission, and this time wrote the French report on the cutlery and tools section. This Exhibition was the first of the international exhibitions, and was on a completely different scale from the earlier ones. As soon as it was over, the Imperial Government in Paris planned one on a similar scale. This was to take place in 1855 with Prince Napoleon as President of the Imperial Commission, and General Morin as Commissioner-General. Le Play was appointed a member of this Commission. The organisation of this Exhibition did not match the ambitious plans, and there was the further complication that by 1855 France was at war with Russia. At the beginning of the year the opening date was finally fixed for the first of May. During the early spring, the official *Moniteur universel* printed optimistic statements about the preparations, but the Exhibition was still not ready when 1 May arrived, although that date had been confirmed as recently as 9 March. Only on 27 April was the opening postponed to 15 May. The official opening ceremony was held on this day, but the Exhibition was still not ready and there was chaos everywhere. Finally, a few days later, Prince Napoleon sacked Morin – and appointed Le Play as Commissioner-General. Thus Le Play suddenly became a public figure, the man brought in to salvage the exhibition and the reputation of his country. His appointment was announced on 22 May, and brought an immediate protest from the assistant director writing on behalf of the senior administrative staff.[1] They obviously did not think General Morin to blame for the problems that had arisen. As part of the reorganisation the Fine Arts Exhibition, which had previously been managed independently, was also brought under Le Play's direction. The English report says, with some irony, that 'the concluding ceremony took place with great success and punctuality, on the 15th of November, owing to the excellent arrangements of M. Le Play, the Commissioner General'. This report also singles out one feature of the exhibition which was part of Le Play's own contribution – that prizes were awarded to foremen, workmen and others even though they were not direct exhibitors.

In October 1861 Le Play was in London organising the French part of the 1862 Exhibition. Prince Napoleon left all the organisation of this to Le Play, only smoothing the way by high-level contacts. When the prince visited the Exhibition he did so incognito, and only Le Play himself was supposed to know who this French Count really was. One plan, by which both the Prince and Le Play set great store, was for groups of workmen from Paris to visit London in order to meet and see the work of their opposite numbers in England. Le Play tried to get this scheme extended to include workers from other parts of France, but Prince Napoleon vetoed this on the grounds that it was hard enough as it was to sell the idea in Paris. The scheme was for the workers to spend a reasonable length of time in London with an interpreter so that they could really have the opportunity of studying English life and workmanship. To this end the Commission made the necessary arrangements with employers and attended to the finances. For the rest, they left the workmen to manage their own affairs. The first party went to London in the middle of July, and included some of the Prince's own employees. By the end of the month there were complaints about accommodation in London, and talk of exploitation. Bitterly disappointed at this setback to their efforts not to behave paternalistically, the Prince wrote to Le Play that he was 'sorry without being surprised', for 'in our unhappy country you have to put people "in leading strings" '. Clearly this breakdown played into the hands of those who argued that everything must be organised from the top, and that you could not trust the workers. The records do not show whether the Prince and Le Play knew that the contacts between the French and British workers had not just been on a technical level – they had stimulated the growth of an international trade unionism.[2] However, both the visits and the workers' committee continued, a tribute to Le Play's patient determination to see that they should. But this happened only after six members of the workers' committee had been eased out. These wrote to the Prince appealing to his well known 'liberal sympathies' to get them reinstated. The Prince drily replied that he demonstrated his 'liberal sympathies' by leaving the workers to run their own affairs. Unfortunately, the matter did not end there, and at the end of August there were further complaints from the workers' delegates.

In the middle of 1863 Prince Napoleon was already writing to Le Play that it was time to start making plans for the 1867 Exhibition, and for this Exhibition Le Play was the executive Commissioner from the start, with the Prince as Chairman. Certain conditions made this Exhibition a great test of managerial skill. It was on a difficult site, and it had to pay.[3] It also had to be bigger than any previous exhibition.[4] In the event, most reports give a mixture of praise and blame. Le Play showed his ability to maintain a high morale among the workers building it, by getting the job finished on time in spite of immense difficulties. He also made a virtue of the need to plan the Exhibition on a large scale by introducing a novel arrangement, which was widely praised, although doubt has been cast on Le Play's claim to have invented it.[5] The main exhibition hall was laid out so that if you went round the circular gangways you saw the same product but for different countries, whereas if you went up and down the aisles you saw the different products of one country.

The criticisms mostly arose from the pressure for profits, which was all too congenial to Le Play's thrifty nature. All the English reports refer to the 'meanness' of the French Commission, both in the arrangements for exhibitors and in the sizes of the awards.[6] Possibly the fact that the Commission refused free passes to foreign journalists helped to make this particular complaint so widespread. There were also complaints about arbitrary decisions by the Imperial Commission. It appears that decrees were passed and rescinded to the confusion of hard-pressed exhibitors. One notable report was by an English journalist, George Sala.[7] Sala had lately been in America, where he had been covering the Civil War, and perhaps this was why he felt able to describe the Paris Exhibition as 'stupendous'. On the other hand he, too, refers to the meanness of the Commissioners; he also thinks they blundered on many points. In an amusing passage he shows how Le Play's pessimism could affect his handling of men. It appears that Le Play was much concerned about entrance payments. He devised a new type of turnstile for use at the Exhibition, and stationed two men at each. According to Sala one man took your money, and the other pushed it through the slot. The idea of having two men was that one should watch the other. Instead suspicion grew that they paired up to cheat the management, and a *sergent de ville* was appointed to watch each pair. However, three turned out to be a perfect team for further frauds and other police and detectives were drafted to watch them. Perhaps from this Le Play learned a principle of industrial relations he had little suspected hitherto.

But with all the criticisms, Sala pays generous tribute to the achievements. In view of the problems that had had to be overcome, 'M. Le Play certainly achieved a success which, impartially considered, may be accounted a triumph'. Sala particularly notices the underlying philosophy which rewarded workmanship and the social skills of industry. The award of prizes to individuals and not just to firms caught Sala's imagination. Of the 1867 Exhibition, Sala writes that he has never reported 'One sight more noble, more comfortable, and more genuine than this; that the rulers of the nations had assembled', not for some diplomatic manoeuvre, but to declare publicly 'that if Jacques Bonhomme had made a good cabinet of walnutwood he deserved to be honoured among men for it'. In addition to the awarding of prizes to foremen and workmen, and others who were not direct exhibitors, Le Play introduced an entirely new set of awards for industrial relations.

This new class, an innovation in 1867, was instituted in favour of establishments and localities which developed harmony between people working together on the same jobs, and which assured to the workers material, intellectual and moral wellbeing. The Jury which made these awards was a weighty body including four ministers, the Archbishop of Paris (Monsignor Darboy, later to be shot by the communards), Monsieur Schneider (proprietor of the famous firm at Le Creusot and President of the Legislative Corps), and representatives of other nations taking part. The British Government, however, refused to nominate a representative to this particular Jury and thus disqualified any British entrants. The Jury, which was entirely of employers, was inclined to take a paternalistic view of industrial relations. But, as on other occasions, Le Play showed that he himself saw beyond paternalism by inviting the trade unions (although still technically illegal) to nominate their own panel and to produce their own report on the competition. In any case, members of the Jury showed awareness of the dangers of their outlook. They said in the introduction to their report that they were looking for 'an intelligent as well as a generous patronage which respects the dignity and the liberty of the subordinate'.[8]

The reporter for the Jury on Industrial Relations was Alfred Le Roux, who was vice-president of the Legislative Corps. In the opening passages of the report he uses phrases typical of Le Play, with whom he was closely associated; these phrases concern the breaking of family ties and the promotion of hate and division as the marks of an industrial society. The Jury was to be concerned with facts and not opinions, and an entrant would first of all be vetted by a juror of his own country. Hence no country could take part which did not nominate jurors. The result is a picture of managerial practices in many parts considered more satisfactory than the average according to criteria largely worked out by Le Play.

The first prize went to von Diergardt, owner of a silk and velvet mill at Viersen in Prussia. This firm had a bonus scheme, a sick club, a pension scheme, a strict but humane system of discipline and free education for workers' children at local schools. These features it shared with most of the prize-winners; but four additional features earned them the top award. A high degree of mutual understanding between management and workers, which had enabled them to settle all disputes within the works was placed first. Then they showed stability of employment; this employer had made great efforts not to reduce his labour force during periods of slump. Thirdly, the firm had a system of loans to employees to enable them to buy smallholdings to reduce their dependence on the company. And fourthly, they made special arrangements for the employment of women. No married women were employed at all inside the factory but attempts were made to overcome any hardship this might cause by farming out work which might suitably be done at home.

Many of the reports tended to concentrate on the contribution of the employer to wellbeing in the local community; but in Belgium the zinc foundry firm of Vieille-Montagne was described as strike-free in a strike-prone country. This firm had begun to train its workpeople for greater participation by representative thrift and welfare committees inside their plants. They also had a system of long-term contracts with their workpeople, and a bonus system which included putting half the bonus into a savings account. Of one United States firm it was stressed that efforts had been made to increase workers' participation and reduce the amount of activities and benefits that were just 'laid on' by the firm. This was W. Chapin & Company, Spinners and Manufacturers, of Lawrence (Massachusetts). They had a range of social security schemes run by the workers. Further, they encouraged the sale of voting shares to the workers. Schneider & Company did not enter the competition since Monsieur Schneider was on the Jury, but one of the French prizewinners was Le Play's own publisher – Mame & Company, of Tours, printer, publisher and bookseller, with a plant capable of producing 20,000 books a day. This was one of the firms about which the report referred to the selection of supervisors, and the contribution this made to improved working conditions. Once again continuity of employment was attempted, and mention was made of a sale by the proprietors of a family estate in 1848 to avoid the dismissal of workers. They had a sick club and a pension scheme as well. The town of Guebwiller was a locality which won a prize. This was an area with a good tradition of industrial relations and local institutions. Here forty years before a local manufacturer, J.-J. Bourcart, had made a famous protest against the employment of children. Bourcart's own firm had now developed a copartnership scheme. Various firms in the town had workers' committees for negotiation with the employers. Other firms had such committees and some, like Auzous's, at Erceville, dealt with all disciplinary matters.

This is a brief survey of some of the more interesting attempts to improve industrial relations brought out in the report. Naturally, the effect is mixed and the judgments are sometimes superficial. Any reader of the literature of the time, such as the novels of Zola, will have been warned to be careful about taking at their face value firms' claims to provide good houses and social services for the workers. With the experience of a century since 1867, too, a modern evaluation would regard concealed additions to wages, such as subsidised pension schemes and housing, as less important than education and selection and schemes designed to foster workers' participation. The additions to wages, in any case, tended to disappear when economic conditions deteriorated. That this was already happening was affirmed by a writer in an article in *La Revue des Deux Mondes*[9] criticising the whole conception of the competition. The author of this article, Louis Reybaud, was a right-wing politician who yet had considerable sympathy for the aspirations of the workers. He took the view that it was unrealistic to expect a few eminent and very busy men to have sufficient time to decide such subtle questions as the terms of the competition posed. He asked how, in any case, works of physical and moral improvement could be judged; and how anyone could be considered such a paragon among his fellows as to deserve the first prize of 100,000 francs.

He also compared the sense of responsibility of the English workers with that of the French. He said that there was a naked war of wages in England, but this was a sign that the workers were free and not kept in the 'stupor of despotism' to be grateful for crumbs from their masters. These 'crumbs', in the form of fringe benefits which might win prizes at this competition, were disappearing under the pressure for higher wages. The result of the struggle in England had been the evolution of
*

some rough and ready methods of negotiation for settling disputes. If the French would do this, says Reybaud, 'the manufacturers would have in front of them regularly elected delegates, and not this turbulent rabble which is as incapable of setting out clearly its demands as it is prompt to back them up by acts of violence'. Reybaud pointed out how bad the old small workshops could be, and how the irresponsibility of the employers had produced the slogan 'products are made for men, not men for products'. This slogan would seem to support the outlook which inspired the competition, but Reybaud thought that the documents considered by the Jury of 1867 as evidence of good employment practices would remain as 'archives of their too short history'.

When the trade union delegates produced their reports[10] they tended to confirm Reybaud's forecast. They supported the idea of such a competition, but disagreed strongly with the way it had been handled; they denounced particularly the awarding of prizes by a jury without a single trade union representative. Not unnaturally the workers' delegates thought a living wage the most important factor in industrial life, and since they did not have this they considered all the so-called improvements in their conditions irrelevant. They gave six reasons why wages were not sufficient: the employer took more than his fair share, the cost of living was inflated by parasitic intermediaries, opportunities for extra income by work at home were disappearing, the labour market was being flooded by too many apprentices, there were taxes on necessities, the workers themselves were their own worst enemies. This last point showed an element of self-criticism which ran all through the workers' reports, and contrasted with the self-satisfaction of so many of the employers' comments. The other points exhibited an interesting mixture of earlier industrial methods – home industry – with more modern declaration of class strife, the attacks on employers and intermediaries. The limitation on apprenticeships was a theme from the earlier stages of industrialisation, which survived into much later stages. On the subject of apprenticeship, self-criticism was again expressed. For the parent, the workers, the children and the employers were all attacked for the current state of affairs. The printers condemned the whole system, saying: 'Apprenticeship is not just a badly directed education it is a shameful exploitation, which imposes on the child during a period of six or seven years a working day of fourteen to sixteen hours, prematurely using up his strength.' The workers' delegates were very much against the employment of women in industry.

The workers' reports showed dislike of the use of the strike weapon.

Some even suggested that it was out-of-date. The Vicomte de Melun, in opening a discussion at the Société d'Economie Sociale, made an interesting point here. Speaking to a gathering of fellow-employers and professional people who were all too apt to say that the workers did not really want to strike but were being misled by a few agitators, he said the opposition to strikes could easily be misunderstood. Kings were always opposed to war, he pointed out, and the attitude of the trade unions to strikes was to be understood in this sense. They did not fight any less wholeheartedly because they regarded this choice of weapon as a last resort. To replace strikes, the workers recommended industrial courts. Recourse to these courts should be voluntary, but they must be given some 'teeth'. Little hope was expressed that the employers would accept them.

On existing laws which restricted the workers' rights, strong views were naturally expressed. There should be no limitations on the right to hold meetings, or on associations, and the *livret*[11] should be abolished. Much was hoped from institutions such as cooperative societies, although there was wide disagreement about their future. On the other hand there were strong reservations about profit-sharing schemes. Workers' councils were needed, although problems here were acknowledged. These were connected with lack of education, and the demand for more education for youngsters and adults came into all the reports. Many of the prize-winning employers had in fact helped to promote education schemes in their own areas; but most workers were not interested in schemes provided by employers. Among proposals for better health provision was a suggestion that industrial casualties should be treated as the casualties of war.

One-third of the trade union reports advocated wage-fixing combined with compulsory arbitration; and above all they expressed a desire for equal partnership with the employers, and more chances of meeting both formal and informal. Alongside this went expressions of great bitterness and suspicion. The engineers, for instance, attacked vehemently many of the institutions which won prizes at the competition. They regarded these institutions as decoys to pacify the workers without meeting their just demands. It would be a considerable understatement to say that the view of the Jury on Industrial Relations did not match the workers' expectations; but it would still be true that Le Play brought the importance of industrial relations before the public, and showed that it was possible to make a factory a better place to work in and an industrial area a better place to live in, and that this was a suitable subject for public discussion at an International Exhibition. When the reports were discussed by the Société d'Economie Sociale, a M. Carlhian, himself an employer, spoke about the tribunals of commerce. If bodies such as these, he said, could resolve disputes between merchants in ways which everyone accepted, some parallel bodies should be found for industry. He was quite clear that these would only work if the workers were convinced that they were brought in as equal partners.

A contrary view was expressed by the General Manager of the Paris Omnibus Company, Monsieur Lavollée. He thought the only inequality in the *Conseils de Prud'hommes*[12] at the time was the state-appointed chairman, and he could not see why the workers did not accept this. After all, he said, they accepted state-appointed magistrates. Monsieur Lavollée was also critical of the workers' reports in general, and could not understand why his colleagues thought so highly of them. He could find nothing new in them, and much progress had been made since 1848 and made by the efforts of politicians acting on behalf of the workers. To this the Vicomte de Melun, who had earlier praised the statesmanship and unanimity of the workers, drily remarked that the politicians had required a great deal of prodding. During the discussion a Belgian lawyer and member of the society, Charles Boddaert, suggested that the experience of England was useful here. He then used an argument that was frequently used by Le Play that the English trade unions had become a force for industrial peace. He emphasised particularly that the unions were large and powerful bodies with a great deal at stake. They would not easily recognise a strike that had broken out as a result of a snap vote on the shop-floor, and since the national executives dispensed the strike pay, unofficial strikes were usually kept in check. Boddaert also referred to the role of the English consumer cooperatives in helping the workers to make the best use of their resources. At the end of the discussion, Le Play said that the opportunity given to the workers to express their views had been fully justified. This was no mere platitude, rather it was a sigh of relief. He could not have been unaware that the invitation to the workers to appoint their own official delegation was giving a recognition to the trade union movement in advance of the legal position at the time. The results could have been disastrous. In the event the workers' delegates behaved with a responsibility which impressed the more open-minded bourgeoisie, and yet spoke with a bitterness that impressed them even more.

There was another group of workers at this Exhibition. These were not delegates but were recruited by the Society of Arts and other public bodies in England to visit Paris and see the work of their opposite numbers there. The idea and the organisation was based on the visit of the Paris workers to London in 1862. The English workers were skilled men and over 2,000 of them had visited Paris by the end of the Exhibition. They came from London, Sheffield, Coventry, Bradford, Newcastle-under-Lyme and Birmingham. Their reports[13] gave a fascinating selection of contrasts between English and French industry. Most of the reports were concerned with technical matters, but some of them had references to industrial relations. For instance, George Howell, a bricklayer and one-time secretary of the London Trades Council, spoke very highly of the work of the *Conseils de Prud'hommes*. On the subject of trade unions he remarked that the French habit of living so much out-of-doors allowed for continuing discussion and propaganda in spite of the legal handicaps to meetings, and that solidarity came more naturally to the French workers than the English. The French guide and interpreter for the English party, a Monsieur Fouché, was a workers' representative on a *Conseil de Prud'hommes*.

Two of the English workers were briefed to bring back reports on social conditions in France. The fact that they were not picked for being sycophantic to the English employers was shown by the comment of one of them on the amount of Sunday work in France. If this was extended to England, he says, it would help 'to bring on the time when capitalists will discover that it is against the laws of political economy to keep mills empty and machinery standing idle during one whole seventh of the week'. This reporter, Robert Coningsby, stressed the high standard of technical education in France. He made the point, again often made by Le Play, that there was a close connection between this and improved industrial relations. Saying that the young French workman was much more likely to attend technical courses (some of them full-time) than his English opposite number, he continued:

It is notorious to all who are acquainted with our factory system, that English foremen are deficient in that theoretical knowledge which alone can ensure economy in human effort. Our mechanics are perhaps superior in physical strength, perseverance, and correctness of manipulation, to the mechanics of any nation in the world: but the want of system in the utilisation of this splendid human material is outrageous.[14]

Coningsby found in France, perhaps partly as a result of the campaigns of Le Play and his friends, more social insurance and more incentives to saving than in England. He doubted the quality of some French charity: 'With us the pauper is too harshly treated, but in France charity seems rather overdone.' The normal working week he found to be longer in France than in England.

During his visit, Coningsby was taken to Le Creusot where most of the directors were friends or pupils of Le Play.[15] He noted what a great feat of organisation this famous industrial complex was; he also noted that the town had good houses and schools and no police. He considered wages low, but then so was the productivity of the workmen; and he noted a core of English craftsmen receiving much higher wages. He found better relationships here than he was accustomed to in England, and a less strict discipline. He was clearly astonished at the ambivalent attitude of the French authorities towards the unions. On the one hand they were hampered by many more restrictive laws than in Britain, but on the other hand they had a place in the factory which this particular reporter clearly could not imagine happening at home. For instance, at Le Creusot he found that if a man was dismissed, his union official could visit the employer and in his presence ask the man if he had any complaints at his treatment. This action had behind it the power of the *Conseil de Prud'hommes* to order the man's reinstatement if the injustice of his dismissal could be established. Like the other English observers this reporter was impressed with the work of the *conseils*, but pointed out that they could only act on individual complaints – 'If more than one man has a grievance, he is not allowed to say "*we* require such and such alterations, but *I* wish for so and so".' He thought the new English system of conciliation which had just received parliamentary sanction and had already been working for some years in Nottingham was superior.

That English workmen understood some of Le Play's aims in the Exhibition was shown by another of them, Richard Whiting, who wrote, '. . . for the first time in the history of exhibitions, labour has obtained a recognition adequate to its importance among human interests'. Whiting touched on a point which had caused sharp divisions of opinion within the Le Play school when he said that in France government action was more readily accepted than in England. He put the superiority of French technical education, which he also noted, down to this. He also considered that apprentices were more carefully supervised than in England.

This study of the situation of the workers in 1867 shows how Le Play provided a framework for discussion of social issues. He was determined that the great exhibitions could be used to promote this type of dialogue, just as much as the technical and scientific. His experience, however, left him doubtful of the value of these exhibitions.

His concluding lengthy report on 1867[16] listed many reasons why the results of the exhibitions did not match the work involved. Hence he suggested that a permament exhibition, situated in a new town outside Paris, should be set up instead. This imaginative scheme was intended to subserve many objects, but especially the educational and social aims which he considered were not being adequately met at present.

The Commissioner-in-General

Le Play was Commissioner-General for the Universal Exhibitions of 1855 and 1867. He might well have been called Commissioner-in-General between those years. Anthony Sampson has written (in *The Anatomy of Britain To-Day*, London, 1965) that: 'Lord Plowden and Lord Franks, the two omnipresent inquisitors, have tiptoed round from committee to committee, tactfully suggesting that all is not quite what it might be.' This description would admirably have fitted Le Play a century earlier. In those years between the Exhibitions he organised or took part in innumerable investigations including one on the state of the coal industry (1858), one on dangerous and unhealthy dwellings (1858), one on employment exchanges, one on the supervision of a public lottery (1856), one on the determination of paternity, one on technical education (1863), one on Sunday leisure, one on the state of the countryside and absentee landlords (1866), one on public works (1858), one on decentralisation and local government (1858), one on the bakery industry of Paris (1857–59) and one on the state of industrial relations in the provinces. The Emperor's letter announcing this last-named investigation shows clear signs of Le Play's influence and uses some of his phrases. It was addressed to all the Prefects and to other officials inside France, and many consuls abroad. It asked for a report on the quality of relationships between employers and employed in each official's area, and the reasons he can discover for the state of affairs. Le Play noted that the Emperor wanted to check the spread of 'hire and fire' in France and did not wish to see the extension of a system whereby 'In case of industrial crisis or illness, the worker ceases to be chargeable on the manufacturer, and has to ask for the means of subsistence from the innumerable charitable institutions which multiply every day, under the influence of a sentiment that is both honourable and stupid.' The point of the enquiry was to find out the factors which made for better relationships, to assess how social security schemes could be promoted through industry, and to collect facts for a policy on the siting of industry.

The response to this enquiry was very disappointing to Le Play. Some of the Prefects did not seem to be aware that there was any industry in their Departments. Many of them were far too optimistic, and wrote that the workers were devoted[17] to their employers, to the establishment and to the government. Others, in Le Play's view the more intelligent Prefects, produced even more disturbing results. They realised that there was a problem, they knew relations were bad – the Prefect of the Bouches-du-Rhône spoke of the unjust claims and the evil doctrines of the workers – but they suggested that the problem was insoluble. The government, Le Play thought, should do something about this fatalistic attitude. He told the Emperor that his enquiries had shown that the workers were just as concerned as the employers about relationships, if not more so, and one-sided strictures were not justified. The Prefects did not seem to have any idea at all of the workers' point of view. Le Play suggested that the causes of good and bad relations were very complex, but security and insecurity were among the most important.

There was evidence that permanent employment was appreciated even where wages were low, discipline strict and work hard; and, vice versa, there was discontent where there was no security even if wages were high and conditions good. Le Play still believed that there were advantages in small groupings of industry in a rural setting, but now said clearly that the main problem was improving relationships in industries which had to be in great urbanised areas. He finally suggested that it was essential to get at the facts and in view of the failure of the enquiry a small expert commission should be set up.

Of the eighty-six Prefects, thirty-five sent in replies on which Le Play commented with phrases like 'inadequate' or 'facts little studied'; in spite of the thinness of the reports and the insensitivity of so many of the Prefects, the broad outline that appears is as expected. In the larger towns and in the larger factories there was most disaffection, which the Prefects usually ascribed to dangerous doctrines among the workers; only three put part of the blame on the employers. Good relations were usually ascribed, where they existed, to local traditions or good employers. One Prefect spoke about secret workers' organisations; two Prefects flatly denied the connection between rural industry and good relations. One Prefect, on the other hand, suggested that industry should be carefully segregated in the towns so that the countryside should not be contaminated by revolutionary ideas. His report, from the

Bas Rhin, was described by Le Play as 'an outstanding reply, although often mistaken'.[18] Although this enquiry does not seem to have been followed up, further enquiries were made in the 1870s. Le Play was in retirement by this time, but the influence of his work on these enquiries was commented on. Through them his ideas did eventually influence labour legislation.[19]

Much earlier in his life (1836–37) he had bombarded the appropriate Ministry in Paris with memoranda advocating the necessity of rapidly developing the coal industry in France. In those days he had made three points: that British prosperity rested on coal, that this had been developed by private enterprise, and that France, unlike both Britain and Russia, could not solve her economic problems just domestically. She had to look to Europe. That last point was one of many which he did not pursue far, although it must appear today as if it would have been most worth pursuing. The other two he had the chance of promoting in the period now being considered. It is notable that in spite of his theoretical advocacy of private enterprise, in practice he always assumed that the state engineers of the Corps de Mines would supervise any developments that might take place in the mining industry. At this time the railways were developing rapidly and many members of the Le Play circle, like Auguste Cochin, were involved in this expansion.

The alternative to either state or private enterprise, the cooperative movement, was much discussed at the time. This is mentioned in different connections elsewhere in this study; Le Play showed some interest in cooperatives. Indeed he showed some support for those that actually existed, while doubting whether cooperation was a suitable method of organisation for large-scale industry. However, it was assumed that he had sympathy for the cooperatives by people like Prince Napoleon, who wrote obviously expecting Le Play to support his own idea of giving some money to help establish consumers' cooperatives.[20] But he devotes considerable space in La Réforme sociale to illustrating the problems of producers' cooperatives, and why he thinks that 'individual initiative is the true principle of social action'.[21] This point is mentioned again in Chapter 5 in connection with Le Play's theory of organisation.

The subject for which Le Play conducted his most sustained campaign was testamentary freedom. His long, repetitive arguments on this subject do not make easy reading, nor is it a subject which impresses as of great historical concern. But it shows Le Play's mind at work on some of the social problems of his time. As the law stood, only a certain proportion of a man's estate could be bequeathed as he wished; the rest had to be shared equally between his sons. Le Play argued that this law, which had been designed to break up the large estates, had had a devastating effect on the smallholdings. Indeed, many large landowners had found means of avoiding its effects; but the small farmers, wine-growers and horticulturalists and some of the small rural industries, on all of which French prosperity depended, were hard hit by the law. He had first made this point in writing in *Les Ouvriers européens* (1855). He was engaged in public debate two years later as a result, curiously enough, of an article in the London *Times*. On previous occasions (*The Economist*, in 1848, for instance) the French law on inheritance had been ridiculed by the English press, perhaps on the basis of evidence furnished by Le Play; but this time *The Times* ran an article on the decline of population in France sparked off by the recent publication of the quinquennial census. This article (the first leader for 15 April 1857) put down the decline in population to the effects of the wars at the beginning of the century and the poverty of the peasantry. On the first point it says that between 1792 and 1815 'the French fought more battles than we have since the beginning of our history'. The poverty of the peasantry is mainly ascribed to the 'enforced division of property'. This, of course, was just what Le Play was saying. A French newspaper invited his views.[22] He wrote that *The Times* had pointed out that the French population trend was running counter to the rest of Europe. Three main reasons were suggested for this – war, social services (alleged to encourage the less fruitful elements in the population) and *partage forcé* (enforced division of inheritance). The Anglo-Saxons (Le Play actually called them *Anglo-normands*!) have no doubt that testamentary freedom is essential to progress, and cannot understand why the French retain it, especially when the harmful effects on the state of agriculture are obvious.

This discussion gave Le Play the opportunity to point to the complexity of social causation. In his view war has only a temporary influence. The decline in the birth-rate was due to a number of factors – social antagonisms, lack of hope for the future, instability in family, workshop and state. *Partage forcé* contributes to all these. It breaks up the smallholdings and small businesses, it also removes the authority of the father who cannot dispose of his property according to the capacity or deserts of his sons. Le Play's idea is of the family as a self-governing unit in which *partage forcé* takes away an important sanction. In further support of his view, he quotes the fact that in other countries such a law has mainly been used with specific objects. For instance, Le Play says, in the British Isles it has been used only in Ireland to break up the Catholic estates, Protestants being exempt. To this theme he constantly returned, arguing that only an obstinate and one-sided egalitarianism prevented a change. He alleged that in an interview in 1858 the Emperor agreed with his view. Be this as it may, the Emperor did set up a high-powered commission to consider the matter – consisting of Le Play, Schneider (the Vice-President of the Legislative Assembly) and the Minister of Agriculture, Rouher. Le Play later wrote that his monograph on the Marseilles' soap-boiler was written as part of this report.[23]

In the light of what is now known about the growth and decline of the birth-rate it is not surprising that Le Play failed to convince his contemporaries that the laws of inheritance were a determining factor. Nor indeed did he convince them that his arguments were factual and those of his opponents ideological, although no doubt the ideology was very important. Montesquieu, whom he often quoted with approval, had argued on the contrary that primogeniture kept down the birth-rate. Levasseur points out that Malthus supports Montesquieu rather than Le Play but that his own researches do not confirm either point of view.[24] Another example occurs in the controversy published by *La Patrie*. Here another *Conseiller d'Etat*, Monsieur de la Guéronnière argues that the Napoleonic code does leave the father some discretion. He can dispose of half his inheritance if he has one child, one-third if he has two, and one-quarter if he has more; and yet most fathers do in fact leave equal amounts to all their children. Emile Ollivier, on the other hand, flatly told Le Play that 'on principle I do not recognise any right of the child on the goods of its father'.[25] The campaign culminated in 1865 when Baron de Veauce collected fifty-six signatories to a resolution for the modification of the laws of inheritance and the increase of the rights of fathers. The result was a fiasco. The resolution received far less votes than it had signatories and was defeated by a majority of nearly 200.[26]

This ignominious defeat did not deter Le Play. Indeed, when he retired from all his official posts with the dissolution of the senate in 1870, he spent much time mounting a campaign on the laws of inheritance. Among organisations for this purpose were the Unions de la Paix Sociale, as they were called. These unions were Le Play's great interest in his last years. They were small local organisations loosely federated through a central annual meeting. Apart from the coordinating office in Paris these unions were independent neighbourhood groups. They received propaganda literature, and any of Le Play's writings, at cost price from the publisher, and distributed some to their poorer neighbours. 'For', says Le Play, 'experience has shown the Unions that, in our age of error, alms-giving in the form of traditional truths is more lacking than that of daily bread.'[27] The traditional wisdom that they propagate is not concerned with political or religious controversies. It is common to the socialist revolutionary who talks about his 'splendid creed' ('le magnifique symbole') and the priest who talks about the 'everlasting law' ('le Décalogue éternel'). There was a strong moral bias in the membership of the unions. To Le Play they were the practical side of his strategy. La Société d'Economie sociale was the theoretical side, promoting empirical social science. *Les Unions* were small groups of practical men aiming to put his discoveries into practice. They were a new form of public work for the 'Commissioner-in-General' disillusioned with public life.

4
The social scientist

By 1856 Le Play the technologist had become Le Play the social scientist; he himself never used the word 'sociologist', being suspicious of Comte. His technical writings had been abandoned, and his first social studies published. He had resigned his professorship, and been appointed to the Conseil d'Etat. He had left the School of Mines and was in the process of forming a 'School' of social research. We have already said that his life divides into two. But to overemphasise the significance of this change is to miss the significance of his life. At all times Le Play was both engineer and social scientist; this point cannot be laboured too much. In the first half of his life he was primarily a technologist, but studied the social implications of technical decisions. In the second half of his life he looked at society through the eyes of an engineer. He fought, we have already noted, the same battle on both fields – the subject must develop through empirical study and not reasoning *a priori*. How closely linked were the engineer and the sociologist is well illustrated by an incident reported by one of Le Play's biographers, Charles de Ribbe.[1] This latter lived in the Rhone valley, scene of a major flood disaster in 1856. The following year he came to Paris armed with a detailed collection of facts about the deforestation of the Alps and the contribution this had made to the flood. He was recommended to see Le Play as a likely ally. He describes how the conversation changed from trees to foresters, and he found himself subjected to a searching enquiry about the way of life and family customs of the inhabitants of Provence. He found later in the conversation that his host was also very knowledgeable about forests. His parting words were: 'It is not just a question of reconstructing the forests, it is a question also of remaking men and families.'

Le Play, not unnaturally, derived his method of study from Descartes. Defending his method, he frequently quoted: '. . . for it seemed to me that I could encounter many more truths in the argument that any particular person might make concerning the matters which were important to him, than in those which men of letters produced in their studies.' Basically, he set out to collect social data, classify this data and then draw out of it some general laws of society. The social survey was already well established when Le Play began to write; and the great French exponent, Dr Villermé,[2] was one of his mentors, and first President of his Society. But previous work had had a more modest purpose, usually the accurate description of a situation in order to advocate the need for reform. The social studies had no generalising objective. But Le Play was, up to 1870 at any rate, more interested in analysis than amelioration, and hence he immediately met a problem novel in his day – how to select the problems to be investigated. 'We have a lot to do', he wrote to de Ribbe in understandable frustration, 'to complete the fundamentals of the science. What I have written rests on the observation of 300 families, and we should have thousands. Our science is still in the imperfect state that mineralogy would be if you had only studied the minerals.'[3]

'Study the facts,' Le Play constantly urged, 'wander around the society you are looking at and get to know it thoroughly.' This doctrine was crucial to his method and to his whole outlook. 'The time is not far distant', he once wrote optimistically, 'when the fact that an author has not moved out of his study will be sufficient refutation of his theory.'[4] The possibility of being able to generalise from large numbers of case studies has, of course, been much debated since and is discussed below. Alfred Marshall said of Le Play's method: 'At its best, it is the best of all.' He argued, however, that a great deal depends on the observer who must combine great skill in selection with sympathy in interpretation. For normal purposes he considered that an 'extensive' method with facts presented in statistical form was more reliable.[5] One of Le Play's followers emphasised the importance of the discipline of his method in the development of social science. Without the method, it was said, 'social science is only like astrology or alchemy, covering its nakedness with a declamatory pomp, serving the most disastrous theories, justifying the most risky efforts, leading to disaster those whom it claims to guide' (Cheysson).

The actual method that Le Play did adopt was to study a culture through a representative family. This method involved two pre-suppositions – one that the family was the basic social unit, and the other that it was possible to devise means of discovering a representative family. This latter should be understood in the light of the conception suggested above, that large numbers of studies would be undertaken. Le Play regarded his own studies as curtain-raisers to the major effort which was to follow. Even so he went to considerable lengths to study the district and the major occupations so that he knew what he wanted when he looked for his representative family. Occupation, number of children, type of dwelling and other such factors were all supposed to be as near the local average as possible. The selection was, in Le Play's hands at least, conscientious. But the monographs that have survived, that is only the published ones, have gone through a further process of selection – their quality as monographs. Most of those that Le Play himself compiled he destroyed. They did not come up to his exacting standards. This selection among the case studies naturally makes it even less possible to claim that the families described are more than shrewdly chosen examples of working-class life at the time. Any generalisations from them are unlikely to be satisfactory.

The families selected were studied in depth and in their environment. If the selection was less satisfactory than has been suggested, it would seem that the actual monograph was far more satisfactory than has sometimes been thought. It involved three distinct operations – the study of the environment, followed by a prolonged series of meetings and conversations with the family, and these involved, thirdly, the collection of as much objective information as possible. It would seem, however, that the process was much more thorough with regard to the French monographs than the foreign ones. In the latter he often acknowledged local assistance (Demidov's agent, Danilov, in Nizhni Tagil, for instance, and a mysterious Monsieur Smith in Chesterfield, possibly a local ironmaster); but this reliance on local help cannot have made for consistency of treatment. Le Play and his immediate collaborators did not stay long enough in some of the foreign towns he studied to do the three months' intensive interviewing which he prescribed.[6]

The 'objective' information in these monographs consists largely of the budgets of family expenditure. These have been criticised on two grounds. One that he is claiming an accuracy for his facts which cannot be supported. Few working-class families would be likely to keep such accurate accounts as the figures suggest, nor is it possible to calculate the value of an allotment (for instance) with the accuracy asserted. The other criticism, that of Durkheim among others, was that such figures in any case tell one nothing of importance about the life of the family. But such criticisms overlook two points. The collection of facts about income and expenditure was in part an interview tool, and is important in the development of interviewing techniques anyway. And, secondly, Le Play did not use the figures to show average levels of production and consumption for a given area or social class. He used them to demonstrate the activities, the welfare (or otherwise), and the priorities in consumption of his representative families. That he was using the family accounts in this way is further shown by the fact that he did not include them in all his monographs.

Le Play needed an assessment of the level and type of consumption of his representative family which was as accurate as possible. For this was his indicator of the material prosperity of society. The family was the basic social unit, society existed for the wellbeing of the family, hence the level of this wellbeing could be regarded as a social thermometer. But this was not just a level of material consumption; stability was at least as important. Hence a high level of stability with respect for custom and ownership, alongside a low level of consumption, could still represent a satisfactory condition. The nomads of the East with their established way of life but low standard of living could be just as prosperous as the new industrial nomads of the West with a highly changeable income and a complete break-up of their traditional way of life. In his last book (W45) he returned to a constant theme when he contrasted the lot of a tin smelter of Bohemia, daily wage 6*d*, with a tin smelter of Cornwall, earning 4*s* a day. The former had security and many fringe benefits; his material condition may have been better than the latter's. With an eighth of the wages, he probably cost his employer more too. As an example of extreme insecurity Le Play often cited a suburb of Paris where the bulk of the population were men, because the women had been left in the countryside as the men were drawn into the city. To bring out the contrast between income and standard of living, in the first edition of the *Workers of Europe*[7] Le Play distinguished between an analysis of the *means* of existence and the *mode* of living. In this edition there are four subdivisions in each monograph: these are physical environment, the family's means of existence, the family's mode of existence and details of the culture being studied. In the second edition[8] there is a greater emphasis on physical environment, and this is used as one basis for classification. The actual arrangement of the studies, however, is according to the stability of the families and populations. No attempt is made to produce a measure of this stability, which nevertheless provides a basis for analysing the results. The following are the headings:

1. Patriarchal families, stable populations: *familles patriarcales, populations stables.*
2. Stem families, stable populations, *familles souches, populations stables.* The phrase *famille souche* causes problems of translation. One writer uses 'stock family', another 'root and branch family'; but 'stem family' is most common, and seems to fit Le Play's idea of a family-

type in which the offshoots leave the main stem and spread themselves, but retain close and defined links. But 'stem' does not convey
the real meaning of the word which would rather be 'stump'.
3. Stem families or patriarchal families, stable populations; *familles
souches ou patriacales, populations stables.*
4. Unstable families, unsettled populations: *familles instables, populations
ébranlées.*
5. Unstable families, disorganised populations: *familles instables, populations désorganisées.*

The following chart gives the numbers of families in the *Workers of
Europe*, W42, in each section:

SOCIETY	FAMILY-TYPE		
	Patriarchal	*Stem*	*Unstable*
Stable	10	12	8
Unsettled	0	3	10
Disorganised	0	1	13

It should be noted that the titles of the volumes of the *Workers of
Europe* do not necessarily correspond with the contents. Thus all the
English families are of the 'unstable' type; but they come in volume III
which is headed '*Familles souches, populations stables*'. It should also
be noted that the 'society' classification is much more subjective than
the family one. The latter is based on stated criteria; the former seems
to be based on Le Play's judgment, and different parts of a country
appear in different classes. The patriarchal family, common in eastern
countries, was the 'extended' family in which three or more generations
and numerous relations lived together under the supervision of the
official 'father'. This was a close-knit unit ruled by tradition. On the
other extreme was the unstable family, the modern western family,
where two generations (parents and children) formed the normal unit,
and there might be no other definite links at all. The stem family stood
between the two, maintained some links between the generations, and
was much influenced by custom; but it escaped the rigidity of the
patriarchal family.

Le Play's case studies are almost all about working-class families.
Although he writes about management and, as a matter of fact, land
ownership, he uses his monograph technique only for workers. He

justifies this simply on numbers. In simple societies almost everyone is a worker, and so the worker's family can be said to be almost a precise image of the society. As societies grow more complex, obviously the workers cease to be the whole; but in Le Play's time it was still possible to say that they constituted the large majority. In simple races, the force of tradition is such that to analyse the behaviour patterns of one family is to understand them all. Le Play illustrates this by telling how, when he was a manager in Russia, he would ask advice of grown men on the threshold of middle age. Before replying, they would wish to consult their fathers. The method is not so simple in more advanced societies. Here the most rigorous enquiry is needed to locate the typical family. Fortunately people were not slow to discuss their affairs with Le Play at any rate. He obviously had a technique for making friends with the selected families, and tells how he got to know them well over a long period. He also emphasises the need of strict impartiality in recording what is said.

The nature of primitive society, according to Le Play, was largely determined by geographical situation. There were three different habitats in which society grew – the field, the shore and the forest. Each had its typical social and family structure. Then a new way of living began to develop mainly in the coalfields of Europe. Characteristically this broke down custom and tradition, replacing the love of stability with the love of innovation. The new type of landless nomad became common. From now on occupation rather than geography conditioned society, and the two classifications (region + work) were put together to form:

savages (*les sauvages*)
herdsmen (*les pasteurs*)
coastal fishermen (*les pêcheurs-côtiers*)
foresters (*les forestiers et les professions annexes*)
miners and foundrymen (*les mineurs et les fondeurs*)
farm-workers (*les agriculteurs*)
factory-workers (*les manufacturiers*)
distributive workers (*les commerçants*)
professional workers (*les professions libérales*)

The word 'conditioned' is appropriate here. Lenin's dictum that man is fashioned in the image of his craft might well have been used by Le Play. Indeed, contemporaries remarked that this conservative observer believed that the means of production determined social processes.

The case studies are arranged, then, according to the stability of the society, and labelled according to occupation. Another classification which is brought in is the type of employment policy as well as the occupational class. These types follow the classification set out above in Chapter 2, and range from serf conditions to 'hire and fire'. The monographs themselves were subdivided in detail to bring out the environment as well as the way of life of the family chosen. A few examples from the monographs illustrate the method most clearly. The second edition of *Les Ouvriers européens* contained fifty-seven of these case studies. All had been published before in some form or other, but were modified to some extent in this collection of those which Le Play considered most satisfactory.

Nicolai Pavlovich R— was a forgeman in an ironworks in the Urals.[9] His was a patriarchal family in a stable society; he was also a serf bound to labour in the iron-works, possessing his own smallholding as well. The family is studied under nineteen headings, beginning with the local geography and ending with special customs to promote wellbeing. The area was fertile, although subject to extremes of temperature. Relations between masters and serfs are different from the purely agricultural regions; the industrial serf does get a wage. Nicolai does live in his own house, having left his father's house when his oldest son got to a marriageable age. His religion is Russian orthodox, but is related to the social security system under which he lived rather than to any religious fervour ('l'énergie du sentiment religieux'). The nature of the arrangements for care in sickness, old age and so on was one of the matters which Le Play investigated carefully in each study. He asked both what provisions were made and how they worked out in the experience of the family studied. In this particular case, the priest had an integral part in the system of care against misfortune which was all financed by the landlord. The same partnership of priest and landlord applied in the education system. Medical provision was much developed around the metal industry. Nicolai had his smallholding and his animals but otherwise no savings. This holding was given to him by the lord when he had to leave his father's home. In addition to free medical aid and free education for his children, he has the use of the forest for timber, hunting, fishing and so on. He is bound to work in the iron-works for four weeks in every five; the fifth week he spends on his smallholding or engaged in one of his numerous sidelines. In spite of the fact that nearly half his food was home grown, over 60 per cent of Nicolai's wages were spent on food. So the pay was obviously very low, and he depended on the earnings of his sons for clothing and recreation.

The three final sections of the monograph deal in more detail with the industry and the system of employment. In this part of Russia there were two types of worker – the industrial and the peasant. The latter were outside workers who provided the ancillary services for the iron-works. They supplied, for instance, timber and transport. This was done as their duty to the lord; they were also merchants and shop-keepers for the village on their own account. The internal work of the forges and mines was done by the industrials, of whom Nicolai was one; and the conditions of work and wages just described were roughly typical of them. His eldest son, on the other hand, was a peasant worker. Le Play describes a certain measure of prosperity, but a prosperity which entirely depended on the harvest. The wages for the industrial work, even including the fringe benefits, were small enough for an experienced man like Nicolai. They were smaller still for the unskilled labourers. Alongside the large concerns employing forced labour were small concerns under communal ownership. The workers in these might be free or they might pay a sum of money as a group to commute their serf dues. Within a patriarchal system, these organisa-tions could be regarded as producers' cooperatives, and were common in light industry. Many people, said Le Play, thought that this was the form that industrial organisation would take in Russia, but he did not agree. He questioned whether these associations would ever be able to build up the capital or the organisation needed for heavy industry.

In addition to land grants and medical services provided by the feudal lord, the patriarchal family contained its own built-in social security. This Le Play constantly pointed out, and is one of the reasons why he was sometimes accused of wishing to restore feudalism. The old, the young, the infirm were the care of the whole family. One of the case studies describes a nomadic family where this also applied as the family moved together. It began to break down when industrialisation made greater scope for the individual. Le Play saw the beginnings of workers' organisations in the associations of immigrant workers that were beginning to form in the towns. Another of his Russian case studies was of a transitional stage between the system of feudal obligations with permanent employment and a system of short-term, free engage-ments. Philip Amelianovich, the subject of this monograph,[10] was himself an agricultural worker in the Oka valley in central Russia. His two elder sons were porters in St Petersburg and were away for long periods, one of them only coming home in alternate winters. The power of the patriarchal family is shown by the fact that there was no question of moving to St Petersburg; their wives and children remained part of their father's household, and they themselves were very much subject to their father's rulings. Not surprisingly, Le Play remarks upon a high illegitimacy rate in this area, although in Russia at the time it was generally low because of the custom of early marriage. In St Petersburg these emigrant porters belonged to one of the workers' associations known as 'Artels'. These were temporary organisations meant to give the migrant worker the security given to the sedentary worker by his family. The Artel was an association of migrant workers in one particular occupation who appointed officials to negotiate terms and conditions of work. These officials also paid the members and detailed them for specific jobs. So they exercised some of the functions of an employer, but were elected by their fellow-workers; they also performed a part of the role of the trade union official, in negotiations with employers, but in addition they fixed and paid the wages of their members. The Artel to which the elder sons of Philip Amelianovich belonged was mainly employed loading and unloading the ships, but did general labouring work as well. During the period of its existence, the members lived, ate, slept and worked together as a community; the treasurer shared out some pocket money regularly, and then all the surplus income at the end of the period. The Artel was a complete unit of social security during its existence. All members were rewarded equally regardless of ability and regardless of health. Efforts were made to ensure that all members pulled their weight; but still, Le Play maintained, a sick worker got complete protection.

This brief outline gives some idea of the way Le Play describes this stable society. Not a rigorous account by presentday standards but a passable photograph, considering the equipment at his disposal, and certainly adequate to bear the comparisons he was to make as he developed his theories of the influence of technical change on social systems. All the Russian case studies are of patriarchal families, but there are two Eastern European examples of the Stem family type. One of these was another forgeman, this time living in Bulgaria, then part of Turkey.[11] Jorgui S— was also a serf, but with fewer fringe benefits, to judge from the fact that none of his children went to school. Nevertheless, Le Play pointed out that for all his poverty he still had more basic security and wellbeing than many Western workers on much higher wages. He depends to a certain extent on the charity of the lord, and Le Play does not discuss what happens if this is not forthcoming. During the winter he is continuously at work at the forge; but this closes down in summer through lack of water to drive the machinery. During this period he does some agricultural and transport work for his lord and some on his own account. Over half his meagre wages is spent on food, and he grows most of what he eats himself. This monograph again ends with a detailed account of the environment. Land tenure is complicated by the efforts to convert the country to Islam some centuries earlier after the capture of Constantinople; and by the tendency to dedicate the land to religious uses. As far as the peasants were concerned, although technically serfs, Le Play says that the actual situation was more like that of a freeman with permanent employment. Rightly or wrongly Le Play finds the position of the Christian workers in firms with Islamic proprietors a very favoured one, with stable employment, relatively good conditions and a large amount of freedom. He points out, indeed, that there was a very small labour turnover among those who were technically free.

This study of the Bulgarian worker is cited as an example of the stem family, but little is said about how this classification is made. In the case of another forgeworker, this time from Sweden (see note 6), the classification is explained in terms of the general family structure of the area. The Swedes have, Le Play says, as much as any European country the three main elements of wellbeing – good natural resources, a strong family organisation and respect for the moral law. But this 'strong family organisation' is not as rigid as the patriarchal system of Russia. There several generations live together in a house, under the rule of the head of the household. The permanent authority of an old man, which this system ensures, stifles initiative and innovation among the younger members. The Scandinavian countries, partly as a result of their peculiar geography, have produced a family type which combines stability and respect for tradition with the flexibility and adaptability required by an industrial society. The stem family retains links between members of the family and a 'hearth' to which they can all hope to return; it also provides care and security for retired members of the family. The main differences between the stem family and the patriarchal family listed by Le Play were:

First, that in the stem family power does not pass from generation to generation gradually, but in a sudden jump from father to heir. Then secondly members of the family do not leave home in groups to form another identical household elsewhere. They leave in successive stages as and when savings have been built up to start their own household. Thirdly, stem family members go to a wide range of occupations, and finally these occupations themselves each provide a wide range of activities. The hold of tradition on the stem family is always weaker than on the patriarchal, but is strongest where conditions are most harsh.

Tradition is weakened for the stem family by a mild climate, fertile soil, or proximity to a main trade route. In 1845, when the Swedish study was written, cottage industry was still widespread. The father of the family described in this monograph, however, worked in the iron industry. Along with forestry, this was one of the traditional industries built up by landlords on the large estates. Other industries were organised in traditional guilds, as existed still in other parts of Europe. These guilds, organised for masters and journeymen and apprentices, survived mainly in clothing, furniture and building where one-man businesses were normal. Finally, there were the new factories, notably in the textile industry and still using water-power, which were increasing in number. Thus Le Play found in Sweden four main types of work organisation – cottage industry, traditional large-scale industries, guilds and the new factories. The new machinery had largely broken the power of the guilds in many occupations, but they could still make problems to anyone setting up manufacture in the towns. Le Play describes the coming of legislation enforcing the 'right to work', but bringing with it some security for the workers. In general the Swedes have, more than any other European country, taken steps to ensure that the problems of industrialisation are mitigated for the workers. Indeed, many of Le Play's later ideas both on the organisation of the family and on the organisation of work came from his studies of Scandinavia. He found there a society between that of East and West. The workers were free, but had some protection. The state interfered but, in Le Play's view, skilfully. Le Play paints an almost idyllic picture of life in Sweden. For here, he alleges, security for the industrial worker is achieved without loss of liberty. But the prosperity and high standard of living is apparent in the older, more rural industrial areas, and especially in the metal industries. The trends of western Europe are apparent in Stockholm itself and in the new textile areas. One of the causes of the satisfactory state of affairs in the iron industry was the combination of industrial work with a smallholding, and hence Le Play constantly recommended this. A particularly satisfactory organisation from the point of view of stability and security was the communally owned furnace set in a forest which the same group of peasants also owned. But here Le Play came up against the familiar conflict of social and economic factors. This type of organisation with its total security and resistance to change was no match for the rising manufacturers. Le Play saw this clearly enough, and expressed this as a major dilemma when he came to work out his theory.

Le Play's first studies were made in the Harz mountains in Saxony.

Here, too, there was a satisfactory organisation, but one that was highly resistant to change. Again a well-established system was being undermined. At the time of Le Play's visits the forests and the iron-works were state owned, and the materials for the mines were supplied to the individual contractors who exploited them. The state administration limited the number of traders and others who were licensed to operate in the area. Housing is secured to the worker by an unusual system in which the state lends him the money to buy the house on a non-repayable loan. The interest of 4 per cent on this loan is, as Le Play says, in effect a rent; but the house belongs to the worker until his death. There is a subsidised insurance scheme for himself and his dependants. There is education for the children up to thirteen or fourteen. There were limitations on the freedom of the worker. As with the mercury miners of Idria described in a later case study, although in a milder form, the administration tried to prevent early marriage in order to control the population. Such attempts, said Le Play, were always self-frustrating. If they succeeded in raising the age of marriage, they merely increased the illegitimacy rate. With some limitations on his liberty, and with hard and laborious work in a harsh climate, the worker of the Harz was free but with an unalienable right to support by the mining administration whatever his health and ability and whatever his trade.

Several English families, both industrial and agricultural, were included in the collections of case studies. These were all shown as examples of unstable families in stable populations. The English case studies show, in fact, much less stability than the others from northern Europe; there is a movement of population going on all the time, but Le Play assumes that a sufficiently large proportion of the population is stationary to absorb the mobile part without the major social problems apparent elsewhere. He also states that the influence of custom, reinforced by a system of effective local government, helps in this absorption. John R— was from Cork, the son of a farm labourer, and himself a skilled cutler in Sheffield. In this he seems to have been fortunate. For elsewhere Le Play makes the point that it is very hard for immigrants (even from the neighbouring countryside of Yorkshire or Derbyshire) to get the higher prestige jobs in the cutlery or steel industries of Sheffield. It was also hard for their sons to get apprenticeships.

If England was regarded by Le Play as a stable society, its employment system was regarded as the most unstable in Europe. In the Harz mountains, the system of employment was that of *patronage*; in England it was 'hire and fire', and with hardly any mitigation. Under this system there was great insecurity and there were few of the 'fringe benefits' of the system of *patronage*, but wages were higher. One of the English workers he described was paid nearly four times the wages of the Harz miner. For the anglophile that he was, Le Play made some trenchant criticism of certain aspects of English life, notably the employment policies and the poor law. This latter he described as 'draconian in appearance, ineffective in fact'.[12] With the switch to coal as a motive force there was a rapid increase in production which led to a shortage of workers and a great increase in wages. This in turn was followed by a slump which left the workers without any wages at all. These alternations of boom and slump 'led to social disorders such as mankind had never before known'.[13] When the English at last overcame their repugnance to government intervention, they passed laws to mitigate the worst effects of industrialisation; but these have proved only palliatives, for there was a deep-seated antagonism established within British industry. This had its roots in the theories of Adam Smith, 'A writer completely ignorant of the practices of the workshops', who pandered to the greed of the employers. Carried to its extreme, the English system meant that the worker had no security beyond the very short period for which he was employed, and this might be as little as an hour. In this system there was no unit of social security, only the 'draconian' poor law to try to prevent a man starving in the street. But the rigours of the system produced their own defences, some of which Le Play described. The passive defences included insurance and friendly societies; the more active defences were the trade unions. Here under force of circumstances, and in default of what Le Play saw as the advantages of 'patronage', he detected the beginnings of the new system of industrial relations which we have called 'consultative'. Another 'defence' was, of course, the conscience of some members of the ruling classes, oddly enough a subject on which Le Play quoted Marx. In spite of a slow start and theoretical objections, the English did draw ahead of the French and the Germans in the matter of social legislation, and this legislation was promoted by wealthy men with social consciences.

The rise of the British trade unions, Le Play regarded as a remarkable example of the tolerance of the government for private initiative, the spirit of conciliation between the classes, and the wisdom of the English workers. He was evidently thinking of the unions of skilled workers, for he gave as the first object of a trade union in Sheffield the limitation of entry to the trade by fixing the number of apprentices. He then went on to describe how the trade unions had forced the employers to discuss wage rates with them. He quoted a document which showed how much

D

progress had already been made in industrial negotiation in England –
'at a conference of manufacturers and workers, held in the Cutlers' Hall
on 13th October 1848, the following price-list for the cutting of rasps
and files was unanimously adopted'. The agreements in the file industry
allowed the dismissal of redundant workers in the case of a slump, but
did not allow a reduction of wages for those at work. Where a union
was well-established, it was usually led by full-time officials who built
up the status and the finances of their union by sound administration.
A good understanding had grown up between the trade union leaders
and the main employers in Sheffield as in most English cities. The trade
unions themselves were keen not to break this understanding, which
was threatened among employers not only by those who opposed the
unions on principle, but also by those who would do anything to
undercut prices. Where this practice was suspected the employers might
inform the unions, who would watch carefully the workers in such a
factory. In an interesting summary, Le Play said that contrary to what
some of his readers might think, the unions were agents of peace in
industry. The new system they were bringing into existence could
be preferable to *patronage* in that it contained within itself a remedy
against the vices of the employer. On the other hand it perpetuated the
principle of the antagonism of the classes.

Of the two Sheffield workers described by Le Play, one, a cutler, was
constantly in and out of work. The other, a joiner in a large steel works,
had regular employment and expected to have until he retired. The
joiner was paid a day-wage, which Le Play said was rare and suggested
that he was especially trusted by his employers. Another English
worker described in *Les Ouvriers européens* was a Derbyshire ironworker,
Dick B—, who was described from information supplied by a Mr T.
Smith.[14] Dick B—, like the Sheffield carpenter, worked in a system of
'hire and fire', but had worked at his firm since it started, and had an
employer who tried to retain his long-service employees. Hence Dick
had never known unemployment. He was paid a day-wage. Apparently
payment by results was unusual in the Derbyshire iron industry at the
time because of the number of incalculable factors that had to be taken
into account. Dick owned no property and had no savings; he spent
most of his income (seven-tenths) on food and drink. Le Play often
remarked that this was a characteristic of English workers; workers in
other European countries were more likely to be buying their own
houses and perhaps a smallholding as well. Dick worked very long
hours, as the furnace was a continuous one, seven days a week and
twelve hours through the day one week, and through the night the next.

Apparently some such furnaces in England did stop on Sundays and festivals, but this particular factory never stopped, and in this it was like continental ones. Dick did not belong to a union. In a final note at the end of the monograph, Le Play says that there was some *patronage*, mainly in the north of England, but that Factory Acts, as well as the development of the unions, had lessened the rigours of the 'English system'. His praise of the Factory Acts[15] might surprise English commentators; but Le Play was well aware of the strong traditions against such legislation in England, and he obviously regarded the establishment of inspectors as a very significant achievement from which more was bound to follow. The other English monographs concerned farmworkers or those who were in effect self-employed, like the London cutler.

In Paris, the shawl weaver (see M112) worked in a similar system to the Sheffield cutler; but with the notable exception that there was generally permanent employment with one master-manufacturer. In the early months of 1857, when the monograph on the shawl-weaver was compiled, there were 729 Jacquart looms in the industry in the Paris area (mostly in and around Gentilly); one-third of these were currently idle, some were employed weaving other material. Most of the looms were sublet to master-workmen who managed a group, sometimes working on one themselves, sometimes wholly occupied in administration. Jean-Marie E—, who lived with his wife and four children at Gentilly, was one of the 172 master-workmen who worked one of their own looms. He had a permanent contract with one manufacturer, and employed a number of weavers. An interesting note on child labour in this monograph tells us that Jean-Marie himself had not started work until he was fifteen; hence he could read and write and do the necessary book-keeping. His wife, on the other hand, had started work very early and had never been to school. She could not read or write, and they were both determined that their own children should stay at school until they had reached a reasonable standard of education. This master-workman did not own his own workshop, which he rented from the manufacturer, but he did own his four looms, and ancillary equipment and tools. On the whole the relations between the manufacturers and the master-workmen were good. There had recently been an increase in wages to match the increase in prices, and this had been granted without argument, in contrast to other industries. Further, most of the manufacturers granted interest-free loans to help buy equipment or tide over a difficult period.

The shawl worker worked a twelve-hour day, fourteen hours from start to finish. The master had to supervise his employees, deal with the manufacturer, probably do most of his own maintenance, and mind his own machine. In spite of the permanence of employment Jean-Marie enjoyed, he was still subject to boom and slump. Permanence of employment, in this case, did not go so far as to guarantee pay during a time of very bad trade, although there was the possibility of the interest-free loan. When there was work both husband and wife often worked a seven-day week. The wife attended the husband's machine when he had to be away from it on other duties; she also saw to the washing of the shawls. The wages of the other workmen were paid by the master, and this, as in other industries, led to many abuses. Clearly the authors of this monograph thought this was a matter for state regulation, and some regulation had been introduced since Jean-Marie became a master. The generally accepted custom was that the master paid the other workmen two-thirds of what he received for the material. But often the ordinary workman had no means of knowing what this was. If he did know what it was, on the other hand, he might insist on his two-thirds even if the master accepted a cut-rate. But the relationship between the master and the manufacturer was influenced by the fact that the master owned his own machinery. This led him to be willing to accept any price rather than keep his machinery idle, and so produced constant rate-cutting in spite of fixed agreements about the amount to be paid. This had improved in theory, since in 1839 the system of payment used today was introduced – namely, according to the number of times the shuttle crossed the machine. This gave a more accurate basis for calculation, especially in 1848 when the climate of opinion became more favourable to making agreements. But the rate-cutting went on. This was especially dangerous, in the author's view, because the constant cutting of agreed rates gave the workers a special sense of grievance; the lowering of their wages also made many of them dependent on public assistance. The authors suggested that payment below the agreed rates should disqualify a manufacturer from winning prizes at an exhibition, and referred to the position of the cutlers in Sheffield, with powerful unions forcing the masters to pay the agreed rate. They were not sure whether this would work without bloodshed in France; they were inclined to think that the government should bring the manufacturers and workmen together, and force them to produce an agreement. The position of the workman, poorly paid as he was and subject to constant slumps, was extremely precarious. The ordinary workman had no relationship at all to the manufacturer, since he was in fact employed by the master under conditions which ensured constant friction.

Le Play's emphasis on 'custom' gained some support from the study of the employment of children in this industry. The operation of the loom required an assistant, doing a job which did not require much effort and so was done by children. The old custom was that no child started work before its First Communion, normally at the age of twelve. Now this was being broken, and the age of starting had gradually been lowered to seven. The authors commented that in view of the bad conditions and long hours it was lucky for the children that slumps were frequent. In this industry the children were unprotected by the law, because most of the workshops contained less than twenty workers. There were hardly any women in the industry since an agreement in 1849 had given them equal pay with the men.

Many supervisors were not as literate as Jean-Marie; and illiterate supervision, which was often both harsh and inefficient, was a subject with which Le Play was much concerned. A quarryman on the outskirts of Paris was Jacques L—, the subject of a monograph by E. Avalle and A. Focillon (M51). Jacques had been a day-labourer working in a 'hire and fire' firm, but he had now been promoted to a supervisory position which ensured regular work for him all the year round. Jacques could not read or write and kept the necessary records of the men under him by giving verbal reports to the proprietor's wife. His promotion was said to be due to his 'skill in all sides of the work, his good conduct, his zeal and the confidence which he inspires'. His salary was more than that of a day-worker, but less than a piece-worker could make when fully employed. The supervisor, roughly equivalent to a chargehand, averaged more because the piece-worker was frequently without work. He worked a ten-hour day, six days a week, with overtime in the summer.

In many parts of France, the system of *patronage* existed in principle, but had been broken down by class bitterness promoted, according to Le Play, by the spread of revolutionary ideas. Considering the economic problems of the extractive industries in France as much as anywhere, this view of Le Play's may well have lacked perceptiveness. At least he brought out the bitterness clearly enough in monographs such as that on the Auvergne silver-miner (M85) of which the facts were collected for him by a Monsieur E. Landsberg in 1850. The 'English system' seemed to be reversed in this area (as, Le Play might have discovered, could happen in England), for the workers did not wish to be tied to one employer for too long. The men worked in small teams of about six who negotiated a price with the employer for a given quantity of silver-bearing rock. Thus there was consultation but in this case it had the character of subcontracting rather than direct employment. Significantly it had been found that the output her head went down when the number in the team was more than six. The firm had initiated many of the benefits of *patronage*, including subsidised insurance schemes, and free schools.

Employed in small factories and with strong craft-traditions were the printing trade workers, and a monograph described a compositor of Brussels (M12). In an atmosphere of considerable unrest and rapid expansion, the printers had achieved a situation of stability and some prosperity. There were two organisations to which the compositors belonged which are of some interest. One was the Société typographique de Secours mutuels. This was a friendly society which provided the usual benefits to members during sickness. The other society was L'Association libre des compositeurs-typographes de Bruxelles. Founded early in 1842 to resist attempts to lower wages, this was a trade union. It was run responsibly according to Le Play, who was not always so sympathetic to the unions. It had 'an influence equally healthy for the workers and the employers', he said. It confined itself to considering conditions of work, and built up a fund to support unemployed members. L'Association libre organised compositors only, but the other branches of the industry had their own society. In addition to the friendly society and the trade union, there was a printers' co-operative society in process of formation. In the case of these skilled workers in a traditional craft, the unit of social insurance had become the workers' organisations themselves. So once again, Le Play showed, almost despite himself, how the growth of a strong union could lead to industrial peace. In a passage on negotiations between L'Association libre and the printing employers in 1857 Le Play described an example of joint discussion on a wage dispute leading to a settlement. Regarding the outlook of the Brussels compositors, Le Play said that the subject of this monograph did not share the common bitterness of his fellows. This bitterness, he suggested in 1858, was due to the ambiguous class situation of the printing craftsmen – between the bourgeoisie and the proletariat. This was one of the contexts in which Le Play showed an awareness of role conflict and its influence on outlooks. This monograph also discussed methods of payment. The piece-workers, who frequently changed their employers, were of two types – those who made the pages and were paid so much a page, and those who set the type and were paid by the amount set.[16] The day-workers (picturesquely called *compositeurs en conscience*) were usually hired by the day, by the hour, or by the publication. This last was normal for printers of weekly magazines. The system of time-payment was usual for the good all-round craftsman, and was becoming general. It was universal among newspaper workers.

In the last two case studies issues are raised which show how near Le Play came to modern sociological insights. On more than one occasion he stumbled on the significance of size and cohesion in the working-group. He did not see the significance of this clearly enough to incorporate it into his theory, but nevertheless it showed up strongly in the silver-mine of the Auvergne where productivity declined as the size of the group increased. Le Play showed himself sensitive to this issue, but even more sensitive to attitudes produced by role uncertainty. This comes up in more than one case study, including that of the Brussels printer. Bitterness about his position on the part of the prosperous rather than the down-trodden worker has often been mentioned; but Le Play anticipated the thought of a century later when he linked this with the ambiguity of the worker's situation. He also discussed (for instance in a study of the Swiss watch industry) some effects of technical change, but again just stopping short of building insights into a theory. Interesting for another reason was the study already mentioned of the Austrian mercury-miner (M8). Here was a case of a stem family in a very disorganised society, but a stem family which began with an unmarried couple. Here was a case of the 'unintended consequences' of an attempt to influence the structures of society.

Anton R— was one of 750 workers in the mines and processing works of the district. The regime under which he lived well illustrated the dangers of *patronage*, for it involved considerable interference in the lives of the workers, mainly designed to limit the number of persons for whom the company was to be held responsible. For one thing, part of the wages was paid in 'truck', in this case rye. But the amount of rye allowed was the same for a married man with a family as for a single man. The main interference with family life was that an employee was not allowed to marry until he reached a certain status in the firm. In spite of his general support for *patronage*, Le Play unsparingly condemned this rule which had the effect of making thirty-two the minimum age of marriage. In fact this rule had little effect on the size of the family, but a great effect on the illegitimacy rate. Anton B— at thirty-six had only been legally married four years, but he had four children of whom the oldest was ten. This rule showed clearly the tendency of *patronage* and why workers often regarded it as an attempt to perpetuate a system of serfdom. The reason for these attempts at family limitation arose from the system of social security itself – the company paid for the medical attention and the education of the children.

The method of payment in these mines was also such as to emphasise the dependence of the worker. He was nominally on piece-work, but in fact the rate was constantly being adjusted so that wages did not vary very much. For the underground workers payment was according to the amount of work done in the shift. On the furnaces, payment was for the refinement of a certain amount of mercury. As has already been said, part of his wages were paid in kind. He received, or bought at a cheap rate, most of his essential foodstuffs from the company. Sick-pay stood at almost as much as ordinary wages, and there were provisions for medical care. The social security benefits were not wholly laid on by the company. In fact they were paid for in a variety of ways, including a small levy (under 2 per cent) on the workers' wages.

In the case studies a distinction is drawn between the disturbed ('ébranlées') and the disorganised ('désorganisées') societies. In volume v of *Les Ouvriers européens* the distinction between stable, disturbed and disorganised is explained. In the stable societies there is suffering but it is not normal or permanent. Custom, a delicate web of norms and links, still holds society together. In the disturbed societies these links are weaker and there is distinct evidence that suffering and division are becoming normal social realities. The stable society is often upset, but returns to a steady state without great difficulty. In the disturbed society social cohesion is constantly under threat both in the home and in the workplace. One of the causes of disturbance is the breakdown of the old systems of social security, such as the guilds, and the failure to replace them with any new one. Le Play notes this tendency in Vienna, although not in all parts of the Austrian Empire. The removal of the opportunity to have two jobs at once, industrial and agricultural, was found in the study of the Rhineland among others. Another cause of problems was the cycle of boom and slump which the development of new inventions seemed to bring with it, thus causing great distress at each period of slump. Social mobility destroys social solidarity, and there is a struggle for wealth at one time and against starvation at another. Customs are broken up, and all motives for working together are removed.

The further stage from the disturbed to the disorganised society is characterised by that great concern of the early twentieth century – rootlessness. The new nomads of Paris do not wander with their families and their flocks. They wander alone, and substitute liaisons for marriages. The new nomad has his intellectual equivalent, the man who plays with destructive ideas. As already noted, the distinguishing mark of all social, personal and intellectual development is division. The disorganised society completes the process begun in the disturbed societies, and produces great suffering alongside great wealth. But, Le Play says explicitly, and this is an element in his thought often overlooked, his researches do not produce evidence of any inevitable decline. The elements of reconstruction can be detected in the most disorganised societies he has studied. Notably stable families do survive in areas most affected by industrialisation. Le Play attempts to analyse the factors which will encourage or discourage the forces of stability. Just as the modern sociologist may write about the influence of the 'innovating personality' in a change-resistant bureaucracy; so Le Play investigates the influence of the person with some sense of direction in the rapidly changing society. He might well have understood Riesman's 'inner-directed' type.[17]

*

5

The social thinker

Le Play's social thought was compounded of a sense of danger, a sense of tragedy and a sense of the future. The sense of danger stemmed from the revolutions through which his country was passing, the sense of tragedy from the sufferings of the Industrial Revolution, and the sense of the future sprang from studies which showed trends that he had to accept without being able to like. The immediacy of these pressures sometimes makes his position seem ambiguous to us. He cannot be pinned down and neatly labelled in terms of twentieth-century outlooks. He confuses us by drawing on obsolete ideas to remedy problems he has accurately diagnosed. It is alleged that he damaged his reputation by drawing premature conclusions from his researches.[1] Indeed the truth of this cannot be doubted, but the social conscience which caused it is also clear. After much original research into social issues, he felt compelled to draw some practical conclusions when his country was in such danger. But nevertheless there are subtle threads in Le Play's thought by which we shall try to find our way.

The first puzzling element in that thought is where he stands with regard to the fundamental distinctions between realism and nominalism, and between the organic and mechanistic approaches. These distinctions have been discussed with great force and clarity by Werner Stark in his *Fundamental Forms of Social Thought*. Stark distinguishes between the view that society has a 'real' existence apart from the individuals that make it up (realism), and the opposite view in which any social category is a 'name' for a grouping of people and their relationships (nominalism). Realism, at least in its obvious sense, is unfashionable today and most of us would consider ourselves nominalists. Society exists for people, not people for society, would be the view. This was not so among some of the early sociologists. Durkheim, for instance, called himself a realist. Le Play certainly would not have done so. He would have agreed emphatically that society existed for the individual, and has no existence apart from the individual. But he equally maintained that the family and not the individual was the basic social unit. More important still, his *summum bonum* was social peace, and his greatest evil was social disorganisation. Thus the avowed nominalism of his attitude is contradicted by the realism of his research objective. He is searching for a unified social organism. This is further supported by a curious element in his thought. He assumed, and constantly emphasised the assumption, that the principles of social action had to be discovered and not invented. Such a view surely leads to realism, however individualistic the author's own view may be. Such a view also, of course, makes possible the use of biological analogy. For an important theoretical objection to the social scientist using parallels from the natural sciences is just on this subject of the relationship between discovery and invention. Physical phenomena are discovered by man, social phenomena are his invention, the product of human creativity. Natural evolution has taken place regardless of the will of the evolving creatures; societies have changed as a result of human decisions. The unsuitability of applying analogies like evolution to social thought becomes less if in fact social and natural studies both start from the same assumption. This Le Play did not say, and he did use analogies from the natural sciences only sparingly; less, in fact, than most of his contemporaries, though he had more logical entitlement to use them. When he did so it was mainly in discussing classification. Like de Tourville after him, he assumed that a system of classification could be built up analogous to that used in the natural sciences. It can be said that his instincts aligned him with later individualistic and nominalistic thinking, but his methods produced some writing nearer to the old world of realism and organicism.

His friend, Emile Cheysson, spoke of the influence of Vico on Le Play. There are not many quotations from Vico in his writings, but Cheysson says he constantly quoted him in his conversation.[2] And Vico, writing more than a hundred years before Le Play, took account of both realistic and nominalistic theories. One reason for Le Play's enthusiasm for Vico was because the latter fought for the autonomy of social science, for its freedom from *a priori* assumptions about the intervention of external forces in history. The body of thinkers who have developed consistent theories out of dissatisfaction with both nominalistic and realistic trends has been called by Stark the 'cultural' school. The distinctive tenet of this school is that society is 'a process'. One might add that Le Play's tenacious realism under attack from his instinctive nominalism is an obvious route to the cultural school. If Le Play did not actually reach the position of this school, it was perhaps because he never quite grasped the concept of 'process'. He did, on the other hand, grasp the significance of the interaction between the society and its environment. S. H. Swinny (in an article in the *Positivist Review*,

October 1917) alleges that Vico, Herder and Condorcet underestimate the significance of the environment; he goes on to suggest that Le Play corrects this.

Most of Le Play's social theory can be seen in his six elements of social change. The first was the perversity of human nature. Le Play's thought was coloured by a deep-set pessimism. The most obvious fact about human nature was its disorder. Le Play constantly used the phrase 'original sin', but not in quite the way the theologians use it, as will be seen later. He constantly attacked thinkers like Rousseau, to whom man was fundamentally good. He claimed to have based his theory of original sin on the results of experience and observation, but his criticisms of Rousseau often appear to contradict his avowed empiricism and his analysis of causation. He writes, for example, 'The more I investigate the cause of our revolutions and the evils they bring with them, the more I find it in the sophisms which infected our nation at the end of the eighteenth century. The most dangerous of these sophisms has been spread by J.-J. Rousseau.'[3] Yet, as a matter of fact, he was showing at the same time in his empirical studies that the ideas of Rousseau had only a limited following; and that the Rousseauite intellectuals (the 'littrés', he called them) had little influence. On many occasions, indeed, he was addicted to emphasising that inventions were more powerful than ideas in changing outlooks anyway. He distrusted equally too much state intervention, and too much *laissez-faire*. In his view overoptimistic opinions about human nature could lead in either of these undesirable directions. Later in the passage quoted above he cites a letter from Rousseau to the Archbishop of Paris, saying that 'man is a being naturally good, loving justice and order'. This was the type of statement which Le Play strongly opposed. As suggested in Chapter 1, he would have been unlikely to call himself an existentialist, but he was very conscious of the human predicament. The irony of man's condition was especially emphasised by Le Play when he discussed successive stages in the development of civilisation.[4] Each fresh stage, from the most primitive use of natural resources through the development of agricultural skills to industrial technologies, involved at least three important factors – an actual increase in human skill, a necessary increase in human education and a potential increase in the security of life. This potentiality increases rapidly as fresh inventions make men less dependent on the forces of nature. Yet in the recent stages of development, actual security has declined for most people. Thus human nature turns an apparent victory over physical nature into defeat. Le Play analysed man's predicament into three major forms of abuse. The first was the abuse of riches. The second was the abuse of knowledge; and the most notable examples of this were the propagation of systematic liberty, providential equality and the right to revolt. The other form was the abuse of power.

One consequence of Le Play's pessimism was his statement of the gap between technical and moral progress. The fact that this has become commonplace since his time should not be allowed to obscure its significance for his writings. Le Play did not refer to this gap with a vague lament, but rather as a measure of what was required from the social sciences. A social theory was needed to match the metallurgical theory he had once taught, and to enable informed social progress to take place. The slowness of social science to do this was all the more remarkable in Le Play's view for he considered the techniques simpler. This is not an issue on which he can be said to have anticipated later ideas. The object of social science research was to discover the elements of stability and cohesion which already existed in society, and how these could be adapted to changing conditions. A main agent of change might be technology; but the fact that this itself changed through *invention* should not lead to the assumption that society could also be changed through invention. This was an illusion; the principles of social well-being did not change. They had to be discovered by accurate observation and statistical comparison of existing societies. Innovation was a word appropriate to engineering, adaptation to society.

In the first edition of the *Workers of Europe* (1855) Le Play wrote with great confidence of the possibilities of applying the principles of the natural sciences to social science. In the second edition (1878) the confidence was still there but the emphasis had changed. Indeed, he was now apologising for the use of the word 'science' at all, saying that this implied invention as well as discovery. Since the social sciences were not to invent there was greater emphasis on discovering worthwhile practices; there was also greater emphasis on the remedial purposes of the study. Both of these were present in the first edition, but took on greater significance in the second. In view of its orientation towards discovery, social research should be easier than technical, but to apply the results was much harder. So was the maintenance of these results. Society is hardly likely, wrote Le Play,[5] 'to be deprived henceforth of the electric telegraph or photography', but it is continually trying to deprive itself of the moral law and 'the fear of God'.

This deep perversity in human nature required a strong antidote, and this was the second element in Le Play's theory of social change. The most powerful social control was the force of custom, and herein lay the distinctive danger of an industrial civilisation. For new technologies and the movements of populations were necessarily breaking down established usages, and in so doing breaking the whole delicate web which held society together. The remedy for this was in the hands of some gifted individuals who instinctively adapted their traditions so that ancient remedies for human perversity were maintained without strangling the new opportunities for a fuller life. These individuals he called the 'social authorities' (*autorités sociales*), and they came from all walks of life. They acted unconsciously, but their influence could be calculated. For instance, they had evolved the 'stem family'.

One of Le Play's objects on his travels was to elicit the views of the social authorities, although he never makes it quite clear how they are identified. They are the opposites of the 'littrés', the 'sophists' who propagate the teachings of Rousseau and aim to bring custom and morality into contempt. The concept of the social authorities is derived from the godlike men (οἱ θεῖοι ἀνθρώποι, Le Play uses the phrase *Hommes divins*) of Plato's *The Laws* (Book 12) – the men who are to be regarded as sacred by reason of their role in society rather than the cult objects worshipped for their supposed powers. These are men whom, by an extension of the analogy of sacredness, to scorn is real blasphemy. In Le Play's thought the concept is really one of 'adjustment'. The 'social authorities' are people whose outlooks and family structure are adjusted to the state of civilisation in which they are living. They have the social skill required to adapt their way of life to technical change without social disintegration. These people are found in all classes, but they become much more rare among those most subject to the pressures of industrialisation. This is the real cause for concern about the future. The 'social authority' is equipped to cope with the insecurity and root-lessness of industrial society, but the 'equipment' is easily destroyed. The survival of this elite can be aided by law and organisation – for instance, house ownership and long-term contracts of employment. The social authorities are hard workers. When Le Play's liberal-minded but antisocialist friend, Claudio Jannet, advocated state limitation of the laws of work, Le Play criticised him on the grounds that such a law would handicap the social authorities.

These people, Le Play says, are the real authors of his books. He has tried to be their secretary. A society's ability to produce such is a measure of its success. A century later, when the dangers of 'adjustment' are becoming all too apparent, the concept of the social authority might be considered a questionable guide to social wellbeing. The age of the public relations executive and the organisation man may well be over-adjusted, but these characters bear little resemblance to the 'social authorities'. In any case the dangers could not have been obvious in Le Play's time. Just the reverse; he contemplated a civilisation that was red in tooth and claw. What this concept does represent, surely, is an effort to find some classification which takes account of social skills and yet is to some degree definable. It is an important part of the pre-history of the study of informal groups. For the social authorities have to be traced by intimate study, the sort of study which leads to the development of hypotheses about group behaviour and leadership. This concept also, as Zimmerman has pointed out,[6] was part of his theory of the immanent causation of social change. Thus there were internal mechanisms producing social change, and the efforts of social authorities to develop more prosperous conditions after the onset of corruption was a good example of this. But these immanent mechanisms were essentially conservative. They helped to tide society over periods of difficulty caused by external forces.

The conflict between security and freedom was the third element in Le Play's theory of social change. His views on this conflict were subtle and have been misrepresented. As a matter of analysis, he saw society functioning normally when security was at its maximum. Part of the craft of authority in any sphere was the provision of security – for the governed, the employed, the family, whatever the social unit might be. Insecurity was a deviance. The social engineer in Le Play emphasised security, and underestimated freedom as a social force. As a matter of opinion, on the other hand, he reacted strongly against tyranny. The humanist in Le Play saw the need for freedom and limits on authority. In his case-studies this view of the relationship between security and freedom was interwoven with another – the fact that current social change was leading to greater freedom, but less security. The serf was secure, although Le Play may have underestimated the serf's ability to starve in a famine. The free industrial worker was constantly threatened with unemployment and eviction from his house. Yet he was apt to regard any measures providing greater security as a threat to his freedom. Skilful leadership, backed by custom, was the route to a reconciliation of the two. At the end of his life, Le Play wrote an introduction to a book produced by some of his supporters.[7] In this he wrote about the insecurity of the workers, and congratulated the authors on putting measures to overcome slump and guarantee a permanent minimum income at the head of their programme.

The perversity of human nature, then, made adjustment to change difficult, especially when a lack of leadership meant the breakdown of traditional measures of security. The fourth element, in Le Play's analysis of social change, was the conditioning of technical and economic factors. One writer[8] has placed Le Play among the 'geographical determinists'. But the use of the word 'determinist' surely begs the question. The conditioning effect of geographical factors was indeed important to him, as has been mentioned already. This subject became even more important in the writings of the Le Play school. In Le Play's own writings geography as a main influence is to be found in his speculative account of the development of primitive cultures. The trend of civilisation was to reduce this influence of geographical factors, such as coal measures, on the siting of industry and thus of new communities. This appeared to have social disadvantages in that these new industrial towns grew up in isolated places. But this could be an advantage, for the existing industrial centres were already over-large. Anticipating later ideas on town-planning, Le Play speculated on the optimum size for a community.

The other geographical influence was that of harsh conditions upon character. More of the 'social authorities' and the 'stem families' were to be found in the mountainous areas of northern Europe than in the plains. Here easier conditions and milder climates produced social institutions with less vitality. But the technical and economic factors also helped to decide the course of history – they made, as it were, the route which a changing culture was likely to follow. Early in his career (1836) he had written from Britain that a visit to Glasgow had shown astonishing developments in the conurbation, and that these developments were having ideological consequences. Both developments had had geographical origins in the presence of coal seams there. The same applied to other parts of the United Kingdom, and Le Play wrote that a Staffordshire coal seam would change France more radically than a new civil code.

The fifth element in Le Play's theory was his use of the phrase 'social peace' (*paix sociale*). This has similarities to the modern phrase 'social cohesion', by which it has been translated where suitable. One of the features of social peace, as Le Play understood it, was that it was the normal condition of all social institutions in a stable society. Le Play did believe in the possibility of identifying a social equilibrium. Indeed, a stable society was one in which cohesion was normally restored after any disturbance, however great, and under similar conditions to those which obtained before. Social division, likewise, penetrated all through society once it had established a foothold. Thus class divisions became exacerbated; so did divisions in the workshop, so did divisions in family life. As society became disturbed and disorganised, so division became the distinguishing mark of all its parts. This division produced an atomising effect. Hence social peace could only be achieved by creating a new situation which would break the vicious circle of division. Social peace, Le Play did not forget, can mask injustice and frustration. But social division was a disease in itself. Not that, Le Play hastily added, industrialisation necessarily produced bad results: 'So, for example, railways, steam-ships and telegraph would have been a powerful help to Saint Paul.'[9]

Social peace is established by a ruling elite who have regard for the common good. New developments confuse this elite and destroy familiar landmarks, thus producing a disturbed society. Where the landmarks are destroyed and the rulers themselves are practising class war, then is society disorganised and divided. The depth of the disorganisation has been mentioned in the last chapter, but Le Play has no truck with theories of inevitable decline. This is the obverse side of his pessimism. He claims that there are forces of reconstruction latent in any society. This is especially interesting in that users of analogies from the natural sciences, as Le Play, often get misled by their own analogies into a doctrinaire determinism that speaks of the 'youth' and 'old age' of any given society. This type of analogy Le Play specifically denounced. In China, he said, you have a stable society; in Australia, he alleged, you have a disorganised one. Which, then, of these societies should be called 'old' and which 'young'?

This leads to the sixth element of social change. In *La Réforme sociale* there is a chapter headed: 'Nations are not fated to inevitable progress or to inevitable decadence.'[10] Such a statement makes it all the more curious that Le Play has been classed as a determinist. Clearly he was concerned to isolate the conditions that lead to 'progress' or 'decadence', which are to be understood in terms of greater or less stability and security. But these conditions did not determine the results. At this point Le Play put great stress on the elite – the 'social authorities' drawn, as we have said, from every class. Where they were strong enough and adaptable enough to hold society together during a period of rapid change, this change would be for the good. This applied to any country, and he claimed that his researches had shown that the character of the rulers decided the character of the country.

Le Play's theory of social change, then, was compounded of the six elements just described: a deep pessimism about human nature, a study of the influence of custom and informal leadership, the conflict of security and freedom, the determination of the route of change by technical and economic factors, the concept of cohesion, the cyclical view of history. The main theme of *La Réforme sociale* was that this theory of social change could be tested by studies of the actual institutions of society, for instance the family, the political unit, and the Church. The reciprocal influence between the main social institutions could also be studied. An example of such a study was that of the relationship between the wellbeing of a society and the wellbeing of its typical families.[11] Moreover, the family 'imprints upon each social organisation its essential character'. On the other hand, law and other elements of social organisation could easily damage the family. Thus the Laws of Inheritance were condemned on the grounds that they weakened the family tie.

In his studies of the family, Le Play developed his scale of family types – from the patriarchal on the one hand through the stem family to the unstable family on the other. The patriarchal family survived in the most traditional societies in eastern Europe and North Africa. It was essentially a multi-generation family, with the rule of the oldest – 'the patriarch'. In principle, a man might never leave the family home, and a woman only to get married. Where in practice many of the men did leave, as with the Russian family described by Le Play where the younger sons were away months at a time working on the docks at St Petersburg, the family home was still a normal point of return. It provided a complete system of social security within the economic circumstances of the family as a whole. But, as Le Play saw, it was not sufficiently adaptable. Indeed, it could be very rigid. Since the head of such a family was likely to be an old man before he reached this position, the system did not encourage initiative. It flourished where experience was more important than adaptability, and where obedience was the highest virtue.

At the other extreme is the two-generation 'unstable family'. This is characterised by an insecure individualism which can produce great prosperity for the able or the lucky. In this family all three-generational ties were broken and the family was no longer a unit of social security. In view of modern studies showing how tenacious are the three-generational links among city families, and how the breaking of these makes for problems when people are moved to new housing estates, Le Play must surely have exaggerated the individualism of the unstable family. Hence the 'pauperism' which he sees as a concomitant of this family type can only have been partly due to the breaking of all links. It must have been partly due to general economic conditions, a factor which Le Play underestimated in comparing these family types. It would appear that he similarly underestimated the effect of economic conditions when he discussed the Laws of Inheritance.

Finally, there is the stem family, this delicate compromise which allows freedom and initiative, but still retains some of the social security aspects of the older family type. In a footnote Le Play discusses his use of the phrase 'famille souche'. He says that his friend, Schaeffle,[12] tells him that the German equivalent 'Stammfamilie' is a word still in current use. The family recognises its common stock to which it retains links. Typically, in the stem family the possessions of the family are not shared but passed to the son considered most capable. In return for this, he is expected to provide a centre for, and assistance to, weak or unfortunate members of the family. The concept of the stem family came under criticism within the Le Play school after his death. Was there really such a marked difference between the patriarchal family and the stem family? As a result of further studies of families supposedly of this type, a distinction was developed between the quasi-patriarchal family and the stem family. But this distinction also came under fire, and fourteen years after Le Play's death Demolins was saying that the stem family idea had been finally demolished.[13] The social scientist that was Demolins finally decided that there was no identifiable family type which would fit Le Play's classification. Some writers, however, kept to the idea. The novelist Henry Bordeaux, for example, used it as a theme for some of his writing. And in one of his essays he claims that this is a family type that is resistant to the forces of destruction, but not resistant to the forces of change.[14] This point is further discussed in the next chapter.

The stem family is still an 'extended' family. The head of the family lives in his father's house, usually follows a traditional occupation, and has several unmarried relations living with him. Le Play also claims that the stem family is more fertile than the other types of family, and argues that this shows its advantage. Including all relations a household often consists of more than fifteen members (there was an average of eighteen in the families he actually investigated). Every family can be studied in relation to five elements – the place of the home and the roles of the wife, the father, the children and the unmarried relations. A stable family required a home of its own or at least security from eviction. Hence Le Play's interest not only in the laws of inheritance but in housing schemes of all sorts. This interest led him into discussions about land societies, building societies, 'workers' cities', and other schemes which were coming into fashion in the second half of the nineteenth century. He tended to assume that actual ownership was good in itself, and did not study the problems this might produce for the worker-householder. However, he did mention the problem of the employer in the newer industrial area who assisted his employees to buy their own land and build their own homes, only to find that they left his employment and became smallholders.

Organisation and wellbeing were closely related in Le Play's view of the family. This arose partly out of his interest in social security. The superiority of the stem family lay in the fact that it provided some elementary security for its members without being too rigid. Wellbeing was also related to consumption but not in a straightforward manner. Le Play did not say that higher consumption was the same as greater wellbeing; on the contrary, he wrote about the discipline of low consumption. There was a considerable puritan strain in Le Play's thought. The important consideration was how the family responded to different economic conditions. Further, the nature of consumption did not just vary with the business cycle, but with other influences as well. Thus a social organisation could be prosperous and demoralised. Zimmerman and Frampton[15] have listed eight hypotheses which underlie Le Play's thought on the relationship between consumption and wellbeing, and which provide his justification for the particular form of his studies. In a phrase like 'the discipline of a hard country', Toynbee and others have developed similar conclusions.

Le Play's views on the role of the parents were paternalistic. Some of his campaigns, including those for testamentary freedom and the decentralisation of government, were largely based on the need to increase the authority of the father. The ultimate sanction of paternal authority was to cut off a son's inheritance. In stable and prosperous societies, he maintained in L'Organisation de la Famille, this authority was upheld. Indeed he paints an idyllic picture in this book of the stem family in the stable community. This picture, it should be said, hardly corresponds with the reality described in the case studies. Nevertheless it presents the father as the custodian of custom. This role was inherited, but could be invalidated by bad performance. Inside the home, the mother was in charge in the families where wellbeing was most evident. Again her role was traditional, her place was in the home; but Le Play did believe that cultural changes were influencing the position of women more than that of men. One of his campaigns was for the rights of unmarried mothers, and against a law which forbade search for the father of an illegitimate child. One of his tests of good employment practices was the provision of suitable work under suitable conditions for those women who needed it. Women were even admitted to the Société d'Economie sociale in the seventies.

Le Play's pessimism about human nature led to his emphasis on custom and tradition as limiting the area of choice and therefore the area of potential disaster. This enhanced the role of the father who was supposed to be the natural channel of tradition to the child who had 'a decided leaning towards evil'.[16] Civil liberty and paternal authority went together, and were likely to collapse together. This was also a key hypothesis in Le Play's view of government. For all his liberal outlook, Le Play was not an egalitarian. Social peace was ensured by a hierarchical system. He complicates the study by blurring the distinction between analysis and opinion. Just as Le Play started as a technologist with a social conscience and this led him to sociology, so it was as a sociologist with a social conscience that he was led into social prescription. We have already seen that this last transformation was not a happy one in that it held back the development of empirical studies; it was unhappy, too, in that it did not suit Le Play's genius. His writings on social theory always read as if they were written with reluctance, under the impulse of a conscience spurred by national crisis, when the writer would be more at home writing analytical social science. Nevertheless his objectivity should not be underestimated, nor his ability to see ahead of his present position. Neither of these abilities was dimmed by this urge towards prescriptive writing. But there is at times an uncertainty as to whether he is saying 'this is' when he actually says 'this should be', or whether he means 'this is what I think the evidence indicates' when he actually says 'this is'.

Le Play is obviously not unique in finding his social fighting with his scientific conscience. However, in his case this struggle explains much of his later writing, its apparent inconsistencies, and how it is that such a wide variety of people have been able to claim his support for their views. His opposition to state intervention applied to personal and economic affairs, and was based on his understanding of the British system. At the same time he bitterly criticised the English economists for leaving human beings to the mercy of economic forces, and he advocated nationalisation of the mines and forests in France (on pragmatic grounds, namely that no one else seemed capable of running them). In terms of controversies then current in France, he was a strong advocate of decentralisation. This meant giving more power to local government. It also involved a strong central government, undiluted by the necessity of frequent appeals to the people, and a local government with the maximum degree of democracy. For the central government he had reservations about universal suffrage, but thought that in France this 'dangerous experiment' should be continued.[17]

Le Play hated violence in all forms. This made him an opponent of revolution. It also made him an opponent of all militarism, and he regarded military adventures as a sign of decadence. He opposed colonialism. 'The system of annexing territories by force without the consent of the people is the great scourge of the west,' he wrote.[18] It would be true to say that the question – does or did it produce violence? – was a main criterion for Le Play in judging any political regime. English historians might think that Le Play had some illusions about the English system; but the fact that the country had not had civil war for a century was sufficient to recommend its system in Le Play's eyes. In general, the ruler must earn the right to govern; he abdicated this right by any form of corruption, and to this rulers were much prone. Le Play would certainly have agreed with Lord Acton's saying about the corruption of power, but he might have wished to change the last word – 'absolute power corrupts *differently*' would be more in keeping with his thought. For he saw special forms of corruption in democratic government, especially unskilful innovation and factionalism. He saw other forms of corruption as characteristic of autocratic government, including undue resistance to change and the tendency to embark on military adventures. If corrupt rulers had abdicated the right to govern, this fact does not give their subjects the right to revolt. For social violence, the problem of democratic regimes, was worse than the international violence produced by dictators. This peace at any price policy on the home as well as the foreign front accounts for Le Play's caution about social reform. We are faced here with a scheme of priorities, with opposition to violence at the top of the list. This makes an oppressive regime preferable to civil war, but illegitimate for all that. No wonder Le Play has proved a useful source of quotation for people of widely differing views.

Le Play's caution about reform extended to his views on education. On principle he believed in universal education, and urged employers to ensure that there was provision for the education of their young workers; in practice he was more cautious and evidently feared the consequences of too much education. Nevertheless, he produced many ideas about educational reform; and this subject became an important one to his followers, one of whom (Demolins) founded the Ecole des Roches on the model of the *avant garde* English public school, Bedales. Le Play himself was not in favour of boarding schools, on the grounds that they weakened parental influence. Although it so happened that he sent his son to one, a matter on which this latter did not follow his example. Indeed, he drily remarked that it took his father, a well-known expert on education, long enough to see through the school to which he had sent him. The aspect of English education that Le Play did admire, on the other hand, was apprenticeship. He did not favour the full-time technical courses which were developing in other parts of Europe. The wrong sort of education, in Le Play's view, could be as damaging as the lack of it. He divided the subject into two parts – academic and social. The former had to be taught, the latter could be taught but was also acquired from experience. This division corresponded to the division in knowledge between technical and moral; and just as technical progress is outstripping moral, so academic education has gone far beyond social. This imbalance is an important source of social problems.[19] For academic education without social produces false ideas which promote the disintegration of society. Both types of education should be oriented to the current needs of society. This is crucial to the formation of policies for higher education. On the other hand, there is only limited scope, he thought, for the development of social education. We have already seen how he advocated courses of social studies at the Ecole des Mines. For the rest, social education was best performed by the family. It could also be carried out by the employer, as in the case of apprentices.

To turn from education to business, here again practices were to be judged in the light of the theories of social change and cohesion. As in government, the man in authority needed to earn the right to be heard. The responsibility of the employer has already been discussed, and is the subject of one of Le Play's books – *L'Organisation du Travail*. In this, as in the third volume of *La Réforme sociale*, he discusses in detail the relationship between the structure of society in general and its influence on particular institutions. Thus a closeknit society with a strong family life can make for an industrial development with the minimum of dislocation and the maximum of personal security. The evidence for this was in his studies of certain parts of Germany and Sweden. But Le Play's nostalgic regard for the small master did not blind him to economic realities; so he faced the problem of what form of industrial organisation was most suitable to the human, the technical, and the economic realities. This varied, in his view, from industry to industry. In general, large-scale industry had the resources, especially opportunities for research, not available to the small business. In some industries this was so compelling a consideration as to override others. Steel and railways were examples of such industries. Where this was so he urged a point often discussed since, the attempt to combine the human advantages of the small firm with the economic advantages of the large one. Wherever possible, however, he favoured the small company. At the end of the day, he would argue, the object of work was virtue rather than riches. But there were other ingredients in his view of work, some elementary role theory for instance.

Sociological theories of role-playing include the concept 'role specialisation'. Naturally this was not a phrase that Le Play ever used, but the underlying facts were noticed by him. Role specialisation is described by Frankenberg[20] as arising in situations where different types of role relation are played with different groups of people. The reverse, role generalisation, is the typical situation in a rural society. There a man may have an *economic* role (employer, for example), a *recreational* role (secretary of the village football team, for example), a *governmental* role (a magistrate) and a *religious* role (a local preacher) to the same group of people. He may also have a *kinship* role (such as that of father) to some of the people with whom he is involved in those other role relationships. Thus the performance of one role may be said to *reinforce* that of another. Relationships are closer and more continuous. Authority in one role supports authority in another. Cross-referencing between roles aids social cohesion, even if perhaps to an extent which the person unaccustomed to role reinforcement would find oppressive. As society becomes more industrialised, the tendency is for roles to become more 'specialised'. The trend is for the individual to play his different types of role in relation to different groups of people.

Le Play saw this trend and discussed the issues involved. He saw that role specialisation could, in the workers' eyes, mean greater freedom. But his concern with social peace made him much concerned with the effects on social cohesion. The limited range of relationships between employers and employed and the increasing separation between work life and home life helped to produce the divided society. Further, one consequence of role specialisation is that it increased the problems of authority. To use another word not used in this sense by Le Play, the manager had greater difficulty in 'legitimating' his authority when it was limited to the employer–employee relationship. The sort of diffusion of this role relationship implied by the company shop and the tied house notoriously increased the power of the employer, and thus eased his problems of 'legitimation'. Hence Le Play's concern with management education was linked to his understanding of the changing role relationship. The amount of skill needed in management increased as the range of role relationships narrowed. The formal development of social skills became vital. In keeping with his general outlook Le Play assumed that large-scale industry was most easily corrupted, and that the supply of adequate management of the right calibre was unlikely to be achieved. Thus he deduced that society needed a mixture of large and small concerns – the former to be technical leaders, and the latter social pace-setters. He appears to assume that the state should ensure a satisfactory balance between the two types of concern by such devices as the allocation of state contracts.[21]

Le Play, we have already said, advocated private ownership where this showed itself able to succeed. But the wellbeing of society must override any doctrinaire ideas of ownership. In France, in his opinion, the administration of the forests and mines had shown that private individuals or firms, were unable to manage them successfully. Hence the state must intervene.[22] However, in the case of the forests state control was only to last until a viable form of private ownership could develop. The wouldbe owner must earn the right to own. A long-term view and a willingness to sink individual self-interests were required in such an owner. Wood was still an important fuel in Le Play's time, so there was a close link between the forestry and metal industries. In his view they should be organised together. If they were being managed efficiently they could be left alone. If not, the state must take over. The smaller veins consisting of rarer metals were best exploited by family enterprises, but here the laws of succession interfered. So Le Play returned to his constant theme that inappropriate social organisation produced disastrous economic results. The decline of the precious metals industry, he wrote, 'cannot be put down to the fruitlessness of the metal-bearing seams; it is due to bad institutions which dry up the fertile sources of action'.[23]

In his writings on industry, Le Play discussed organisation. He took the view that different types of industrial organisation were suitable for different industries, and the word 'suitable' must be understood in the light of his assessment of the wellbeing of those engaged in the industry. To discuss his views on such issues as nationalisation in terms either of modern politics or of classical economics, for instance, would be to misunderstand his approach completely. Inasmuch as he had prejudices on the matter, they were influenced by the tendency of authoritarian regimes to interfere unduly in industrial affairs; but he was equally clear about the effects of extreme *laissez-faire*; so he condemned many aspects of British industrial life, but praised the Factory Acts. The clue to his attitude on this, as on so many other matters, is the phrase used earlier – 'a technologist with a social conscience'. The extractive industries needed above all long-term planning, and hence an organisation with the capital and the will to undertake this had to be found. In England this had proved possible by a partnership of the large landowners, who owned the mineral rights, and the mining companies, to whom they granted leases for extraction and in whom they themselves invested. In the German states, Hanover for example, the state had replaced the landowner in a similar partnership. This had advantages because it facilitated long-term planning; it also made for better industrial relations because the state was more interested in safeguarding its citizens against the fluctuations of trade. However, Le Play stressed that this was the case in small states, and that these really had the character of regional government rather than over-centralised national government. In France, there was a lack of sufficient advance planning which had had disastrous results on the coal and mineral industries, hence he advocated state or regional control.[24] For most forms of manufacturing industry, on the other hand, he advocated private enterprise limited by the principles of *patronage*. *Patronage* ideally had its roots in the adaptation of local customs to new industrial situations. Hence it should gain a steady acceptance by both sides in industry, and where this happened the state should not intervene. For any intervention would be likely to be clumsy and damaging to the delicate links built up by custom. On the other hand, some state intervention was necessary where no such links had survived industrialisation. For light industry and for commerce other forms of organisation, such as cooperative societies, might be relevant.

Here it would seem appropriate to insert a word on Le Play's attitude to the cooperative movement, for this illustrates the pragmatic nature of his thought, and a further example of conflict between economic and social desirability. He took little interest in the consumers' cooperatives which developed so rapidly in England after the Rochdale pioneers in 1844;[25] but he had considerable acquaintance with producers' co-operatives, to which he gave a guarded encouragement. Some of these organisations of producers were survivors of ancient communities and federations. Thus he lists group holdings in the iron industry in various parts of Europe dating from the Middle Ages, along with examples that had grown up more recently in other industries, especially in France and England. While sympathetic to these newer ventures, he doubted whether many of them would survive because of the general diffuseness of their organisation. He took the view that only a limited number of workers would be suitable for cooperative production because of the special qualities required.[26] Gaumont, in his history of cooperation in France,[27] has shown how Le Play himself did not give much open support to the cooperative movement, but many of his followers did.

Nevertheless, he supported 'self-help' among workers, and when Prince Napoleon was asked to subscribe towards a new producers' cooperative society, it was to Le Play that he wrote for advice. Le Play's reply is unknown, but in fact in 1864 the Emperor himself showed some support for the cooperative movement, and in the same year an imperial investigation showed that workmen worked better in cooperative associations.

In 1867 legislation was introduced to facilitate the formation of cooperatives. In spite of this general support, Le Play expresses some disillusion in *La Réforme sociale*. Naturally, also, he and his followers were only interested in the practical aspects; they were impatient of the idealistic vision of the cooperative movement. There were also some who said that cooperation was an illusion. A successful venture, the argument ran, soon turned into a joint stock company.

The practice of *patronage*, described above, was not intended just to be paternalistic. An analogy with the rich man's patronage of the artist was also intended. Further, it should be stressed that Le Play counselled discretion on the employer's part. One of Le Play's friends said that he 'remarked that it [*patronage*] produced all its fruits only if the patron took care to conceal his action and to awaken with regard to the workers a feeling for their own initiative'.[28] This discretion was all part of the business of earning the right to be heard and he condemned 'indiscreet' patronage, as witness the mercury firm in Austria. The view of the employer was to treat labour as a commodity to be bought and sold in the market-place like any other material. It was because Le Play disliked this so strongly that he so often criticised the classical economists who had made the market-place view socially acceptable. He was equally opposed to the socialists, and on the same grounds. He did not believe that conflict between employers and employed was inevitable.

His lack of a theory of conflict might well be regarded as Le Play's main weakness. He was concerned to establish good informal contact between employers and employed based on a common outlook on life. And he still regarded this as possible in spite of studies which showed a breakdown in good relations in country after country. On principle, government intervention should only underpin or make possible the restoration of satisfactory social links based on custom; but where the situation was bedevilled by serious conflict, the government should intervene even to the extent of dispossessing the proprietors. Indeed, government action and trade union power he saw as second-best developments which were yet made necessary by the events. As a technologist writing to employers, he was concerned above all with their responsibility towards their workers. If he still lived in the past, and thought that these 'responsibilities' could be restored by exhortation, he also saw the trends of the future and drew attention to them. He did much to create a climate of opinion within which joint consultation could develop.

In *L'Organisation du Travail*, Le Play lists six essential needs of the worker. The first was permanent contracts, both between the employer and the worker and vice versa. The second was a complete understanding between the two on wages. This was an optimistic suggestion, but was intended to prevent exploitation and maintain peace at the same time. Custom was to settle wages, rather than bargaining or the authority of the employer. The third was local diversification. Le Play noticed the problem, so often discussed since, that it was dangerous for a region to be overdependent on heavy industry. There was need to ensure that in any area a balanced industrial development took place. Heavy industry alone made the district liable to chronic unemployment, and meant a lack of any suitable employment for disabled men or for women. The fourth need was the provision of suitable means of saving. Some of this should be compulsory, in the form of obligatory insurance schemes. Le Play and members of the Société d'Economie sociale had deduced from their studies that the bulk of workers' savings was through compulsory saving. They lived through the rapid increase of both compulsory and voluntary schemes by savings banks, cooperative organisations, mutual benefit societies and insurance companies. But, clearly, only a limited number of people made adequate provision for their future needs voluntarily. The fifth and sixth needs have been discussed under Le Play's view of the family – they are protection from eviction, and protection for women.

Reconstruction is the main theme of Le Play's social thought. Hating revolution, he developed a pattern of reform by encouraging what his researches had convinced him were the more cohesive elements in society. There is a sense in which his analysis was revolutionary and his prescription ultra-conservative, and this may well be the clue to the problem of understanding his political philosophy. Something of this was suggested in a letter written to Le Play from an Austrian supporter comparing his views with those of Marx.[29] Perceptively this letter says that starting from a similar basis and with a similar analysis, Max postulates the building of a new society, Le Play the remaking of an old one. Has, the writer asks, Le Play a convincing answer to the retort that this reconstruction is impossible? Those who suggest he has are told, 'Le Play wants to teach us to swim when we feel the water up to our necks.' Le Play did not demur to the suggestion that he and Marx had a common starting point. In his reply he criticised Marx's claim that the accumulation of capital necessarily damaged the relations of the workers and the bourgeoisie. He went on: 'As a conclusion, he arrives at the common ownership of property. While we are reproached for going back to the Middle Ages to find there the elements of social reconstruction; he postulates the model for the society of which he dreams in the organisation of certain Hindustani Communities, whose memory is lost in the darkness of the ages.' In view of this quotation it would be easy to write about the dangers of underestimating Marx; but Le Play certainly did not underestimate the divisive forces operating in the new economic conditions. Nor did he have any illusions about the trend of opinion. In 1868 he wrote to Père Hyacinthe that the young now think Proudhon too modest when he called property 'theft'. They think he should have said 'murder', and against this 'error' Le Play prescribes 'clearer thinking'.

Perhaps the closest to Le Play's views in England were the tories of the radical–tory alliance. Men who by nature viewed the state with suspicion, but did not hesitate to call upon it to set right the evils of unbridled individualism, and thus joined with the radicals in promoting the original Factory Acts. Le Play had a strong pacifist streak, and disliked violence in any form. This pacifism made him condemn unsparingly the military adventures of the Empire as well as revolution. But he had a deeper reason for opposing this latter, even against an unjust and tyrannical regime. For he took the view that it is in the nature of revolution to destroy the delicate, informal threads which make life tolerable while retaining and even strengthening the oppressive external structures of society. That the external structure was maintained others besides Le Play have pointed out. While rival groups shot one another in the streets, the same civil servants continued to operate the same codes of laws. This was less true in 1848, when the shortlived Provisional Government did bring in some reforms which survived the various counterrevolutions and became permanent. But even after 1789 it was the oppressive laws, for instance those against trade unions, which tended to become permanent as opposed to rudimentary efforts to smooth over the social transition. In any case, Le Play said, the political revolution was of minor importance beside the technological revolution which largely produced it. What were the really significant events of the 1790s, he once asked, the struggle for power in France or the development of new machinery across the Channel? More than once he suggested that France lost out in the industrial race through a fascination for the details of political doctrines. On this matter of his attitude to revolution, Le Play has been the subject of many different interpretations. The comments of Saint-Beuve have already been quoted. Perhaps he is best seen as a link between pre-industrial society and the welfare state. He might not have welcomed the latter, and he would certainly have cried 'decadent' to its successor, the affluent society. But his social conscience which led him into social science led him out again, groping for a social theory which would satisfy his stern demands.

If his politics are hard to pin down, so is his religion. Victor Brants says that Le Play convinced himself of the truth of the Catholic religion by 'simple analysis of the facts'. Charles Gide sees him as a religious but unclerical reformer; among his proposed reforms was a reduction in the numbers of clergy, with correspondingly increasing spheres of activity for the laity. Paul Ribot describes him as a humanist, interested in the Decalogue but not the New Testament. Baudin points out his strong dislike of religious orders and clerical celibacy which undermined his view of the family. It was the parish priest of Saint-Sulpice at the time of Le Play's death, the Abbé Riche, who wrote that he came to the practices of religion in his old age.[30] After he died, some obituary writers suggested that his religion was one of the Old Testament – his claim to discover social truth by observation was, they pointed out, contrary to Catholic teaching about revelation.

Between his politics and his religion there is his pessimism, his bitter attack on the facile optimism which he saw to be misleading opinion at the time. This pessimism made him advocate restrictions on power in politics, and the upholding of custom rather than state action. Religion was the sanction for this custom and the most satisfactory restraint on power. His religion was a social cement. Men, as he often liked to say, had two needs – daily bread and the moral law. Religion was a necessary support underpinning the moral law. Le Play's view of religion did not imply any personal relationship with the Almighty, nor did it contain any supernatural content beyond the use of the word 'God' as a vague sanction for his ethics. Only at the very end of his life did he become what is known as a 'practising Catholic'. For the rest of his life his religion was universalistic. He specifically said[31] that the Chinese practised monotheism and the moral law more than the French. The clergy, like others in positions of leadership, had to earn the right to be heard, and he constantly criticised weaknesses in the organisation of the Catholic Church in France.

An attempt to produce a theological interpretation of Le Play was made by a liberal Capuchin, Ludovic de Besse.[32] As a result of his studies Le Play taught, he writes, 'that true social reform ought to consist in organising the correction of original sin'. De Besse had evidently been inspired by Le Play to some thoughts on the sociology of religion. He discusses the gap between the Church and the industrial masses, and suggests among other reasons that the break-up of the traditional guilds (*corporations de métiers*) has robbed the clergy of the opportunity to speak to the specialised needs of the workers.

The phrase 'original sin' is obviously linked with Le Play's pessimism, but as an inspirer of action and not (as sometimes) to lead to quietism. Indeed, as Einaudi has pointed out,[33] consciousness of original sin is one of the marks of the elite for Le Play. A man may be a *de facto* ruler but not a member of the elite because he has lost awareness of original sin and the necessity of observing the ten commandments. However, in his correspondence with de Curzon towards the end of his life, Le Play drew an interesting distinction. This was between what he called 'original sin' and 'original vice'. The former was the concern of the theologians. The latter was, he claimed, discoverable by social observation. It was corrected by moral teaching and experience. This stress on experience was one of Le Play's links with the old world; it led him to say that the young were more subject to 'original vice' than older people. Hence the danger of granting authority to those who were too young or too optimistic. They were not yet part of the true elite.

So this chapter has attempted to trace Le Play's thought as he moved from social investigation to social prescription. The central question to him was how to control the forces of social change so as to maintain social peace. He was examining and re-examining his material in the light of this question. On the one hand he was balancing his own experience of violence, on the other hand he had discovered much in the collection of his case studies which suggested needs and aspirations society was failing to fulfil. Since his theory of social change involved a deep pessimism about human nature, he concentrated on the corruption he saw in every institution examined. He shared the technical self-confidence of his time, while persistently reminding people that social skills had actually declined at the same time as technical knowledge was increasing.

6

The followers

The Le Play School

Le Play had a special genius for collecting able collaborators. His own personality together with his ability to bring together technical and social issues attracted people to him, and many of those who aligned themselves with his views had European reputations. The phrase 'Le Play School' was first used in the early 1850s. This has been called 'the first sociological school of thought in history',[1] and 'the first to formulate correlations between places and the different characteristics of social life'. In 1856 was founded the Société internationale des Etudes pratiques d'Economie sociale. The name has changed, but the society still exists, and Le Play's ideas and influence have spread through it. The first President was Dr Villermé, himself one of Le Play's predecessors in the field of social studies. Many famous people subsequently led the society – Michel Chevalier, Daru, Wolowsky, Melun, Charles Robert, de Lesseps. The society was founded to promote the scientific study of social facts and among its objectives was the training of a corps of observers. Most of the members were amateur social scientists, conscientiously collecting facts. In a similar way amateur astronomers and biologists were active at the time, extending the frontiers of knowledge and setting the scene for advances that were to come later. Le Play's society discussed case studies such as those printed in *Les Ouvriers Européens* and others modelled on them. They also discussed how to improve the research method. Until his death Le Play himself was Secretary-General and arranged the discussions, which were usually led by people who shared his outlook. So the minutes of the society contain much material on the views of Le Play and his school. At a meeting in 1862, there was an appraisal of progress to that date.[2] At this meeting Le Play spoke about his aims and methods. He suggested that the social survey was made necessary by social division. He went on to summarise the outlook of the school by saying: 'Friends of progress, but dreading disorder and sterile agitation, we summon onto the ground of experience, fertilised by study and discussion, all the men who wish to render our country free, great and prosperous.' The main features of the method of observation were then outlined and discussed. The conditions of success were described as the winning of the confidence of the family to be studied, scrupulous accuracy, and lack of bias in reporting the results.

In 1864 the Society decided to widen its discussions, and to try to relate the observational techniques it had developed to broader issues of social policy. The issues thus investigated included a wide range of topics. As an illustration some of those which followed directly from the industrial studies are described below. At the first meeting after this decision was taken (18 December 1864) a Colonel Favé read a paper 'On the means of organising free apprenticeship for the poor adolescent'. Colonel Favé was quite clear that apprenticeships should be made more readily available by means of state subsidies for training schemes, and state grants to parents to compensate them for the wages the boys would otherwise be earning. He thought this was an economical proposition for the state for four reasons. The first was that the boy, and his parents before his marriage, would not be chargeable on public funds once he had completed his apprenticeship. The second was, similarly, that after his marriage he would be able to support his family. The third was that he would add to the nation's resources; and the fourth was that he was not so likely to add to the nation's crime.

Colonel Favé then went on to discuss reasons why this was best done by the state. Like Le Play he distrusted state intervention on principle, but thought that private charity was inadequate in practice. Two of the most distinguished members of the society – Melun and Wolowski – championed private societies such as L'Oeuvre des apprentis et des jeunes ouvrières de la ville de Paris which had supported twelve to thirteen thousand apprentices of both sexes. The Vicomte de Melun, a great patron of voluntary social services, supported this. He went on to say that the traditional apprenticeship was, in any case, in decline. Articles were a dead letter, and neither party really accepted a binding obligation. Both speakers advocated an extension of full-time education. The Vicomte de Melun thought the problem was not one of idle children, but of children who worked too hard too soon.

Another discussion on apprenticeship was held on 21 February 1869. The discussion also brought out the decline of articles of apprenticeship which were becoming hard to enforce, and centred round four demands put forward by the workers for the reform of apprenticeship. The first demand of the workers was for a further limitation of the number of apprentices in relation to skilled workers. The speaker regarded this as incompatible with liberty and the needs of an expanding industry. The

E

second demand was to make twelve the minimum age of entry to apprenticeship, and that only for those who could read or write. Of this demand the speaker entirely approved. It is curious to find that the workers demanded this provision, which enabled the brighter children to leave school earlier; once incorporated in the law, this provision was to come under heavy fire from the workers, and indeed seems anomalous today. The third demand of the workers was for shorter working hours and part-time education. This also the speaker approved of, although he thought it might be difficult to enforce. Finally, the workers demanded a certificate of competence for the successful apprentice. They did not demand financial assistance for the parents of the sort that the society had discussed at the 1864 meeting. Le Play spoke on the subject of the limitation of hours. He agreed that legislation should not be necessary to force employers to limit the number of hours during which they could work women and children; but there had been a breakdown of custom on these matters. So he thought there should be legislation, but subject to annual renewal to ensure a regular check on the position.

In 1874 there was another discussion on apprentices. J. Dumas, the President that year, ran a voluntary apprentice society (La Société des Apprentis). He was a champion of the need to raise the prestige of the craftsman; and he advocated that a general education should continue together with craft teaching during apprenticeship. A member of the Société d'Economie sociale, Monsieur Legentil, had just prepared a report on apprenticeship in Paris and he outlined this to the meeting. He brought up the argument, often heard since, about the danger of dead-end jobs. The young office-boy, he said, learns little and spends most of his time on errands which are 'a sort of authorised vagabondage' and he has no chance of promotion unless he is well educated. It came out in discussion that in 1874 the number of apprenticeships was declining – mechanisation was increasing the proportion of semi-skilled jobs. Dangers to apprentices resulted from bad organisation of industry, bad conditions of employment, lack of education, the atmosphere of the workshop, bad examples from older men. The laws of 1841 and 1851 had provided some protection, and some further protection was included in a law under discussion. The new law would enforce holidays and abolish night work. One interesting feature of the new law was the introduction of part-time study. As were other members of the society, Monsieur Legentil was much more concerned with the extension of full-time education. He doubted the practicability of part-time study for the apprentices or for the firms. He was keen on an extension of *patronage* so that someone was responsible for the general guidance of the apprentice, who had no one apart from the voluntary societies to champion him. The *Conseils de Prud'hommes* might be the right sort of bodies to protect them; but these only represented employers and adult workers. They did not, for instance, include representatives of parents as such.[3]

At a meeting on 13 January 1867 Wolowski was elected President. This Polish exile who lived in Paris most of his life was one of the more unusual members of the society. A keen republican, he had not made his peace with the Emperor; he was not part of the 'establishment' like some leaders of the society. On the other hand he was a supporter of the classical economists. He was also a humane student of industrial affairs and in his presidential address he said: 'Never forget, while you admire the marvels of industry, to research into the conditions under which they are produced, to see if they do not show signs of the tears they have caused to flow.' There followed a discussion around a monograph of a Grenoble glove-worker which covered many subjects including the employment of women. An English member, C. F. Audley, shared Le Play's dislike of women having to work in factories. Henri Ameline, who developed Le Play's thought on many matters, supported this but said that where they were employed there should be equal pay. Other speakers disagreed, and Wolowski himself would allow women to work in factories subject to legal safeguards. Le Play repeated his arguments for finding suitable work for those who really needed it.

In January 1870 Charles Robert, a Protestant, was elected President of the Society. Robert was an ardent promoter of cooperative schemes, and especially copartnership and profit-sharing. In his presidential address he said that the trend of the times was to peace between the nations and war between the classes. This underlined the need to hasten researches and plans aimed at genuine conciliation. Le Play was away ill from this meeting; but subsequently he warmly supported Robert, and suggested that the whole of the following session should be devoted to the question of profit-sharing. In fact the siege of Paris and the Revolution sabotaged this suggestion, and when they did meet again, in November 1871, it was to spend two meetings discussing a sociological study of the Prussian Army.

In the 1870s the Society had a series of meetings to discuss the existing situation in industrial relations. In 1872, for instance, Amédée Burat read a paper on the coal-mines of Blanzy. Burat thought highly of the efforts of the company at that time, but these same mines were condemned for paternalism by Paul Bureau thirty years later. The company had been founded at Montceau-les-Mines in 1834. The district was a thinly populated semi-desert, high up and with harsh winters. Hence there was a strong incentive to set up a regime of *patronage* to attract and hold labour. This was one practical argument for *patronage*. It did draw labour to such remote areas. It was popular with some workers, even if the more self-conscious did regard the system as emphasising their dependence. The discussion on Blanzy raised some controversial questions. One was the provision of shops by the company. When this was criticised as making the workers undesirably dependent, the company replied that they were trying to prevent the workers being exploited by parasitic traders in their isolated township. Again, the provision of houses was criticised, but here the company said their policy was not to rent houses but to give their workers an interest-free loan for house-purchase. Once his house was paid for, the worker was free to leave the company. No doubt many of the workers were in debt to the company, and the debt took a long time to pay off. So the company had some hold over them; but at the same time the company suffered from much absenteeism in the summer when the workers were busy on their smallholdings. The company had a careful selection and promotion policy. The attempt to put the right men in the right jobs was noted on the credit side. On the other side was the fact that the company retained the right to withdraw privileges from those who were considered not to have deserved them. These 'privileges' included a number of social security measures – cut-price food (at the company shops), medical and relief services, cheap fuel, pensions at sixty, half-pensions for widows at fifty – and amenities. The amenities included the upkeep of the town, its church, chapels, schools and hospital. The system here described is typical of what Le Play called *patronage*. There is no reason to suppose that the employers consciously asked themselves, 'How can we ensure the subordination of our labour force?' Sufficient question was, 'How can we man a colliery in such an area?' For an answer they turned to the precedents of a more primitive form of society, but at least they caused the workers to complain, when they did complain, of their excessive humanity and not of their inhumanity. They did not create a race of industrial nomads in a social desert. They tried to create a settled, balanced community. Further, in this particular case, the directors lived in the community. They were no absentee masters. If they did not see beyond *patronage* to a more developed system, they at least ensured that development would one day occur by building seven schools for the children of a labour force of 3,600 workers.

Another meeting which discussed industrial relations specifically was addressed by an engineer from Lyons, Jules Michel.[4] He spoke about a paper mill at Annonay and a marine cement works at Teil. Two significant points came out in the first case. The employer had made it his business to try to promote a better community spirit inside and outside the mill on the grounds that 'man does not live by bread alone', and that this saying had a special relevance to the promotion of satisfactory human relations. The other point was that he had tried to attend to the 'bread' first. There were three bonus schemes in operation. One was a group bonus based on production, the second was a bonus based on economies effected, and the third was an individual bonus paid for length of service. The second of these three is the most interesting. The search for an incentive scheme for workers on jobs for which normal production bonuses would not apply is often regarded as a twentieth-century quest. Here is an example of an employer in the 1870s who was operating such a scheme.

The two factories under discussion had one thing in common – they were both in isolated positions, and the employer was necessarily involved in matters outside the factory, such as housing. There the resemblance ended. The paper mill was run with the cooperation of the employees, and some attempt to involve them at many points. The cement works was run autocratically, with low wages, but some social services, and an employer who relied on his personal touch to keep the peace in his factory. The speaker remarked that this type of relationship might succeed, but it could not last indefinitely. Le Play was missing from this meeting through illness, but one of his persistent themes was that industry could not contract out of the influence it had on its workers' lives. It had that influence in any case, and it had a duty to see that the influence was used beneficially – Michel echoed this thought of Le Play when he said in conclusion: 'Is not the true aim of industry to help the families of the workers whose cooperation it claims to live suitably and to develop their moral and intellectual culture?'

At another meeting, held in 1876[5] a Monsieur Lehaussois spoke at length about the history of La Société d'Economie sociale, now twenty years old, and its influence so far. Part of his speech was devoted to industrial relations, and he gave three examples of the influence of the society here. One was the industrial relations competition of 1867.[6] The international jury had used the principles set out in *Les Ouvriers européens* and *Les Ouvriers des deux mondes* as criteria for their decisions. Secondly, he quoted a factory owner who had told him that he had learnt, from discussions at the society, the principles of management which he had tried to work out in his factory. No doubt many factory owners could have said this: but it needs to be emphasised that nowhere did members of the Society commit themselves to any set of principles other than the general guides set out in *L'Organisation du Travail*. 'Feel your way, humanely', would have been Le Play's advice; he never suggested a rigid code for management. Hence the speaker must have meant that the factory owner had been inspired with a valid perspective on management by the Society, not that he had learnt a set of rules there. And Monsieur Lehaussois's third point was that a recent report on the state of industry showed the influence of the Society.

Monsieur Lehaussois also made two perceptive points on the changing role of the employer in society and the changing significance of industrial relations. He added that the Society planned monographs on these matters. The employer had ceased to be the 'patron' of a small group of workpeople. He was becoming a significant part of the government of the country. In 1876, he was saying, the chairman of a large concern wielded an influence on the whole structure of society analogous to that of a minister of state. This power was different in kind from the power of the old employer. During this century employers of labour had gained a place in the shaping of their country's progress previously held by government, the Church, the outstanding thinkers. A different, but equally significant, change was taking place in the conduct of industrial relations. The area of disagreement between employer and employed was ceasing to be over purely industrial questions, and was beginning to include every sphere of human concern – industrial, social, political, religious. The workers' leaders back in 1830, the speaker pointed out, did not preach atheism. One might think that the changes in the role of the employer and the changes in the conduct of industrial relations had more in common than the speaker suggested. Like Le Play, it seems that he could not bring himself to see the logic of his own insights. Paradoxically one could say that he tells us what he did not know himself, namely that industrial conflict had become a governmental matter; that the two sides ranged against each other in this conflict were both already led by men having political importance – an importance that carried with it social, religious and moral implications. At a meeting of the Society the following year, one of the leaders of the first International was to underline this very point.

Meanwhile, another interesting character addressed the Society the following month[7] – Emile Cheysson. Cheysson is not often mentioned among Le Play's successors; he did not contribute to the progress of social science like de Tourville or Demolins; but in many ways he was the most like Le Play himself. A director of the great works at Le Creusot, he was a distinguished engineer with many interests in social studies and social services. In 1884, two years after Le Play's death, he started a course of social studies at L'Ecole des Mines where, like Le Play, he eventually became vice-principal. So popular did he become that when at a function in 1906 to celebrate the centenary of Le Play's birth he casually referred to his own coming retirement, he nearly sabotaged the meeting. (The principal had to intervene hastily to explain the rigidity of the age-limit rule.) Meanwhile, to La Société d'Economie sociale in 1876 he spoke about 'permanent employment' and spoke, he said, at Le Play's special request. Le Play and he regarded this as the most important issue in industrial relations. If casual labour could be abolished, other improvements would follow. The traditional suspicion of the workers for permanent contracts as reminiscent of serfdom was not mentioned by Cheysson. He sees the other side of the coin, the fear of unemployment among the workers. Like more modern writers, he sees this fear as influencing the outlook of the workers on most matters; every industrial question has been bedevilled by giving the workers a sense of insecurity. The price of 'free' labour is unemployment, pauperism, hatred. 'The employer hires and fires at will, the workers regard the employer as an enemy and the factory as a temporary misfortune. The large firm and the state industries do not set as good an example as they might.'

Some teach 'resignation', Cheysson continued. To them instability, pauperism, unemployment and strife were unavoidable in an industrial civilisation. But this was surely not so; it was a question of attitude. Some employers had decided not to make a fortune through the misery and degradation of those they regarded as 'collaborators'. This was all of a piece with Le Play's emphasis on saving; the main purpose of the thrift was to ensure that the employer could retain his labour force during a slump. The role of the government was neutral unless an employer was shown to be seriously failing in his responsibility. The engineering students whom Cheysson taught can never have been allowed to forget that the first task of the manager was the wellbeing of his men. At a later meeting Cheysson was to be one of the members of the society who argued for finding as much common ground as possible with the socialists of the First International. In suggesting specific areas of collaboration – the search for a basis for permanent contracts, the improvement of conditions for women, the support of self-help and cooperative schemes – he demonstrated the sincerity of his undoctrinaire approach. He also reported that an American Commission investigating the question of strikes had listed 'permanent employment' as the first of remedies.[8] The other recommendations were also in line with Le Play's thinking – long service bonuses, company-assisted pensions, and a committee of appeal against the decisions of officials.

Another interesting member of La Société d'Economie sociale was Michel Chevalier. Prosecuted as a Saint-Simonian under the July Monarchy, Chevalier represented an aggressive industrialisation in which all classes should have a stake. Much less interested than Le Play in trying to bring back some supposed period of social peace, he was just as interested in schemes for improved industrial relations. On the whole he took the view that increased industrial activity and free trade would of themselves raise the standards and status of the workers. He is known in England for his negotiation of an Anglo-French trading agreement. (Incidentally, during his year of presidency of La Société d'Economie sociale, the minutes record the absence of the President from one meeting as he was busy with plans for an undersea tunnel from France to England.) Eighteen seventy-eight was a year in which Le Play's influence was shown in many directions, including official reports and legislation. It was also a year when reaction against his ideas was strong. For the Paris International Exhibition of that year did not exhibit *patronage* in industry, nor were social studies emphasised. These were brought back in subsequent exhibitions in 1889 and 1900.

In April 1882 the society held a major conference on social and industrial questions. This was the meeting (mentioned above in Chapter 1) which was to have been Le Play's comeback, and for which he carefully planned the programme. In fact, it took place soon after his death and was his memorial; but his programme was retained. At this meeting a message to the society was read out by Emile Cheysson, who said Le Play had written this two years before when he thought he was dying. The message characteristically urges a 'wise economy' on the society which should live within its income. It asks members to be rigorous in their judgment of monographs and not to publish inferior ones, and that a school for social peace should be set up. He hopes:

> . . . that the same spirit always controls our meetings; that we are concerned with social facts, with exact observation and not with *a priori* theories; that politics and personalities should always be strictly barred. That we abstain from voting on the conclusions of reports, leaving it to each member to draw his own conclusions.

Once again Le Play emphasised that they were helping to build up a body of thought, not a ready-made system.

The Conference had six main speakers, all but one members of the society. Cheysson himself spoke on workers' houses, then Jules Michel spoke on *patronage*. As in his previous talk to the society, Michel stressed the need for fair wages before anything else. He said that the worker 'ought to find in the remuneration of his work the means of living, of bringing up his family, of satisfying his indispensable moral and intellectual needs', for Le Play's followers 'fair wages' were to be fixed well above the subsistence level. After wages, he regarded security as the most important consideration. This could be provided in a variety of ways that produced various benefits, but its importance was that it was a duty to the workers. The workers, Michel said, had as much right to be provided against risk of unemployment as the shareholders had to be paid a dividend. The role of La Société d'Economie sociale was to be constantly throwing out ideas for the development of better employment practices, and promoting the interchange of ideas between companies.

Sedley Taylor spoke on profit-sharing, and for one who was so interested in the subject he had nothing but failure to report. The earliest scheme he knew of was John Scott Vandeleur in Ireland. This was very successful until the founder gambled away the capital and hastily emigrated. But, said Sedley Taylor, the initial success had shown the possibility of profit-sharing to others. Among the other schemes he mentioned, he spoke a final epilogue on the profit-sharing of Briggs & Company, the much-publicised but ill-fated scheme in the British mining industry.

One new factor in industrial relations which interested some members of the society and appalled others was the increasing organisation and power of the trade union movement as represented by the First International. This stemmed from a meeting in London in 1864. Starting with a variety of influences, the First International was soon dominated by Marx. The first discussion La Société d'Economie sociale had on the matter[9] was introduced by Maxime Gaussen, who had been an employers' delegate to the Luxembourg Commission of 1848. He outlined the history of the series of congresses the International had held, and suggested that the four most significant aims were: the promotion of atheism, political equality and the abolition of inheritance, equality of the sexes, the victory of labour over capitalism. Where Cheysson picked out the objects with which members of the society might feel they had something in common, Gaussen underlined those

*

they were likely to reject outright. He was inclined to see a plot to promote strikes and riots in every country. But Gaussen also said that the needs and condition of men in society must be taken seriously. Those who refused to do this were condemned by the rise of socialism.

Clearly members of the society were likely to regard the First International as the result, not the cause, of conflict between the classes. On this point Le Play himself was clear in theory. The conflict arose from the corruption of the ruling classes and false teaching among the working classes. But there are many signs that Le Play was not so sure of this in practice. Perhaps to clarify his views on the subject, he invited Charles Limousin to speak to the society about the Congress of 1876.[10] Limousin was a veteran French workers' leader and delegate to the International, which he later left. He spoke of the progress in understanding between the classes, of which this particular meeting gave two signs. First, 'you have wanted, you members of the ruling classes, to have on social questions the opinion of a member of the lower classes'; and the 'second is in the rise in dignity of the class to which I belong, of which this honour done to me is proof. It is a step in the road to equality and the end of classes.' No comment from Le Play is recorded on that statement. Limousin went on to make a familiar point in a curious manner: 'Yesterday,' he said, 'you rose in the world by ennoblement, today by enrichment. . . . Now the new fact, in my opinion, is the presence among you of a representative of a group of men who have come out of the masses without enrichment.' Later in his speech he said that socialists believed in 'laws' as much as the classical economists, but thought that these 'laws' should be manipulated for the common good; it was the business of government to see that this happened. He showed a shrewd understanding of Le Play's point of view by suggesting that this was common ground between them.

In outlining the views of the International, Limousin diplomatically emphasised the points with which his hearers might agree. He mentioned the demand for limitations on the work of women together with equality of pay, and in passing stressed the great bitterness caused by the competition of the cheap labour of the convents. He listed also: abolition of legal disabilities on trade unions, development of co-operative societies, parliamentary representation for the workers, reform of bodies like the *Conseils de Prud'hommes*, more technical education, better provision for retirement, the recruitment of peasants into the trade union movement. He also said that thanks to the disabilities imposed upon them by the laws, the French workers lacked the experience and hence the statesmanship of their English counterparts.

The conciliatory nature of his talk did not prevent a fierce attack from members of the society – Rondelet accused him of leaving out all the important opinions of the International, and Gaussen launched a diatribe against socialism. Other members of the Society doubted whether there was any common ground between themselves and the socialists. But two meetings later they were once more discussing their 'common ground'.

In the last years of Le Play's life two significant figures joined his 'School'. One was Edmond Demolins (1852–1907), already mentioned in this study, who was secretary of the society and a rising young academic. The other was the Abbé Henri de Tourville (1842–1903). This latter was ordained to a parish in Paris in 1873, and was already associated with Le Play. His health broke down in 1881 and thenceforth he wrote his books in the family castle in Eure. These two became increasingly impatient of the moral and exhortatory element among Le Play's followers. It was Demolins who said that the master himself had set back the progress of social science by attempting to draw premature conclusions. He and de Tourville attempted to turn the Society into a purely scientific one. They began to develop a more accurate system of classification, to re-examine some of Le Play's studies, to forge new instruments of investigation. These efforts split the Le Play School. It is important to understand the nature of the split. It was not about matters of political or social reform, for people of varied opinions found themselves on both sides of the division. It was not about whether the subject should be treated 'scientifically'. Those on both sides of the split agreed that it should. They also agreed that the collection of monographs was an important activity. The split was about the relationship between analysis and prescription, the significance of conclusions that could be drawn from the type of evidence collected, the role of the social scientist.

De Tourville and Demolins left La Société d'Economie sociale in 1885, and founded La Société internationale de Science sociale. In January 1886 appeared the first issue of *La Science sociale* with an article by de Tourville under the title, 'La science sociale est-elle une science?' In this and the three subsequent issues de Tourville sets out his view of the present state of social science. For a few years from 1892, the society ran another more popular periodical called *Le Mouvement sociale*. The first issue of this periodical explained how the Society had dissolved and re-formed itself in order to live down a suspicion that had cropped up that there was some political bias to their work. In spite of this desire to be seen to be free of political bias, the society still had the development of private as opposed to state initiatives among its objectives. On the surface the difference between the two rival societies is hard to see. For La Société d'Economie sociale continued to publish monographs, in fact the last issue of *Les Ouvriers des deux mondes* did not come out until 1912. So both societies had something of the mixture of social studies and social amelioration among their purposes. No doubt those who formed La Société de Science sociale were the more rigorous; but it is hard to avoid the conclusion that the split had as much to do with personalities as with methods, even if the familiar reason for such a split (a recall to the principles of the master) was always the one given. Indeed, thirty years later, when a reunion of the two societies was under discussion, one speaker recalled what he called the intransigence of de Tourville's friends in the early days.[11]

De Tourville did not conduct much fieldwork himself, rather he spent his time analysing the work of other members of the school. In the course of this he revised and considerably expanded the framework for social facts which Le Play had worked out. Philippe Périer has reproduced the de Tourville system under twenty-five headings.[12] Among these the section on workers' families is interesting for two reasons. One is the fact that this still makes a separate section. Landowning, managerial and professional families are apparently classified under the occupation of the breadwinner; the workers' families are classified by the structure of the family itself. The other interesting point is that this structure classification has been changed. The same writer has described how the very cornerstone of Le Play's family classification was knocked out by his followers. He, it will be remembered, grouped the families he studied into three main structural types – patriarchal, stem and unstable. The three were then used as the basis of a typology which included the condition of the society. After Le Play's death the stem family was the subject of intensive research, which covered both new families who appeared to be of this type and existing families which had already been studied.

Périer points out that Le Play treated the family as an economic unit; his disciples tried to treat the family as a social unit. As an organisation for the holding of property and the security of dependents, the stem family stood between the other two types of family. When you come to look at the social, and particularly the educational, functions of the family the distinction becomes a problem. Within ten years of Le Play's death both types of research had cast doubts on the stem family. A fresh look at an existing family that had been thus classified by Le Play had demonstrated that *in intention* they were a patriarchal family. That they were not so in fact was due to their impoverishment. Le Play had missed the reality by looking too closely at the facts. At the same time de Rousiers came back from the United States to describe a family type there which enshrined all the qualities that Le Play had ascribed to the stem family, but with a different economic organisation.[13] This type came to be called *famille particulariste*. Périer has a fascinating paragraph suggesting how the word *particularisme* came to be used in this sense. At the time, he says, it was only used in two meanings – a political one used of the German states, and a theological one used of a view of Christ's death as only for the elect. He suggests that it was a theologian (Père Schwalm in *Science sociale* for April 1893) who first used the noun as one with which he was already familiar. Be that as it may, the individualistic, dynamic, self-reliant basic social group was henceforth *la famille particulariste*, and the word *particularisme* had a new significance. But the element of geographical determinism remained in an effort to trace the north European *particularistes* to the necessities of the life of a coastal fisherman.

So the classification of working-class families was henceforth to be determined by social relationships, and the intention as well as the outward form of these relationships was to be taken into account. This produced the four family types: patriarchal, semipatriarchal, particularist, unstable. The other interesting element in the classification was *patronage*, the system of employment. This was divided into seven types, analysed by the following considerations: role of the proprietor, method of organising the work, workers' share of profits, social security arrangements. The typology would work out as follows:

IDENTIFICATORY ELEMENTS		
	Direction *by employer*	Partici- *pation by worker*	Social *security*
Classification[14]			
Patriarchal	High	Low	High
Community holding	Low	High	High
Master craftsman	High	Low	(Depends upon family type)
Small proprietor	High	Low	
Cooperative concern	Low	High	
Large proprietor	High	Low	
Joint stock company	High	Low	

Thus de Tourville followed and elaborated Le Play's theory of industrial relations. He continued to view the social security element as of considerable importance, but placed the workers' share in the prosperity of the enterprise alongside this.

The Le Play influence

There is no space here to trace the subsequent development of the Le Play School. It would be fair to say that the initial impetus was not maintained, and that the moralising overtones became stronger. It would also be fair to say that Le Play was attacked by powerful critics soon after his death. Emile Durkheim[15] was already twenty-four years old when Le Play died. He was soon to start the course of lectures which made him famous and which opened up fresh avenues for the development of sociology. He criticised the Le Play method on two grounds. Firstly that it is impossible to generalise from the case studies which tell us much about the individual family, but little about the society in which it is placed; and secondly that this *sociographie microscopique* involved the collection of a mass of uninteresting detail. Other French critics have attacked the case study method on similar grounds. For instance Simiand took the view that the monographs could not be said to do more than illuminate the way of life of the family studied. They could not, in any case, be used to show the relationships between cultural variables. Nowadays most people would share this view. Nevertheless, a great deal of sociological effort has gone and is going into the collection of case studies. Le Play's monographs were of particular families, but showed their relationship with their environment and developed hypotheses about this. He only attempted one monograph of a wider community, and this was not very successful. But he forecast that future studies would look into every different type of community. In this he pioneered. It is easy to cry 'naïve' to some of this pioneering; but it contained, as has been shown, the seeds of many considerations which became important later.

The direct influence of his work was more limited. For half a century and more after his death, the main stream of academic sociology concentrated on general issues. Furthermore, in many European countries the political involvement of so many of his followers did not encourage people to take his work seriously. An American commented that Le Play's name drifted into obscurity because the conservatives in France moved towards a more authoritarian point of view, the workers towards Marxism.[16] In Britain, as in France, a small group of significant social science pioneers took their cue from Le Play. During Le Play's lifetime he was friendly with some members of the Society of Arts in London, and he described the National Association for the Promotion of Social Science as a 'daughter society'. Later in the century eminent members of the Royal Statistical Society were acknowledging their indebtedness to Le Play. Charles Booth was Chairman of a meeting in 1893 at which he strongly commended the study of Le Play,[17] as did Professor Marshall. At this meeting Henry Higgs said that the study of workmen's budgets by the Department of Labour was ascribed to Le Play's influence. He listed English social scientists from Petty to Booth, and then went on to say: 'But, after all, there is nothing here – nor, so far as I am aware, in America either – which will compare in fulness and scientific completeness with Le Play's conception of a family budget.' He then attempts to give a statistical rationalisation to one of the problems of the Le Play method by saying: 'The ideal family for the purpose of this microscopic study is that represented by the greatest ordinate mean – in less technical terms the family which has the greatest number of other families similar to it in the field of choice.'

Later de Rousiers spoke about the division in the Le Play School, ascribing it entirely to a division between social reform and social science. It could be described, he said, as a division between those who aimed at 'the amelioration of the people' and those concerned with 'the amelioration of the method'. Three years later a book was published by 'The Economic Club' under the title of *Family Budgets*. The introduction is signed by Charles Booth, Ernest Aves and Henry Higgs, and begins: 'This little book is the result of an effort to study family life in Great Britain through details of family expenditure, and from this it takes its title "Family Budgets". It follows humbly, and at some distance, in the footsteps of Le Play.' In 1897 the newly founded *American Journal of Sociology* printed a translation (vol. 2, pp. 662ff) of the Le Play method of social research. Even before this, in 1889, the Board of Trade had published thirty-four family monographs following Le Play's method.[18]

Thus the name of Le Play was being used in Britain and the United States. This use was mainly as propaganda. Those who advocated detailed, empirical study and the use of natural science techniques in the social sciences were saying, in effect: 'Le Play has already done this on a large scale in France.' There is not much evidence that he was widely read, or that his work was closely followed up. As has already been said, little of it was available in English. Sargant had published an account of the *Workers of Europe*,[19] and parts of two of the case studies had appeared in journals. Gouverneur Emerson had translated *The Organisation of Work*. That was all by the end of the century, although some of the writings of Demolins and de Rousiers were translated at about this time. There was, however, one group of Englishmen who did read and quote Le Play. Soon after his death Patrick Geddes[20] was in Paris and attended Demolin's lectures. He, as he repeatedly said, found the Le Play system a revelation. He saw in it a systemisation of his own thoughts. He picked up the geographical factors and built his own system on his simple interpretation of place, work, folk. Geddes is widely known for his work on town-planning, but he wrote and lectured on a range of sociological subjects. For instance in 1908 he gave a course of London University Extension Lectures on the 'Sociology of Labour' for which almost all the recommended reading was books by Le Play and his School. Geddes' best-known collaborator was Victor Branford, and together they founded the Sociological Society in 1902.[21] Yet another member of the group was A. J. Herbertson, Professor of Geography at Oxford. Through him Le Play influenced the development of field studies in the discipline of geography. Indeed, Mogey makes the point that it is in educational method rather than social research techniques that Le Play had his greatest influence in Britain. In 1920 the Institute of Sociology, as it was by then called, moved to new headquarters which were called Le Play House, and this name was given to the publishing activities of the society.

Ten years later the Le Play Society was formed. This broke away from the Institute of Sociology on similar grounds to those given for the split in France – closer adherence to the methods of the master. The Le Play Society was dedicated to detailed locality studies on the lines prescribed by Geddes – place, work, folk. During the thirty years of its existence the society conducted seventy to eighty studies in various parts of Europe. Thus for some years there were actually two institutions in Britain which carried the name of Le Play. Both have now died; an important survivor of the initiatives of Geddes, Branford and their circle is the *Sociological Review*. However, the name of Le Play came back into currency in the English-speaking world with the rapid development of sociological studies in the United States which began around 1925. Some of the relevant writings have already been mentioned. Sorokin gave considerable space to the Le Play School in his study of sociological theory. Then Zimmerman in 1935 published his book *The Family and Society*, which drew heavily on *The Workers of Europe*, and included a précis translation of volume I. Elton Mayo was another American writer, quoted above in Chapter 1, who drew on Le Play. Finally in the 1950s the 'extended family', as it is now called, became the object of study. Mogey revived Le Play's concept of the stem family to describe the pattern of a family life which includes more than two generations. He refers to Le Play's work, but makes it clear that the family type which he is describing is not to be identified by an emphasis on inheritance. In a footnote he says that the extended family pattern 'has been repeatedly rediscovered in urban working-class districts'.[22]

This brief sketch of Le Play's influence has concentrated on the English speaking countries. But in many other countries an impetus was given to study by direct observation. In Portugal a member of the Le Play School was elected to the professorship, left vacant when Salazar became prime minister. In Germany both Schaeffle and Engel (the statistician) directly used Le Play's work, and the former built his lectures around the family case study method. So did Pobedonotstser in his course in Russia in 1890. Numerous mentions of Le Play's influence can be found in other countries. For instance Kubali and Kosemihal mention his influence in Turkey; as does Iribarne in Spain.[23]

The Le Play interest

If the Le Play influence on us is problematical, his interest for us is not. A glance at his writings is fascinating on many counts. As a source book of social history, for instance, he gives some unusual glimpses of social behaviour and its determinants. As an engineer he formed and developed both research and teaching methods in his subject. As pioneer advocate of management education he showed his astonishing ability to foresee what was to come. As a painstaking observer he has a significant place in the prehistory of sociology. As a man of many social campaigns he provides interest and insights on subjects as diverse as industrial relations, education, family life and regional government.

Many times in this study it has been emphasised that Le Play's ideas and insights led further than he would go. To the end, his picture of a factory as it should be resembled his idealised picture of a primitive village with a lord and his retainers sharing a common prosperity. Custom rather than law was supposed to govern relationships and a custom which involved mutual obligations. The theoretical objections to this picture did not concern Le Play; *patronage* was an analogy from the world of the arts, and after all the artist who owed his ability to practise his art to patronage did not noticeably sacrifice his individuality or independence. He knew well enough that the system of *patronage* rarely existed and still more rarely succeeded; but his 'picture' prevented him accepting the logic of the facts he had collected. While he criticised charitable efforts to improve the workers' lot as mere 'palliatives', he himself hoped for the establishment of industrial practices which the 'original sin' he believed in so strongly was all too likely to sabotage. On this matter his views were already outdated. But on other matters his views were well ahead of his time. The importance of management education, the need to look beyond the formal organisation of the workshop to the informal structures, the need for managers to earn the right to be heard, the importance of making the factory a better place to work in, the acceptance by industry of some responsibility for the society it was shaping, all these are issues that few people thought to raise before Le Play. Few people again had thought it necessary to make the detailed and personal enquiries to establish the views of the workers. In setting out these views, Le Play showed his objectivity. He might think the workers were 'misled', he did not misrepresent what they told him. The picture he has left behind is completely different from ordinary travellers' accounts, or expressions of opinion by those who thought they knew what others thought. We can see Le Play visiting a factory, studying matters technical but at the same time trying to assess which workmen could most aptly be described as typical, engaging them in long conversations and giving them a tip for the trouble, meeting them in a pub afterwards and then visiting them at home. We can see him constantly using the information thus gained to urge government and employers to face facts. This meant framing their policies so as to make the worker feel his interests were being considered and justice was being done. We can see him, too, urging the social scientists to work with these facts, to abandon their strongly speculative bias.

The way in which Le Play stood between the old, pre-industrial, world and the new is well illustrated by the list of problems which interested him. Some have such a modern sound it is hard to realise that Le Play was ventilating them a century and a quarter ago. In addition to those mentioned in the last paragraph, there are the human consequences of technical change, the organisation of apprenticeships, the problems of immigrant labour. Other concerns of Le Play echo a world that is past, the 'customary' relations between employer and employed, the provision of a smallholding for the worker to fall back on in time of slump. He saw clearly the link between professional management and enlightened industrial relations. This led him to favour an autocratic political system, for in his experience schools for professional engineers were promoted by Frederick the Great and the Napoleons. On the other hand his impatience of petty restrictions imposed by men who did not understand industrial realities led him to the opposite view. Hence his ambivalent attitude to state intervention.

Industrial conflict has since proved more intractable than Le Play hoped and his way of thinking has been squeezed out by the facts of that conflict. The more 'thoughtful' employer has tended towards *laissez-faire* in the democratic countries, and a 'corporate' view of society in undemocratic ones. The more 'thoughtful' worker has tended towards Marxism in any country. But the study of industrial relations has often followed lines that Le Play laid down. Chapter 1 of this study began by citing Elton Mayo. It is no coincidence that Mayo quotes Le Play. The impulse towards the objective study of industrial practices came from Le Play. He provided the first rudiments of a method and of a classification. It is clear that they were rudiments, but they started a process which has ranged widely since. By Mayo's time the study of industry had become much more systematic, but in the years between Le Play's death in the 1880s and the experiments of the Harvard Business School in the 1920s many industrial studies had been produced. Some of these show the direct influence of Le Play. He had a special facility for collecting capable men round him and giving some direction to their work. The example of Emile Cheysson has already been given. Apart from social scientists who collected facts about industrial relations, innumerable French engineers were imbued with ideas of management which stemmed from Le Play. If he can hardly be called a formative thinker, he can certainly be called a formative character.

Thus many modern sociological concerns find roots in Le Play's work. The study of the informal group has been mentioned. He realised the existence of this, although he did not know how to investigate it. He pointed out the significance of the actual working group, though his tools were too blunt to go further. In Chapter 4 his insights on the influence of technical change on social systems were mentioned; so was the subject of group cohesion. In his studies of industrial workers the relationship between role theory and stratification is glimpsed. For instance, he showed how the role ambiguity of the socially mobile Belgian printers influenced their behaviour and their strong left-wing views. Implicit in his analysis of this situation was the modern preoccupation with 'reference groups' – groups to which you do not belong but which much influence your behaviour. His approach to social statistics has also remained a matter of controversy. But perhaps most interesting is the problem so often raised in connection with his case studies – how far can general principles be deduced from them? It may well be asked why his grand conception of a massive collection of facts, from which general theories would follow, failed. This conception has recurred in various branches of sociology much more recently. It has been assumed, tacitly or openly, that the adding of case study to case study will unlock new social truths. At the moment the emphasis has shifted to comparative studies, and the study of individual social systems is assigned a more modest role. One day the question raised so long ago by Le Play may be finally answered, whether the collecting of case studies can produce general answers. In any case, Le Play's critics might heed the retort of George Homans in a different context: 'No one who studies a group will go far wrong if he gets close to it, and by whatever methods are available observes all that he can.[24]

Le Play looked at a divided society, and tried to find some conclusions from his studies that would cure these divisions. His twin concerns for order and social security have interested both those who looked for a corporate state[25] (some of his followers were strong supporters of the Vichy regime in France, as the minutes of the Société d'Economie sociale show) and those who interested themselves in the welfare state (like Geddes) or the New Deal (Baussan). Standing on the edge of the establishment, heavily occupied but not so heavily consulted, his aptness for confusing prescription with description has already been noted. It is curious, however, that his zeal for social security should earn him the reputation of wishing to restore the feudal system. Perhaps a modern analogy would be with those in eastern Europe who are trying to restore liberalism, without trying to restore capitalism. However, some of Le Play's followers did want to put the clock back. To them, it must be remembered, he was an advocate of social peace at any price; he was a social philosopher who had frittered away half his life with technological interests. For us his significance might well be just the reverse. But he did stoutly uphold another modern preoccupation that scientific progress had outpaced moral advance.[26]

Henry Bordeaux, in a book quoted earlier, said that Le Play's predecessors in the eighteenth century had studied man and not men. They had come to the conclusion that man was naturally good, corrupted by institutions. Le Play studied men. He did not go on from there to develop the tools for which social scientists were looking, and this fact places him at the end of what might be called the prehistory of sociology. Most modern teaching starts with some reference to the methods of Durkheim and the ideal types of Weber. Le Play stopped just short of such insights. He was a craftsman of social science rather than a mastermind. In the end the technologist with a social conscience became the sociologist with a technical background.

THE LE PLAY FAMILY

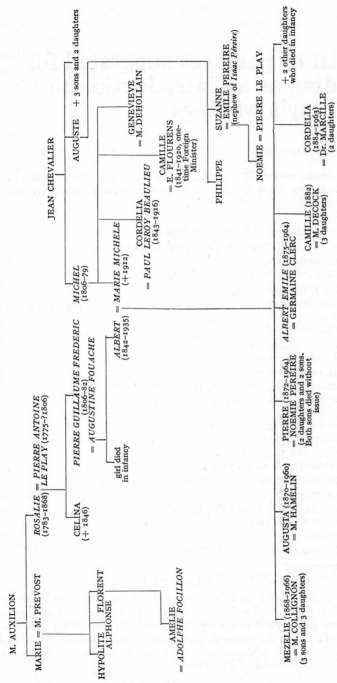

Those in italics are mentioned in the text.

A list of passages suggested for reading as an introduction to Le Play's writings

1. AUTOBIOGRAPHICAL

Les Ouvriers européens (W42), vol. i, pp. vii–xii, 17–48, 395–438. This is Le Play's life as he remembers it, and is not always accurate. It is a moving account of the apprenticeship of a social scientist.

2. METHOD
   either: *La Méthode de la science sociale* (W40),
   or: *Les Ouvriers européens* (W42), vol. i, pp. 208–39.

3. SOCIAL STRUCTURE AND ELITES
   Les Ouvriers européens (W42), vol. i, pp. 380–92.

4. SOCIAL PEACE AND SOCIAL DISORDER
   Les Ouvriers européens (W42), vols. ii, pp. ix–xxiii; iii, pp. xii–xxxix; iv, pp. xix–xxxviii; v, pp. ix–xii; vi, pp. xvii–l, 30–3.
   La Constitution de l'Angleterre (W38), vol. ii, pp. 235–70.

5. WORKING CONDITIONS AND RELATIONSHIPS
   Les Ouvriers européens (W42)
   Russia: vol. ii, pp. 132–41 and 215–30.
   Germany: vol. iii, pp. 125–29, 198–203; vol. v, pp. 83–7.
   Great Britain: vol. iii, pp. 309–63, 432–36.
   Italy: vol. iv, pp. 170–8.
   France: vols. iv, pp. 437–514; v, pp. 178–87, 456–75.
   Austria: vols. v, pp. 33–41; vi, pp. 25–30.
   Belgium: vol. v, pp. 135–48.
   Switzerland: vol. vi, pp. 57–77.
   In general: *L'Organisation du travail* (W51), pp. 135–67.

6. THE FAMILY
   L'Organisation de la Famille (W50), pp. 2–110.
   La Réforme sociale (W54), vol. i, pp. 383–93.

7. THE STATE
   La Réforme sociale (W54), vol. iii, pp. 11–24.

8. THE CHURCH
   La Réforme sociale (W54), vol. i, pp. 193–225.

As this book goes to press a Le Play Room is being established in the Catholic University of Paris. This will have a complete collection of his books, and of the periodicals and writings of the Le Play School. To it are being transferred the records of the Société d'Economie et de Science sociale (from the Faculté de Droit in the University of Paris), and some of the unpublished manuscripts listed below as in the possession of the Le Play family.

Bibliography

Le Play's own writings are numbered with the prefix W for ease of reference. The monographs, either written or sponsored by Le Play, have a prefix M.

Technical Writings

W1   'Aciers': *Exposition de 1849, Rapport du Jury central.* Quatrième Commission, sec. 3, Paris 1850.

W2   'De l'Affinage par cristallisation du plomb et de l'argent', *Annales des Mines,* 3rd ser. vol. x (Paris 1836) 381–406. This documentation of an English process was considered a significant contribution to the development of metallurgy.

W3   Some articles in *Album de l'Exposition universelle,* edited by le baron Léon Brisse, 2 vols. Paris 1856–7.

W3a 'Analyse d'une Substance associée à l'Amphibole . . .', *Annales des Mines,* 2nd ser. v (Paris 1829) 187–8.

Annales des Mines (Paris). Le Play was co-editor of this periodical 1832–40. The following is a list of references to his own articles which appear here under their titles:

Second series: v (1829) 187–8.

Third series: i (1832) 159–60; ii (1832) 501–45; v (1834)175–236; vi (1834) 297–380, 477–522; vii (1835) 185–96; x (1836) 381–406; xiv (1838) 491–502; xv (1839) 447–54; xix (1841) 267–386.

Fourth series: iii (1843) 583–714; iv (1843) 411–28; ix (1846) 113–306; xiii (1848) 3–219, 389–666.

Fifth series: iii (1853) 463–640.

BOULANGERIE. The following series of reports on the bakery industry of Paris were presented by Le Play to the *Conseil d'Etat*:

W4   *Question de la Boulangerie du Département de la Seine . . .,* 1857–58.

W5   *Question de la Boulangerie du Département de la Seine . . . Deuxième Rapport . . .,* 1859–60.

W6   *Projet d'Avis de la réforme de la Boulangerie de Paris et des Départements,* 1859, released 1862.

W7   *Question de la Boulangerie de Paris et des Departements,* 1862.

W8   *Projet de décret relatif à la Boulangerie de Paris et des Départements,* adopté par les sections réunies, 1859, released 1862.

W9 *Projet d'Avis relatif à la Boulangerie* . . . adopté . . ., 1859, released 1862.

W10 *Coutellerie et Outils d'Acier*, Paris 1854. This is Le Play's account of the cutlery section of the London International Exhibition of 1851, and is reprinted from vol. vi of the *Travaux de la Commission française*. Le Play was a member of the jury of the cutlery section and as such he had a part in drafting the official report also.

W11 *Description des procédés métallurgiques employés dans le Pays de Galles pour la fabrication du cuivre*, Paris 1848, reprint from *Annales des Mines*, 4th ser. vol. xiii, 3–219, 389–666. German trans. by C. Hartmann: Quedlinburg 1851.

W12 *Disposition nouvelle de tiges de sonde employée en Prusse*, Paris 1839, reprint from *Annales des Mines*, 3rd ser. xv, 447–54.

W13 *L'Encyclopédie nouvelle*, publié sous la direction de P. Leroux et J. Reynaud, Paris 1834–41. Le Play wrote the following articles in this:

Vol. i (1834): Affinage, Aimant, Air, Airain, Albâtre, Alcali, Alliage, Alun, Amalgamation, Ambre, Analyse chimique, Antimoine, Argent.
Vol. ii (1836): Arsenic, Asbeste, Asphalte, Angite, Axinite, Azur, Baierine, Baryte, Barytine, Baryte-calcite, Basalte, Bases, Bayen (French chemist, 1723–97).
Vol. iii (1840): Brèche, Bronze, Cadmium, Carbone, Carrières, Cavernes.
Vol. v (1839): Etain.
Vol. viii (1841): Soie (also published separately), Statistique (also published separately), Zinc.

W14 *Le Magasin pittoresque*, Paris 1833–(1914). Le Play wrote regularly for this journal in its early years; it was listed by Perdiguier as suitable reading for 'Les Compagnons de Devoir'.

W15 Malinvaud: 'Notice Nécrologique sur M. Malinvaud . . .', *Annales des Mines*, 3rd ser. xiv (Paris 1840) 491–502.

W16 *Mémoire sur la Fabrication et le Commerce des fers à acier dans le nord de l'Europe*, Paris 1846, reprint from *Annales des Mines*, 4th ser. ix, 113–306.

W17 *De la Méthode nouvelle employée dans les forêts de la Carinthie pour la fabrication du fer*, Paris 1853, reprint from *Annales des Mines*, 5th ser. iii, 463–640.

W18 *Observations sur le mouvement commerciale des principales substances minérales entre la France et les puissances étrangères*, Paris 1832, reprint from *Annales des Mines*, 3rd ser. ii, 501–45. See also Samuel-Lajeunesse 1948.

W19 *Observations sur l'Histoire naturelle et sur la richesse minérale de l'Espagne*, Paris 1834, reprint from *Annales des Mines*, 3rd ser. v, 175–236; vi, 297–380, 477–522.

W20 *Recherches statistiques sur la production et l'élaboration de la soie en France*, Paris 1839, reprint from *l'Encyclopédie nouvelle*.

W21 'Sur la fabrication de l'acier en Yorkshire', *Annales des Mines*, 4th ser. iii (Paris 1843) 583–714.

W22 'Sur le mode d'action dans la cémentation des corps oxydés . . . en metallurgie', *Annales des Mines*, 3rd ser. vol. xix (Paris 1841) 267–386. The substance of this had been published earlier in *Les comtes rendus de l'Académie de Sciences*, ii, 1836, pp. 68 ff.

W23 'Sur la Préparation de l'acide sulfurique fumant dans le nord de l'Allemagne', *Annales des Mines*, 4th ser. vii (Paris 1835) 185–96.

W24 'Sur les Expériences . . . par le Gouvernement sarde . . . du fil de fer', *Annales des Mines*, 4th ser. iv (Paris 1843) 411–28.

W25 'Tourmaline (de Mont-Rose)', *Annales des Mines*, 3rd ser. i (Paris 1832) 159–60.

W26 *Voyage dans la Russie méridionale et la Crimée*, 4 vols. Paris 1840.

> Vol. i, written by Demidov, described the journey and its objectives. It was illustrated by Raffet.
> Vol. ii, written by various members of the party, described human remains, fossils, botany, geography, geology etc. In this volume Le Play wrote a section on the flora of the Donets Valley.
> Vol. iii, described the fauna.
> Vol. iv was written by Le Play, with appendices by his collaborators. This described the mineral resources and industrial prospects of the Donets Valley.

> Vol. i has been translated into English, 2 vols. (London 1853); also into Italian (Turin 1841). Vol. iv was translated into Russian by Schurovsk in 1854, with a supplement on recent developments in the area.

W27 *Vues générales de Statistiques*, Paris 1840, reprint from *L'Encyclopédie nouvelle*. Le Play also wrote the bulk of the official reports on two of the International Exhibitions, see:

W28 *Rapport sur l'Exposition universelle de 1855*, Paris 1857.

W29 *Rapport sur l'Exposition universelle de 1867*, Paris 1869.

Manuscripts

W30 *Ecole d'Administration.* Some letters and one report by Le Play, Arch. Nat. F^{17} 4142–5.

W31 *Expositions universelles.* There are about 400 cartoons in the Archives nationales on the Exhibitions in which Le Play was concerned. The following have letters or notes by Le Play himself: $F^{12}3167^{ABC}$, $F^{12}5005$–6.

W32 *Des Fôrets considérés dans leur Rapports avec la Constitution physique du Globe et l'économie des sociétés,* MS, undated, with Le Play family.

W33 *Richesse minérale de la Propriété de Nijné-Taguil* . . . 1851–2, Paris 1856, MS at the Eisenbibliothek, Schaffhausen.

W34 *Sur la Question commerciale de la Mer Noire* . . . *et du Commerce extérieur de la France,* 1837, MS at Bibl. de l'Institut de France.

W35 [Le Play's Tour of the German States, Belgium and France], Paris 1829, MS at Paris: Bibl. de l'Ecole des Mines.

W36 *Leçons* (Lecture notes at the Ecole des Mines), 3 vols. Paris 1840–56, Bibl. de l'Ecole des Mines. There is also a copy of the notes taken by a student (? le comte L. Zugo) in the possession of the Le Play family.

W36a *Voyage de M. Le Play dans le Midi de France et dans le Nord-Ouest de l'Italie – 2ième lettre,* Paris 1838, MS at Bibl. de l'Institut de France.

W37   *Voyage en Normandie et Bretagne,* 1831, MS with Le Play family.

Social studies

W38   *La Constitution de l'Angleterre,* 2 vols., Tours 1875.

W39   *Instruction sur la méthode d'observation dite des monographies de familles,* Paris 1862. New edn revised by A .J. Focillon, Paris 1887.

W40   *La Méthode de la Science sociale,* Tours 1879.

W41   *Les Ouvriers des Deux Mondes.* This series of monographs was started by Le Play. He edited and contributed to the first four volumes: i, 1857; ii, 1858; iii, 1861; iv, 1862. The titles of the monographs are listed below. The later volumes appeared as follows (after Le Play's death): v, 1885; 2nd ser.: i, 1887; ii, 1890; iii, 1892; iv, 1895; v, 1899; 3rd ser.: i, 1904; ii, 1908; iii, 1912 (also issued in separate parts).

W42   *Les Ouvriers européens,* Paris 1855; 2nd edn, 6 vols. Tours 1877–79. Precis trans. of vol. i in C. C. Zimmerman *Family and Society,* London 1936. In the list of monographs below and in the text above, the references are to the 2nd edition unless otherwise stated.

W43   Preface to E. Demolins, *Le Mouvement communal et municipal au Moyen Age,* Paris 1875.

W44   Preface to C. Jannet, *Les Etats-Unis contemporains,* Paris 1876.

The Monographs

A list of the case studies in the two collections mentioned above (W41 and W42) by country, each entry gives:

Occupation of the head of the family, in French and English.
Name of the town or district.
Book reference.
Name of compiler.
Reference to map (facing page 9) where applicable.

The case studies only include a small proportion of those actually written. Le Play rigorously excluded those that fell below his standards, and only published just over one-tenth of those he prepared himself. Each monograph includes sections on the following: Environment, the family studied, religion and morals, health and hygiene, the status of the family, property, 'fringe benefits', work, food, house and belongings, recreation, history of family, customs and societies, income and expenditure for year, and a number of supplementary sections describing the social and industrial institutions of the district in which the family lives. Between the first and second edition of *Les Ouvriers européens* the later sections were changed considerably and in keeping with Le Play's later interests; the earlier chapters remained substantially the same, only some of the figures were modified; for instance the attempt to calculate a capital value for the fringe benefits was abandoned.

ALGERIA

M1 *Bordier berbère*, peasant farmer. Beni Yaissi. W41: 2nd ser. ii, 53. A. Geoffroy.

M2 *Pasteurs nomades*, nomadic shepherds. Sahara. W41: 2nd ser. i, 408. A. Geoffroy.

M3 *Paysan colon*, peasant. Sahel. W41: 2nd ser. ii, 92, summary only. M. Cos.

M4 *Paysans en communauté*, peasants with group-holding. Tabou-Douchd-El-Baar. W41: v, 459. Vincent Darasse.

AUSTRO-HUNGARY

M5 *Charbonnier*, charcoal burner. Judenburg-Carinthia. W42: iv, 31, summary only. Also 1st edn 129. Le Play. Map ref. 28.

M6 *Compagnon-Menuisier*, joiner member of guild. Vienna. W42: v, 1. Also 1st edn 121. Le Play and Saint-Léger. Map ref. 31.

M7 *Fondeur d'Argent*, silver smelter. Schemnitz. W42: iv, 1. Also 1st edn 116. Le Play and A. Saglio. Map ref. 19.

M8 *Mineur*, miner. Idria, Carniola. W42: vi, 1. Also 1st edn 134. Le Play. Map ref. 44.

M9 *Paysans à corvée*, serfs. Hatvan, Pesth. W42: ii, 272. Also 1st edn 110. Le Play. Map ref. 7.

BELGIUM

M10 *Ardoisier*, slate quarryman. Luxembourg. W41: 3rd ser. ii, 233. Emile Savoy.

M11 *Commis*, clerk. Brussels. W41: 3rd ser. ii, 197. Th. Théate.

M12 *Compositeur-typographe*, compositor. Brussels. W41: ii, 193; and W42: v, 103. J. Dauby. Map ref. 33.

M13 *Conducteur-typographe*, printing machine-minder. Brussels. W41: 2nd ser. iii, 369. Le chevalier de Moreau.

M14 *Cordonnier*, shoe-maker. Iseghem. W41: 2nd ser. v, 137. Gillès de Pélichy.

M15 *Cordonnier*, shoe-maker. Hainault. W41: 3rd ser. ii, 1. C. Genart.

M16 *Coutelier*, cutler. Namur. W41: 2nd ser. iii, 413. C. Genart.

M17 *Garnisseur de canons et fusils*, munitions worker. Liège. W41: 2nd ser. v, 1. Armand Julin.

M18 *Mineur*, miner. Borinage. W41: 3rd ser. i, 211. le père G. C. Rutten.

M19 *Pêcheur côtier*, coastal fisherman. Blankenberg. W41: 2nd ser. ii, 109. Victor Brants.

M20 *Tisserand*, weaver. Gent. W41: 2nd ser. iii, 173. le comte F. van den Steen de Jehay.

M21 *Tourneur-mécanicien*, turner. Seraing. W41: 2nd ser. ii, 1. Urbain Guérin.

BULGARIA

M22 *Forgeron, fer*, forge-worker in iron. Samakowa, Sofia. W42: ii, 231. Also 1st edn 104. Le Play and A. Daux. Map ref. 6.

CAMBODIA

M23 *Manœuvre-Coolie,* labourer. Pnom-Penh. W41: 2nd ser. v, 437, summary.
A. Delaire.

M24 *Petit fonctionnaire,* schoolmaster. Pnom-Penh. W41: 2nd ser. v, 437. E.
Delaire.

CANADA

M25 *Compositeur-typographe,* compositor. Quebec. W41: 3rd ser. ii, 59. Stanislas
A. Lartie.

M26 *Paysan,* peasant. Saint-Irénée. W41: v, 50. Gouldrée-Boilleau.

CHINA

M27 *Paysans en communauté,* peasants with group-holding. Tche-Kian. W41: iv, 83.
L. Donnat.

M28 *Pêcheur côtier,* coastal fisherman. Chusan Archipelago. W41: 3rd ser. i, 61,
summary only. G. E. Simon.

EGYPT

M29 Fellah. Karnak. W41: 3rd ser. i, 289. Georges Legrain.

ENGLAND

M30 *Coutelier,* cutlery worker. London. W42: iii, 273. Also 1st edn 188. Le Play.
Précis translation in *Quarterly Journal of Economics* iv (Harvard 1890) 467. Map
ref. 15.

M31 *Coutelier,* cutlery worker. Sheffield. W42: iii, 318. Also 1st edn 194. Le Play.
For an excerpt from the accounts given in this monograph and a comparison
with similar studies, see *Journal of the Royal Statistical Society* lvi (London 1893)
277–8. Map ref. 16.

M32 *Fermier,* farmer. Jersey. W41: 3rd ser. i, 1. François Escard.

M33 *Fondeur à la houille,* smelter. Derbyshire. W42: iii, 400. Also 1st edn 206.
T. Smith. Map ref. 18.

M34 *Manœuvre-agriculteur,* farm labourer. Nottinghamshire. W41: i, 373. J. Devey.

M35 *Menuisier,* joiner. Sheffield. W42: iii, 17. Also 1st edn 208. Le Play. Map ref 17.

M36 *Nourisseur de vaches,* cow-herd. Surrey. W41: i, 263. E. Avalle.

M37 *Tanneur,* tanner. Nottingham. W41: 2nd ser. iii, 269. U. Guérin.

FRANCE

M38 *Agriculteur,* farmer. Pas-de-Calais. W41: 2nd ser. v, 283. Yan' Keravic.

M39 *Ajusteur-surveillant,* foreman-fitter. Guise. W41: 2nd ser. iv, 1. U. Guérin.
An account of the copartnership scheme and model village of Guise.

M40 *Allumeur de Réverbères,* lamp-lighter. Nancy. W41: 2nd ser. iv, 177. Chassignet.

M41 *Auvergnat-brocanteur,* dealer. Paris. W41: iv, 283; also W42: vi, 372, summary
only. P. Gautier. Map ref. 57.

M42 *Aveugle accordeur de Pianos,* blind piano tuner. Paris. W41: 3rd ser. i, 89.
Jacques des Forts.

M43 *Bordier,* tenant farmer. Quimper. W42: iv, 336; also 1st edn 230. A. Duchatellier. Map ref. 25.

M44 *Bordier-émigrant,* migrant farmer. Bourguignon, Aisne. W42: vi, 84; also 1st edn 236. De Barive. Map ref. 46.

M45 *Bordier-vigneron,* tenant vine grower. Genillière, Charente-Inférieur. W41: iii, 207; also W42: vi, 143. P. A. Toussaint. Map ref. 47.

M46 *Bouilleur de Cru,* vine-grower and distiller. Charente. W41: 3rd ser. i, 133. P. de Maroussem.

M47 *Brassier de Vignobles,* vineyard labourer. Casaubon, Gers. W42: iv, 369, summary only. D'Abadie de Barrau. Map ref. 30.

M48 *Brigadier de la Garde républicaine,* police sergeant. Paris. W41: v, 261. Joseph Paviez.

M49 *Brodeuse,* embroideress. Vosges. W41: iii, 25. A. Cochin.

M50 *Cantonnier-Poseur,* platelayer. Paris. W41: 3rd ser. i, 435. C. E. Louis.

M51 *Carrier,* quarryman. Paris. W41: ii, 63. L. Avalle and A. Focillon.

M52 *Charpentier,* carpenter. Paris. W41: i, 27; and W42: v, 424. Le Play and A. Focillon. This contains an account of the *Compagnons de Devoir.* Map ref. 39.

M53 *Charron,* wheelwright. Montalaire, Oise. W41: 2nd ser. i, 133. Bertheault.

M54 *Chiffonier,* rag-picker. Paris. W42: vi, 257; also 1st edn 272. Le Play, E. Landsberg, A. Cochin. Map ref. 49.

M55 *Compositeur-typographe,* compositor. Paris. W41: iv, 241. A. Badier.

M56 *Cordonnier,* shoe maker. Paris. W41: v, 145. Urbain Guérin.

M57 *Corsetière,* corset-maker. Paris. W41: 3rd ser. ii, 377. Mme P. Lebrun.

M58 *Cultivateur-maraîcher,* market gardener. Deuil. W41: 2nd ser. i, 228. Urbain Guérin.

M59 *Débardeur et piocheur de craie,* lighterman and chalk-worker. Paris. W41: ii, 447; also W42: vi, 442. T. Châle. Map ref. 52.

M60 *Décapeur,* descaler. Hérimoncourt, Doubs. W41: ii, 233. C. Robert.

M61 *Décoreuse de porcelaine,* girl who enamels china. Limoges. W41: 3rd ser. i, 391. L. de Maillard.

M62 *Ebéniste parisien de haut-luxe,* cabinet-maker. Paris. W41: 2nd ser. iv, 53. P. du Maroussem.

M63 *Etameur sur fer-blanc,* tin-worker. Commentry. W41: 3rd ser. ii, 433. Fénélon Gibon.

M64 *Eventailliste,* fan-maker. Saint-Geneviève. W41: v, 109. Duvelleroy.

M65 *Faïenciers,* earthenware dealers. Nevers. W41: 2nd ser. i, 177. E. de Toytot.

M66 *Ferblantier-couvreur,* tin-smith. Aix-les-Bains. W41: ii, 9; also W42: iv, 183. Le Play. Map ref. 22.

M67 *Fermiers à communauté taisible,* farmers with group holding by custom and not by contract. Nivernais. W41: v, 1. V. de Cheverry.

M68 *Fermiers montagnards,* hill farmers. Loire. W41: 2nd ser. iv, 397. P. du Maroussem.

M69 *Fileur en peigné et régleur de métier*, textile fitter. Marne. W41: 2nd ser. v, 73. Urbain Guérin.

M70 *Fondeur*, melter. Vandenesse, Nièvre. W42: v, 304, summary only; also 1st edn 242. Le Play. Map ref. 42.

M71 *Gantier*, glove-worker. Grenoble. W41: 2nd ser. i, 465. E. de Toytot.

M72 *Instituteur primaire*, teacher. Eure. W41: iii, 327. A. Roguès.

M73 *Jardinier-plantier*, market gardener. Montauban. W41: 3rd ser. ii, 299. F. Escard.

M74 *Lingère*, needlewoman. Lille. W41: iii, 247; also W42: vi, 302, summary only. L. Auvray. Map ref. 56.

M75 *Maître-blanchisseur*, master-laundryman. Paris. W42: v, 372; also 1st edn 266. E. Landsberg. Map ref. 38.

M76 *Manœuvre à famille nombreuse*, labourer with a large family. Paris. W41: iii, 373; also W42: vi, 327. Courteille and Gautier. Map ref. 50.

M77 *Manœuvre-agriculteur*, farm-labourer. Champagne. W41: i, 69; also W42: v, 323. E. Delbet. Map ref. 37.

M78 *Manœuvre-agriculteur*, farm-labourer. Louvigny, Sarthe. W42: vi, 122, summary; also 1st edn 224. A. de Saint-Léger. Map ref. 54.

M79 *Manœuvre-agriculteur*, farm labourer. Morvan, Nièvres. W42: v, 259; also 1st edn 218. Le Play and St-Léger. Map ref. 36.

M80 *Manœuvre-vigneron*, vineyard labourer. Yonne. W41: iv, 195. E. Avalle.

M81 *Maréchal-ferrant*, farrier. Louvigny, Sarthe. W42: v, 409, summary only; also 1st edn 260. Le Play. Map ref. 43.

M82 *Métayer*, tenant farmer. W41: 2nd ser. i, 341. Le baron d'Artigues.

M83 *Métayer*, tenant farmer. Corrèze. W41: 2nd ser. v, 501. Abbé Tounissoux.

M84 *Métayers en communauté*, tenant farmers in group-holding. Charente. W41: 2nd ser. iii, 1. P. du Maroussem.

M85 *Mineur*, miner. Barbecot, Puy-de-Dôme. W42: v, 150; also 1st edn 248. Le Play and E. Landsberg. Map ref. 34.

M86 *Mineur de houille*, coalminer. Pas-de-Calais. W41: 2nd ser. v, 253, summary. Yan' Keravic.

M87 *Monteur d'outils en acier*, steel tool fitter. Hérimoncourt. W41: ii, 285. C. Robert.

M88 *Mouleuse en cartonnage*, toy-maker. Paris. W41: 2nd ser. iv, 173. P. du Maroussem.

M89 *Ouvrier-employé de la fabrique coopérative de papiers*, worker in cooperative paper-mill. Angoulême. W41: 2nd ser. iv, 272. U. Guérin.

M90 *Papeteries*, a general study of a paper-mill. Limousin. W41: 3rd ser. i, 507. P. du Maroussem.

M91 *Paysan*, peasant. Labourd, Basses-Pyrénées. W41: i, 161; also W42: v, 192; see also: W50: 111–289. Le Play and Saint-Léger. Map ref. 35.

M92 *Paysans*, peasants. Laonnais, Aisne. W41: iv, 377. M. Callay.

M93 *Paysans corses*, peasants. Corsica. W41: 2nd ser. ii, 433. M. Bigot.

M94 *Paysans en communauté*, peasants in group-holding. Lavedan. W41: i, 107; also W42: iv, 445. Le Play. Map ref. 27.

M95 *Paysan et maçon émigrant*, migrant peasant and mason. Creuse. W41: 2nd ser. ii, 229; summary. L'Abbé M. Parinet.

M96 *Paysan métayer*, tenant farmer. Bouches-du-Rhône. W41: 2nd ser. ii, 173. D'Estienne de Saint-Jean.

M97 *Paysan paludier*, peasant on the salt marshes. Batz, Loire-Inférieur. W41: 2nd ser. i, 1. A. Delaire.

M98 *Paysan-résinier*, peasant. Lévignac, Landes. W41: v, 316. U. Guérin.

M99 *Paysan et savonnier*, peasant and soap-boiler. Basse-Provence. W41: 1st edn iii, 67; also W42: iv, 390. A. Focillon. Map ref. 26.

M100 *Pêcheur-côtier*, coastal fisherman. Martigues. W41: 2nd ser. i, 285. F. Escard.

M101 *Pêcheur-côtier*, coastal fisherman. Etretat. W41: 2nd ser. ii, 153, summary. C. Vallin.

M102 *Piqueur sociétaire de la 'Mine aux Mineurs'*, official in a cooperative mine. Monthieux. W41: 2nd ser. v, 365. P. du Maroussem.

M103 *Porteur d'eau*, water carrier. Paris. W41: ii, 321. E. Avalle.

M104 *Serrurier*, locksmith. Paris. W41: 2nd ser. v, 347, summary. N. Fanjung.

M105 *Serrurier-forgeron*, locksmith. Paris. W41: v, 201. Le vicomte Jacques de Reviers.

M106 *Serrurier-forgeron*, locksmith. Paris. W41: 2nd ser. v, 317. N. Fanjung.

M107 *Tailleur d'habits*, tailor. Paris. W41: ii, 145; also W42: vi, 387. A. Focillon. Map ref. 51.

M108 *Tailleur de silex*, flint cutter. Loire-et-Cher. W41: 2nd ser. ii, 337. F. Gibon.

M109 *Teinturier*, dyer. Saint-Junien, Haute-Vienne. W41: 3rd ser. ii, 257. L. de Maillard.

M110 *Tisserand*, weaver. Mamers, Sarthe. W42: vi, 193; also 1st edn 254. Pélisson and Saint-Léger. Map ref. 48.

M111 *Tisserand*, weaver. Sainte-Marie-aux-Mines, Haut-Rhin. W41: iv, 363; also W42: vi, 228, summary. L. Coguel. Map ref. 55.

M112 *Tisseur en Châles*, shawl weaver. Paris. W41: i, 299. F. Hébert and E. Delbet.

M113 *Usine hydraulique d'Eclairage et de Transport de Force*, a study of a hydro-electric power station. W41: 3rd ser. ii, supp. 1. P. du Maroussem.

GERMANY

M114 *Armurier*, gunsmith. Solingen. W42: iii, 153; also 1st edn 152. Le Play. Map ref. 13.

M115 *Bûcheron usager*, woodman. Lorraine. W41: v, 387. Pariset.

M116 *Fondeur*, iron-melter. Hundsruck, Rhine. W42: iv, 68; also 1st edn 146. Le Play. Map ref. 20.

M117 *Luthier*, musical instrument maker. Mark-Neukirchen, Saxony. W42: iv, 107, summary. J. Dall' Armi. Map ref. 29.

M118 *Luthier*, musical instrument maker. Mittenwald, Bavaria. W42: v, 88, summary. J. Dall' Armi. Map ref. 40.

M119 *Mineur, argent et plomb*, silver and lead miner. Clausthal, Hanover. W42: iii, 99; also 1st edn 140. Le Play and Saint-Léger. Map ref. 12.

M120 *Mineur*, miner. Ruhr. W41: 2nd ser. ii, 245. L. Fèvre.

M121 *Tisserand*, weaver. Godesberg, Rhine. W42: v, 60; also 1st edn 158. A. de Saint-Léger and A. Cochin. Map ref. 32.

M122 *Tisserand*, weaver. Munchen-Gladbach. W41: 3rd ser. i, 336. V. Brants.

M123 *Vignerons*, vineyard labourers. Alsace. W41: 2nd ser. iii, 69. Charles Hommell.

ITALY

M124 *Agriculteur, ouvrier*, farm labourer. Romagna. W41: 2nd ser. v, 234. Comtesse Marie Pasolini.

M125 *Fondeur de plomb*, lead smelter. Tuscany. W41: iii, 413. F. Blanchard.

M126 *Métayer*, tenant farmer. Florence, Tuscany. W41: i, 221; also W42: iv, 121. U. Peruzzi. Map ref. 21.

M127 *Mineur*, miner. Tuscany. W41: iv, 331. F. Blanchard.

M128 *Mineur de soufrières*, sulphur miner. Sicily. W41: 2nd ser. ii, 281. Hippolyte Santangelo-Spoto.

M129 *Paysan agriculteur*, peasant. Foggia. W41: 2nd ser. iii, 213. Hippolyte Santangelo-Spoto.

M130 *Paysan métayer*, peasant. Tuscany. W41: 2nd ser. v, 188. J.-P. Assirelli.

M131 *Tisseur*, weaver. San Leucio. W41: 2nd ser. iv, 323. Hippolyte Santangelo-Spoto.

M132 *Vigneron précariste*, vineyard worker. Rome. W41: 2nd ser. ii, 1. Urbain Guérin.

MOROCCO

M133 *Menuisier charpentier*, joiner. Tangier. W41: ii, 105; also W42: ii, 398. N. Cotte. Map ref. 9.

NETHERLANDS

M134 *Pêcheur-côtier, maître de barque*, fisherman. Marken. W41: iv, 105; also W42: iii, 204. S. Coronel and F. Allen. Map ref. 14.

M135 *Tisserand*, weaver. Hilversum. W41: 2nd ser. iii, 143. S. Coronel.

NORWAY

M136 *Fondeur, cobalt*, cobalt melter. Buskerud. W42: iii, 54; also 1st edn 98. Le Play and A. de Saint Léger. Map ref. 11.

M137 *Pêcheur côtier*, fisherman. Lapland. W41: 2nd ser. iii, 126, summary. F. Escard.

REUNION (Indian Ocean)

M138 *Mulâtre affranchi*, freed mulatto slave. W41: iv, 159. L. Simonin.

RUSSIA

M139 *Armurier*, gunsmith. Toula. W41: 2nd ser. i, 112. A. Peretz.

M140 Bachkirs, *pasteurs demi-nomades*, nomadic herdsmen. Mochmet, Urals. W42: ii, 1; also 1st edn 49. Le Play and Saint-Léger. Map ref. 1.

M141 *Bordiers émancipés*, freed peasants. Near Spassk. W41: 2nd ser. i, 57. A. Wilbois.

M142 *Charpentier et marchand de grains des laveries d'or*, joiner and grain-dealer in a gold refinery. Nizhnii Tagil. W42: ii, 142; also 1st edn 86. Le Play. Map ref. 4.

M143 *Forgeron et charbonnier des usines à fer*, forgeman. Laia. W42: ii, 99; also 1st edn 78. Le Play. Map ref. 3.

M144 *Paysans et charrons à corvée*, serfs and wheelwrights. Tachli. W42: ii, 47; also 1st edn 58. Le Play and Saint-Léger. Map ref. 2.

M145 *Paysans et portefaix émigrants à l'Abrok*, peasants and migrant porters, commuted serfs. Eractor. W42: ii, 179; also 1st edn 69. Le Play and Saint-Léger. Map ref. 5.

SPAIN

M146 *Métayer*, tenant farmer. Santander. W42: iv, 247; also 1st edn 176. Ratier, A. Paillette, S. Suazez. Map ref. 23.

M147 *Mineur-émigrant*, migrant miner. Spanish Galicia. W42: v, 249, summary only; also 1st edn 182. Le Play and P. Cia. Map refs. 41 and 41 bis.

M148 *Pêcheur-côtier maître de barque*, coastal fisherman. Saint Sebastian. W41: i, 403; also W42: iv, 291. Saint-Léger and E. Delbet. Map ref. 24.

SWEDEN

M149 *Forgeron de fer*, iron forgeman. Dannemora. W42: iii, 1; also 1st edn 92. Le Play and Saint-Léger. Map ref. 10.

SWITZERLAND

M150 *Horloger*, clock-maker. Geneva. W42: vi, 34; also 1st edn 164. Le Play. Map ref. 45.

M151 *Horloger*, clock-maker. Geneva. W42: vi, 70, summary; also 1st edn 170. Le Play. Map ref. 53.

M152 *Savetier*, cobbler. Basle. W41: 2nd ser. iv, 225. C. Landolt.

SYRIA

M153 *Paysans en communauté*, peasants collective holding. Busra. W41: ii, 363; also W42: ii, 304. E. Delbet. Map ref. 8.

TUNIS

M154 *Parfumeur*, perfumer. Tunis. W41: iii, 285. N. Cotte and S. El Haraïri.

U.S.A.

M155 *Métayer de l'Ouest*, tenant farmer. Texas. W41: 2nd ser. iv, 101. Claudio Jannet.

M156 *Mineur des placers*, gold miner. Mariposa. W41: iii, 145. L. Simonin.

F

Social and political theory

W45 *La Constitution essentielle de l'humanité*, Tours 1881; 2nd edn, Tours 1893.

W46 *L'Ecole de la paix sociale*. Tours 1881. A booklet describing the history, method and outlook of the social peace movement. This was his last publication before his death.

W47 *L'Erreur sous l'ancien régime et la révolution*, Tours 1878. Reprinted from ch. 69 of *La Réforme sociale*.

W48 *Les grandes Vérités sociales d'après Le Play*, Paris 1880. A pamphlet summarising Le Play's ideas.

W49 'La Liberté du testament et la prospérité de l'Angleterre', *Annuaire de l'Union de la Paix sociale*, Paris 1875.

W50 *L'Organisation de la famille*, Paris 1871; 2nd edn, Paris and Tours 1875; 3rd edn, Tours 1884; 4th edn, Tours 1895; 5th edn, Tours 1907. In the 1st edn appendices with case studies by Le Play, Cheysson and Jannet. Other collaborators wrote appendices for the later editions.

W51 *L'Organisation du Travail*, Tours 1870; 2nd edn, Tours 1870; 4th edn, Tours 1877; 5th edn, Tours 1888; 7th edn, Tours 1906. English trans. by Gouverneur Emerson, Philadelphia 1872. Spanish trans. by Don Luis de Oliver de Riera, Tours 1895.

W52 *La Paix sociale après le désastre*, Tours 1871; 2nd edn, Tours 1876.

W53 *La Question sociale au XIXe siècle*, Tours 1879; reprint of Epilogue to W42.

W54 *La Réforme sociale en France*, 2 vols., Paris 1864; 2nd edn, 2 vols. Paris 1866,; 3rd edn, 3 vols., Paris 1867; 4th edn, 3 vols., Tours 1872; 5th edn, 3 vols., Tours 1874; 6th edn, 3 vols., Tours 1878; 7th edn, 3 vols., Tours 1887; 8th edn, 3 vols., Tours 1901. This book was described by Montalembert as 'the most original, the most courageous, the most useful, and altogether the most powerful book of the century'. The quotations in the text are from the *seventh* edn.

W55 *La Réforme en Europe et le Salut en France*, Tours 1876. This book contains the programme of Les Unions de la Paix sociale. There is an introduction by H. A. Munro Butler Johnson, M.P.

Prefaces to:

W56 Delaire, Alexis, *Les Unions de la Paix sociale*, Paris 1882.

W56a Delor, Adrien, *La Corporation des Bouchers à Limoges*, Limoges 1877.

W57 Galembert, le comte Louis-Charles Marie de Bodin, *Essai sur le suffrage universel, direct avec scrutin de liste*, Paris 1875.

W58 Un Group d'Economistes, *Programme de gouvernement et d'organisation sociale d'après l'observation comparée des divers peuples*, Paris 1881. This book was written under Le Play's guidance; see de Ribbe's edition of his letters, W78, p. 68 n.

W59 Rouillot, l'abbé F. J., *Les Etudes sociales*, 2e sér. Paris 1881.

W60 Roux, Xavier, *Les Utopies et les Réalités de la Question sociale*, Paris 1876.

L'Union de la Paix sociale, Correspondence:

W61   No. 1 *L'Urgence de l'Union en France.* Lettre de M. le comte de Butenval, réponse de M. F. Le Play, Tours 1872.

W62   No. 2. *L'Accord des Partis politiques.* Lettre de M. Lucien Brun, réponse de M. F. Le Play, Tours 1872.

W63   No. 3. *Le retour au vrai et le rôle du clergé.* Lettre de Mgr Isoard, réponse de M. F. Le Play, Tours 1872.

W64   No. 4. *La Question sociale et l'Assemblée,* Tours 1873.

W65   No. 5. *Le Salut de la France* by Lord Denbigh, Lord Montagu and M. F. Le Play, Tours 1873.

W66   No. 6. *La Presse périodique et la méthode à propos de L'œuvre de* M. F. Le Play, E. P. de Curzon, Tours 1873.

W67   No. 7. *Prélude aux Unions nationales et locales,* Tours 1874.

W68   No. 8. *La Méthode expérimentale et la loi divine.* Lettre de M. P. Pradié, réponse de M. F. Le Play, Tours 1875.

Periodicals, Selections, Letters

PERIODICALS AND ANNUALS

W69   *Bulletin de la Société internationale des études pratiques d'économie sociale,* Paris 1864–83. Edited by Alexis Chevalier, this contained the minutes of the meetings of the society. Summaries of these minutes are also to be found in the earlier volumes of W41.

W70   *L'Economiste français,* a fortnightly edited by Jules Duval, published a report of the proceedings of the society in the following issues: vol. i, no. 3, 10 Jan. 1862, and no. 4, 25 Jan. 1862.

W71   *La Réforme sociale,* Paris bi-monthly, founded by Le Play in 1881. In 1931 became *La Revue d'Economie sociale et rurale.* In 1936 amalgamated with *La Science sociale* (founded by Le Play's followers in 1886) to become *Les Etudes sociales* now (1968) published termly. Another periodical of the Le Play School was *Le Mouvement social,* founded in 1892 and merged with *La Science sociale* in 1896.

W72   *La Société internationale des études pratiques d'économie sociale,* a brief history with many quotes from Le Play.

W73   *Les Unions de la Paix sociale: Annuaires,* Paris 1875–80. Each volume begins with an article by Le Play on current affairs.

SELECTIONS

W74   *Textes choisis,* selection and preface by Louis Baudin, Paris 1947.

W75   *Oeuvres de Frédéric Le Play,* Paris 1941.

W76   *Frédéric Le Play: Economie sociale,* ed. F. Auburtin, Paris 1891.

W77   *Frédéric Le Play d'après lui-même,* sel. and ed. F. Auburtin, Paris 1906.

LETTERS

W78 *Le Play d'après sa Correspondance*, ed. C. de Ribbe, Paris 1884.

W79 *Le Play, Voyages en Europe, 1829 a 1854*. Letters, ed. Albert Le Play, Paris 1899.

W80 [Letters from Le Play to Jean Reynaud, 1849–57], see W71, vol. ii, 1898, pp. 869 ff.

MANUSCRIPTS

Le Play's unpublished correspondence is to be found in La Bibliothèque de l'Institut de France, Les Archives nationales (with his official dossier), and with Madame Le Play. L'Ecole des Mines has two of his letters, so does the University of Keele.

Studies of Le Play and his work

ALLARD, PAUL. *Frédéric Le Play et la Normandie*, Evreux 1906, reprint from *La Revue catholique de Normandie*.

ANGOT DE ROTOURS, le baron. 'Le Centenaire de Frédéric Le Play', *La Revue Hebdomadaire*, Paris, June 1906.

—— 'L'Origine et la Formation normande de Le Play', *La Réforme sociale*, Paris, Sept.–Oct. 1925.

ANSELIN, RÉMY. 'Tardieu chez Le Play', *Eclair de l'Est*, Nancy, 23 June 1935.

—— 'Une Bonne Recrue', *La Voix des Faucilles*, July 1935. In June 1935 André Tardieu, who had just caused a sensation by announcing his retirement from public life due to disillusionment, spoke at the A.G.M. of the Société d'Economie sociale with Pierre Le Play in the Chair. Of the many press reports, the two above say something about Le Play as well.

AUDLEY, C. F. 'The working-classes of Europe', *Journal of the Society of Arts*, iv (London 1856) 189–96.

AYMER DE LA CHEVALERIE, le comte H. M. *Le Play, son système réformiste, ses ouvrages* . . . Paris 1877.

BAUDIN, L. *Précis d'histoire des doctrines économiques*, Paris 1942.

BAUNARD, LOUIS. *La Foi et ses Victoires*, vol. ii: Quatre Maîtres de la Science sociale: Joseph Dros, Frédéric Bastiat, Alexis de Tocqueville, Frédéric Le Play. Paris 1884.

BAUSSAN, G. *De Frédéric Le Play à Paul Bourget*, Paris 1935.

BESSE, le père LUDOVIC DE. *Le Clergé de France et Frédéric Le Play*, San Remo 1909.

BORDEAUX, HENRY. *Paysages romanesques*, Paris 1906, pp. 33 ff. 'Le Play au Luxembourg'.

BOUCHIÉ DE BELLE, EDMOND. *Les Origines de la Science sociale*, Paris 1907; Bibliothèque de la Science sociale, nouvelle série fasc. 36.

BOURQUELOT, F. and MAURY, A. *La Littérature française contemporaine* (1827–1849). vol. v, Paris 1854, contains a bibliographical note on Le Play.

BOUTMY, E. M. 'Le Play et la Réforme sociale', *Revue nationale*, xxi (Paris 1865).

BRANFORD, V. V. and GEDDES, P. *The Coming Polity*, 2nd edn enlarged, London 1919. An interpretation of the Le Play method.

BRANTS, VICTOR. *Frédéric Le Play. Notice sur sa vie et ses travaux.* Louvain 1882, reprint from the *Revue catholique de Louvain*.

—— 'Les Etudes pratiques d'économie sociale', *Revue catholique de Louvain*, Jan. 1882.

BROOKE, M. Z. 'La Théorie de Le Play sur les relations industrielles', *Etudes sociales* no. 64–65, Jan.–April 1965, pp. 1–11.

BUREAU, PAUL. *Introduction à la méthode sociologique*, Paris 1923.

CANTU, C. 'L'Oeuvre de Le Play', *La Réforme sociale*, ix (Paris 1885) 113–23.

CARNE, DE GASTON. 'F. Le Play', *Le Contemporain*, Paris 1882, pp. 1014–26.

CATINEAU, P. H. *Réforme sociale: Deux Lettres à M. F. Le Play*, Paris 1873.

CHAMPAULT, P. 'La Science sociale d'après Le Play et de Tourville', *La Science sociale*, 2e période, fasc. 109, Paris 1913.

CHANSON, M. P. 'Le Play et le Corporalisme', *L'Organisation corporative*, Paris, July 1943.

CHEYSSON, EMILE. *Frédéric Le Play – L'Homme, la Méthode, la Doctrine*, Paris 1896, reprint from *La Quinzaine*, Paris 15 Jan. 1896.

—— 'Frédéric Le Play, sa methode, sa doctrine, son école,' *Comptes rendus de l'Académie des Sciences morales et politiques*, Paris 1905. Reprinted in *Oeuvres choisies*, Paris 1911, vol. ii, ch. 8. See also ch. 1, 'Mon Testament social'.

—— and TOQUE, ALFRED. *Budgets comparés des cents monographies de familles . . .* Paris 1890, reprint from *Bulletin de l'Institut internationale*, v.

CHULLIAT, CHRISTIAN. 'Le Play et Durkheim', *Recueil d'Etudes sociales*, Paris 1956.

CLEMENT, MARCEL. 'Quelques remarques sur la Méthodologie sociale de Le Play', *Recueil d'etudes sociales*, Paris 1956.

COCHIN, AUGUSTIN. *Les Ouvriers européens. Résumé de la méthode et des observations*, Paris 1856, reprint from *Le Correspondant*.

—— *La Réforme sociale en France*, Paris 1865, reprint from *Le Correspondant*.

COLLIGNON, P. *Frédéric Le Play, sa conception de la paix sociale*, Paris 1932. This contains a list of organisations for social wellbeing inspired by Le Play.

CURZON, EMMANUEL PARENT DE. *Frédéric Le Play*, Paris 1899. An assessment of Le Play's social doctrines containing extracts from his writings and letters showing his outlook at the end of his life.

—— *M. Le Play, La Réforme sociale*, Poitiers, 1873.

—— 'Confucius, Le Play', *Revue de France*, Paris 1880.

—— 'La Réforme sociale', *Revue de France*, Paris 1881.

—— 'Les Ouvriers européens et la science sociale', *Revue de France*, Paris 1879.

CURZON, HILAIRE DE. *Emmanuel de Curzon*, 1811–1896, Poitiers 1931. Ch. 9 describes his relationship with Le Play.

DAUPHIN-MEUNIER, A. 'Frédéric Le Play et René Worms', *Etudes sociales,* nouvelle, sér. ii, nos. 29–30, Paris, December 1955.

DELAIRE, ALEXIS. F. *Le Play et l'Ecole de la Paix sociale*, Lille, undated; reprint from *L'Action populaire*, 4th ser. no. 51.

—— *Le Play et la science sociale*, Paris 1895.

—— *M. F. Le Play, sa vie et ses travaux*, Paris 1882.

DELALONDE, l'abbé STANISLAS-FRANÇOIS-ANDRE. Two articles on Le Play's work in *Semaine Religieuse*, Rouen 1878.

DELATOUCHE, RAYMOND. 'La Vie de Frédéric Le Play', *Les Etudes sociales*, nouvelle sér. no. 27, Paris March 1955.

DEMOLINS, EDMOND. *L'Etat actuel de la science sociale*, Paris undated.

—— *M. Le Play et son Oeuvre de Réforme sociale*, Paris 1882; reprint from *Le Correspondant*, lxxxi, Paris 1878.

—— 'La Science sociale depuis F. Le Play, Essai de classification des Sociétés humaines', *Science sociale*, 2e période, fasc. 10–11, Paris 1905.

—— with PINOT, ROBERT and DE ROUSIERS, PAUL. 'La Méthode', *Science sociale*, 2e période, fasc. 1, Paris 1904.

DESCAMPS, PAUL. *La Sociologie expérimentale*, Paris 1933.

—— *Résumé de l'Histoire de la science sociale*, Lisbon 1941.

DIEUX, le père MARIE-ANDREE. *Henri de Tourville d'après ses lettres*, Paris 1928.

—— *Personalité et Communauté*, Paris 1947.

DIMIER, L. *Les Maîtres de la contre-Révolution au XIXe siècle*, Paris 1907.

DUPIN, le baron CHARLES. *Institut impérial de France. Rapport . . . Prix de statistique fondé par M. de Monthyon . . . donné . . . à l'ouvrage portant pour titre*: 'Les Ouvriers européens par M. Le Play, Paris undated; reprint from *La Séance publique de l'Académie des Sciences*, 28 January 1856.

DU SAUSSOIS, A. F. *Le Play*, Paris 1884; from *Galerie des hommes utiles*.

EINAUDI, LUIGI. 'The Doctrine of original sin and the theory of the elite in the writings of Frédéric Le Play', *Essays in European Economic Thought*, trans. and ed. Louise Sommer, Princeton, 1960. Trans. from 'Il peccato originale e la teoria della classe eletta in Frédéric Le Play', *Revista di Storia economica*, i, no. 2 (Turin 1936) 85–118; repr. *Saggi bibliografici e storici intorno alle dottrine economiche*, Rome 1953, pp. 307–43. A particularly interesting and perceptive study with a bibliography describing those works of Le Play which Einaudi possessed.

ELWOOD, C. A. 'Instruction in the Observation of Social Facts according to the Le Play method . . .', *American Journal of Sociology*, ii (Chicago 1897) 662–79.

ESCARD, PAUL. *Comment travaillait Le Play*, Paris 1907, reprint from *La Réforme sociale*, Paris 16 May 1907.

—— *La Méthode de Le Play jugée par un économiste anglais*, reprint from *La Réforme sociale*, Paris 1 February 1900.

—— *Frédéric Le Play*, Arras 1903; reprint from *Science catholique*, Arras 1903.

—— *Question sociale*, Paris 1912. Ch. 6 is on the doctrine of Le Play.

FARMER, PAUL. 'The social theory of Frédéric Le Play', *Teachers of History: Essays in Honor of Lawrence Bradford Packard*, Cornell 1954.

Fête du centenaire de F. Le Play et XXXVe congrès de la Société internationale d'économie sociale, Paris 1907; reprint from *La Réforme sociale* 1906–7.

FOCILLON, ADOLPHE-JEAN. 'Le Play, le fondateur de l'Ecole de la Paix sociale' *La Réforme sociale*, iii (Paris 1881) 474–82.

—— 'La Méthode scientifique d'observation', *Revue des Questions scientifiques*, Paris, July 1879.

FONTENAY, M. R. DE. 'Les Ouvriers européens de M. Le Play (Première lettre . . .)', *Journal des Economistes*, 2nd sér., xxix (Paris, May 1856) 210–27.

—— 'Les Ouvriers européens de M. Le Play (Deuxième lettre . . .)', *Journal des Economistes*, 2nd sér. xxx (Paris, June 1856) 382–402.

GARDEREAU, DON EUGENE. 'Frédéric Le Play', *Le Monde*, Paris 10 May 1879 (critical).

GOUY, JULES. *Appréciation de l'Oeuvre de Le Play*, Nancy 1885.

GRANDMAISON, J. LE COUR. 'Ceux qui ont vu clair', *Figaro*, Paris 4 November 1940.

HAMMERSTEIN, L. VON. *Le Play und die richtige Methode der sozialwissenschaft*, Stimmen aus Maria-Loach, Bd. 19, 1877.

HEERE, W. R. *Frédéric Le Play*. Groningen 1926.

HERBERTSON, DOROTHY. *The Life of Frédéric Le Play*, ed. V. V. Branford and A. Farquarson, Ledbury 1950. Written in the 1890s, Ch. 1–4 were printed in the *Sociological Review*, vol. xii, 1920 and vol. xiii, 1921; and the whole was printed in vol. xxxviii, 1946; and finally reprinted in a limited edition in 1950.

HIGGS, HENRY. See *Quarterly Journal of Economics*, iv (Harvard June 1890) 408 ff.

—— See also *The Journal of the Royal Statistical Society*, vol. lvi, London 1893, pp. 255 ff.

—— See *Réforme sociale*, Paris 1900, p. 236.

IRIBARNE, MANUEL FRAGA. 'La Influencia de Le Play en la sociologia española del sigle', xix, *Recueil d'Etudes sociales*, Paris 1956, p. 29.

JANNET, CLAUDIO. *Quatre Ecoles d'Economie sociale – I. Le Play*, Geneva 1890.

—— 'L'Organisation du Travail d'après F. Le Play', *La Réforme sociale*, Paris 1889, ii, pp. 611 ff.

JOLY, H. *Génies saines et Génies malades*, Paris 1928, pp. 105–50.

KÖSEMIHAL, N. S. 'L'Ecole de Le Play et son Influence en Turquie', *Recueil d'Etudes sociales*, Paris 1956, pp. 35–47.

LACOIN, M. M. 'Frédéric Le Play, Ingénieur au Corps des Mines', *Recueil d'Etudes sociales*, Paris 1956, pp. 49–56.

LACOINTA, J. *Le Play*, reprint from *Le Correspondant*, Paris 25 April 1882.

LAFARGE, R. 'Frédéric Le Play et Michel Chevalier', *Le Limousin*, Paris 1908.

LAFFITTE, PIERRE. *Vers une socio-économie mathématique: Proudhon, Le Play, Mayo et les Economistes*; reprint from *Annales des Mines*, Paris March 1963.

LAVERGNE, LEONCE DE. 'Economie rurale – les ouvriers européens de M. Le Play', *Revue des Deux Mondes*, Paris 1 February 1856.

LEFEBURE DE FOURCY, M. See *La Réforme sociale*, v, (Paris 1883) 29–44.

—— See *Annales des Mines*, 8th ser., mémoires, ii, Paris 1882.

LEGUEU, F.-F. *Les Précurseurs: F. Le Play*, Paris 1943.

LEMOS, MIGUEL. *Le Positivisme et l'Ecole de Le Play*, Le Mans 1891. One of a series of leaflets on Positivism by Lemos.

LE PLAY, ALBERT. 'Souvenirs intimes sur Frédéric Le Play', *Les Etudes sociales*, Paris March 1955; repr. *Recueil d'Etudes sociales*, Paris 1956, pp. 3–13.

LEVILLAIN, LEOPOLD. *Les Caractères de la Famille stable d'après Le Play*, Paris 1910.

LEROY-BEAULIEU, PAUL. 'Le Play', *Journal des Débats*, Paris 25 June 1882; repr. *Réforme sociale*, Paris 1882, p. 70.

—— 'Le Play et son Oeuvre', *Réforme sociale*, Paris 1888, p. 1.

Livre de Centenaire de l'Ecole polytechnique, vol. i, Paris 1895, and vol. iii, Paris 1897. Both these volumes contain many refs. to Le Play, see especially vol. i, pp. 499–509 and vol. ii, pp. 466–77.

LORRAIN, F. *La Problème de la France contemporaine*, Paris 1879. This contrasts the theocratic school with that of Le Play.

LUCE, SIMEON. *F. Le Play, La vieille France . . .*, reprint from *La Réforme sociale*, Paris 1891, p. 26.

MAISTRE, EDOUARD. *Le Play*, Montpelier 1937.

MASCAREL, ARNOLD. *La Famille-souche selon Le Play*, Paris 1895. This is a defence of Le Play's classification against the Science Sociale school.

—— *Un nouveau commentaire de F. Le Play*, Paris 1899; reprint from *La Réforme sociale*, also reprinted in Curzon 1899.

MAZEL, H. 'Le Procès de la Révolution française', *Revue des Questions historiques*, xl (Paris 1886) 95. Contrasts studies of the *ancien regime*.

—— See *Mercure de France*, lxii, (Paris 15 July 1906) 266.

MELINE, PIERRE. *P. G. F. Le Play—l'oeuvre de science*, Paris 1912.

MICHEL, ANDREE. 'Les Cadres sociaux de la Doctrine morale de Frédéric Le Play', *Cahiers internationaux de Sociologie*, Paris 1963, pp. 47–68.

MOGEY, JOHN. 'La "Science sociale" en Angleterre', *Recueil d'Etudes sociales*, Paris 1956, pp. 57–64.

MONTESQUIOU, le comte LEON DE. *L'Oeuvre de Frédéric Le Play*, Paris 1912.

NOILHAN, HENRI. 'Actualité de la Méthode d'Observation', *Recueil d'Etudes sociales*, pp. 65–72.

Nouvelle Biographie générale, xxix, Paris 1859; entry on Le Play by 'L. L-T.'.

PÉQUIGNOT, L. *Frédéric Le Play*, Besançon 1888.

PERIER, PHILIPPE. 'L'Evolution d'une théorie de la "famille-souche" au "particularisme" ', *Recueil d'Etudes sociales*, nouvelle sér. no. 28, Paris 1956, pp. 73–87.

—— 'Le Play et ses Disciples face aux Entreprises coloniales', *Les Etudes sociales*, no. 75–6, Paris, January–June 1968, pp. 7–20.

Petit Journal; unsigned article on the Le Play centenary, 7 June 1906. Numerous other papers carried articles on this day.

PIDAL, marquis L. DE. *Del Método de observation en la ciencia social*: *Le Play y su escuela*, Madrid, 1899.

—— *Discursos de recepcion leidos ante la Real Academia de Ciencias morales y politicas*, tom. 4, Madrid 1875.

Polybiblion (Paris). Reviews of Le Play's books can be found in the following volumes: v (1870) 190; vi (1871) 192, 287; ix (1873) 106; xii (1874) 178; xiv (1875) 407; xvii (1876); xx (1877); xxxi (1881); and obituary in xxxiv (1882) 537.

PRIEUR, PROSPER. *Henri de Tourville*, Paris 1911. This contains some letters from Le Play to de Tourville, and an account of the split in the Le Play School.

QUÉRARD, J. M. *Le Quérard*, vols. i and ii, Paris 1855–56, entry on *Les Ouvriers européens*, pp. 410–11 by H. Rey.

RAMIERE, le père HENRI. *L'Ecole de la Réforme sociale*, Tours 1875.

Recueil d'Etudes sociales publiées à la Mémoire de Frédéric Le Play, Paris 1956. Foreword by Roger Grand. This collection of studies published at the time of the centenary of the Société d'Economie sociale, contains some of the most interesting printed studies of the life and work of Le Play. The articles are listed here under the names of their authors.

La Réforme sociale et le Centenaire de la Révolution, Paris 1890.

REUILLAR, GABRIEL. 'Le Play, apôtre de la Réforme sociale', *Paris-Normandie*, 22 August 1956.

REUSS, ALFONS. *Frédéric Le Play in seiner Bedeutung für die Entwicklung der sozialwissenschaftlichen Methode*, Jena 1913.

REY, H. Review of *Les Ouvriers européens* in *Le Moniteur universel*, 26 July 1856.

RIBBE, CHARLES DE. See *La Réforme sociale*, vii (Paris 1884) 113–27, 161.

RIBOT, PAUL DE. *Du rôle social des idées chrétiennes suivi d'un exposé critique des Doctrines sociales de M. Le Play*, 2 vols., Paris 1879. The second vol. consists mainly of a long critique of Le Play's views written from the point of view of a right-wing catholic.

RICHE, L'abbé A. *Le Play*, Paris 1891. A booklet by the parish priest of Saint-Sulpice. Le Play had a flat in his later years across the road in the old vicarage. He called Riche 'mon directeur spirituel' in a letter to Curzon written on 22 November 1881.

ROBERT, JEAN-PHILIPPE. *Deux Humanités*, Paris 1947. A very useful summary of the methods and classification of Le Play and his followers. Robert is the pen-name of Philippe Périer, q.v.

—— 'Nul n'est prophète en son pays', *Etudes sociales*, Paris September–October 1938.

RONDELET, ANTONIN. 'F. Le Play et l'Ecole de la Paix sociale', *Revue brittanique*, Paris, April 1882, pp. 457–92.

—— 'M. Le Play: Mémoire', *Revue du Monde catholique*, xv (Paris 1 May 1882) 209 ff.

ROSCHER, M. W. *Geschichte der national Oeconomik in Deutschland*, Munich 1875. Contains strong emphasis on the importance of *La Réforme sociale*.

ROUSIERS, PAUL DE. 'Le Play and Social Science', *Annals of the American Academy of Political and Social Science*, iv (Philadelphia 1893–94) 620–46.

—— with DEMOLINS, EDMOND. *Société internationale de Science sociale*, Paris, undated.

—— *Unions de la Paix sociale fondée par Le Play*, Angoulême 1884.

ROUX, PAUL. *Précis de Science sociale. Méthode et Enquêtes*, Paris 1914.

SAINTE-BEUVE, C. A. *Nouveaux Lundis*. 1st to 5th edns Paris 1867–81, vol. ix, pp. 161–201. These articles were first published in the *Constitutionnel* for 5, 12 and 19 December 1864. They were written as a result of two conversations Sainte-Beuve had had with Le Play.

SALOMON, GOTTFRIED. 'F. Le Play', *Encyclopaedia of the Social Sciences*, vol. ix, London 1933, pp. 411–12.

SAMUEL-LAJEUNESSE, R. *Grands Mineurs français*, Paris 1948, ch. 9, 'Frédéric Le Play était aussi un mineur!' Includes Le Play's article 'Observations sur le Mouvement commercial . . .' (W18).

SARGANT, WILLIAM LUCAS. *Economy of the Labouring Classes*, London 1857. Contains a critique of Le Play's methods, uses *Les Ouvriers européens* (W42) as its principal source.

Saturday Review. The following issues contain reviews of Le Play's books – xxxi (3 June 1871) 699; xxxii (23 December 1871) 821; xxxviii (3 June 1875).

SCHAEFFLE, A. E. F. *Das Gesellschaftliche System der menschlichen Wirthschaft*, Tubingen 1867.

SECRETAN, PHILIPPE. 'Création de la Société d'Economie et de Science sociale en 1856', *Etudes sociales*, nouvelle sér., ii, no. 28, Paris September 1955.

—— 'Le destin d'un grand sociologue: Frédéric Le Play', *Les Etudes sociales*, nouvelle sér., no. 73–4, June–December 1967, pp. 6–15.

—— 'Le Play et les Historiens de son Temps', *Recueil d'Etudes sociales*, Paris 1856, pp. 89–97.

—— 'Le Play et son Ecole', *Revue des Deux Mondes*, September–October 1956, p. 310.

SOREL, ALBERT. *Pages normandes*, Paris 1907.

SOROKIN, PITIRIN A. *Contemporary Sociological Theories*, New York 1928, ch. 3: 'Frédéric Le Play's School'.

SWINNY, S. H. See the *Positivist Review*, London October 1917, a review of Branford's *The Coming Polity*. This review says that the book upholds the view that Comte and Le Play are not antagonistic but complementary, 'a thesis that has often been maintained in the pages of this review'.

—— 'Sociology: its successes and its failures', *The Sociological Review*, xi, no. 1 (London 1919) 3.

—— 'The Sociological Schools of Comte and Le Play', *The Sociological Review*, xiii, no. 2 (London April 1921).

THOMAS, LOUIS. *Frédéric Le Play*, Paris 1943.

THUILLIER, G. 'Economie et société dans la pensée de Le Play en 1844', *La Revue Administrative*, no. 89, Paris September–October 1962, pp. 481 ff.

—— 'Le Play et la Réforme sociale,' *La Revue Administrative*, nos. 5–6, Paris 1958, pp. 249–59.

TOURVILLE, HENRI DE. *La Nomenclature sociale d'après Le Play*, Paris 1887. De Tourville developed Le Play's thought, and from it produced a system for classifying social facts based on Le Play's method.

TRENEY, XAVIER. *Les Grands Economistes des XVIIIe et XIXe siècles*, Paris 1889: ch. 48, Le Play.

TWINING, T. See the *Journal of the Society of Arts*, iii (London 1855) 675–6.

VACHEROT, E. See *Réforme sociale*, Paris 15 June 1883, p. 593. This is a report of a speech at the annual meeting of *La Société d'Economie sociale*. Vacherot upheld Le Play's method but denied his doctrine. This point of view is criticised by de Curzon (1899).

VALLAT, XAVIER. See *Libertés francaises*, Paris December 1956.

VIGNES, J. B. MAURICE. *La Science sociale d'après les principes de Le Play et de ses continuateurs*, 2 vols., Paris 1897.

WELLS, A. F. 'Social surveys and sociology', *The Sociological Review*, xxviii (London 1936) 274–94, an article critical of Le Play's method.

WENCKSTERN, A. VON. 'Le Play', *Jahrbuch für Gesetzbehung*, Berlin 1893. This deals mainly with Le Play's family studies. Wenckstern was at the time on a mission to Tokyo University.

WERTH, MARIA. *Die Kritik des Industrialismus bei Sismondi und Le Play*, Köln 1928.

Westminster Review, iii (London 1858) 251; criticism of Le Play's methods in a review of Sargant 1857.

WRIGHT, CARROL. See *La Réforme sociale*, Paris 1906, p.594. Wright was Commissioner of the Department of Labor at Washington which had produced over 6,000 monographs. In this article he says that he owes his technique to Le Play.

ZIMMERMAN, C. C. 'Frédéric Le Play as a social change theorist', *Recueil d'Etudes sociales*, Paris 1956, pp. 99–107.

—— 'Quelques remarques sur Frédéric Le Play', *Etudes sociales*, nouvelle sér., ii, nos. 29–30, Paris December 1955.

—— with FRAMPTON, M. E. *Family and Society*, London 1936; 1st edn, New York 1935. The second half of this book is a translation in summary of vol. i of Le Play's *Les Ouvriers européens*.

MANUSCRIPTS AND PRESS-CUTTINGS

LE PLAY, JEAN ALBERT (1842–1935). *Souvenirs 1842–1925*.

—— *Nouveaux Souvenirs* (1934). These two highly personal documents were written by Le Play's son in his old age and privately circulated round the family, in whose possession they are.

OBITUARY AND OTHER NOTICES

The following national newspapers printed notices about Le Play on one or more dates between 6 and 22 April 1882, the more informative articles are indicated by the date in brackets:

Ami du Peuple, Citoyen, Civilisation (8 April), *Clairon* (6 April), *Constitutionel, Correspondant* (7 April and 25 April), *Corsaire, Courrier du Soir, Courrier républicain, Défense, Démocratie*, 19e *Siècle, Electeur républicain, Estafette, Express, Figaro* (9 April), *Français*,

France (14 April), *France illustrée* (22 April), *France Nouvelle, France Populaire, Gaulois* (10 April), *Gazette de France, Gil Blas, Henri IV, Journal des Débats, Justice, Lanterne, Liberté, Marseillaise, Mémorial diplomatique, Monde* (12 April), *Monde illustré, Moniteur universel* (8 April), *Mot d'Ordre, Napoléon, National, Opinion nationale, Ordre, Paix, Paris, Paris Journal, Paris Passy, Parlement, Patrie, Petit Caporal, Petit 19e Siècle, Petit Moniteur Universel, Petite Presse, Petit Quotidien, Petite République française, Presse, Peuple français, Radical, Rappel, République française, Réveil, Siècle, Soir, Soleil, Télégraphe, Temps, Union, Unité nationale, Univers, Univers illustré, Vérité, Ville de Paris, Voltaire.*

There were also 111 entries in local papers of which the following were most informative:

Le Journal de Marseille (9 April), *La Gazette du Midi* (9 April), *L'Union de l' Ouest* (12 April), *La Décentralisation, Lyon* (12 April), *Le Sémaphore, Marseilles* (13 April), *Journal de Roubaix* (18 April), *Le Courrier de la Somme* (6 April).

Among foreign newspapers the most interesting reports were in *The Times* (7 April), *Le Messager Franco-Américain*, New York (8 April), *Le Journal de Roma* (16 and 19 April), *L'Economiste Catholique*, Bruxelles (12 April).

Notes

References to the Bibliography (pp. 143 ff.) are abbreviated: (a) by a number with a prefix for works written or sponsored by Le Play; (b) by author's name and date of publication for writings about him.

Chapter 1   The technologist with a social conscience

1   Herbertson 1950. A small example of this unreliability is in the datelist on p. 116 where one entry reads: '1848. Resigned Chair to devote himself to social science.' The Chair referred to was at the Ecole des Mines, which he held, as a matter of fact, until 1856. He eventually resigned this Chair on appointment to the Conseil d'Etat. What happened in 1848 was that he became also vice-principal of the School.

2   E. Mayo, *The Social Problems of an Industrial Civilisation*, London 1945.

3   See Bibliography W74.

4   J. Chase, *The Proper Study of Mankind*, London 1957.

5   'Frédéric Le Play est aussi mineur' Ch. 9 of Samuel-Lajeunesse 1948.

6   Founded in 1793 during the most hectic period of the French Revolution and later developed by Napoleon, L'Ecole Polytechnique soon became and remained one of the most famous centres of higher technical education in the world. Le Play's estimate was not so flattering. The school itself stands at the hub of the system of the *hautes écoles*, which are not university institutions, but have similar prestige. The Ecole Polytechnique assured its successful pupils a career in the government service, civil or military; but the main bias in the early days was military; and this no doubt increased Le Play's reservations. Indeed, just after his time (1832) the School was placed under the authority of the Minister of War. The organisation of the School was paramilitary with a uniform and a system of marking examinations according to a military rank (e.g. sergeant and corporal instead of 1st and 2nd class). In its emphasis on corporate life, the School went to the opposite extreme from the University of Paris. There were several reorganisations, but from the beginning the students lived in small lodging-houses in the charge of a house tutor. Among numerous writings about the School, *Ecole polytechnique, Livre de Centenaire*, vol. 1, Paris 1895, gives short biographies of all the famous ex-pupils including Le Play and De La Vauterie (mentioned later in the text).

An analysis of the backgrounds of the pupils can be found in 'Les Elèves de l'Ecole polytechnique de 1815 à 1848', in *Revue d'Histoire moderne et contemporaine*, v (Paris 1958) 226 ff. Emile de Girardin, *De l'Instruction publique*, Paris
G

1838, gives a summary of the courses as they were soon after Le Play was a student.

7   'On ne m'a jamais parlé de ce grand-père, je ne sais ni ou ni à quelle époque il est mort. Je sais seulement qu'il y eut séparation entre les deux époux et qu'ils ne se revirent jamais.' In his writings Le Play always says that his father died when he was five. Apart from this he never mentions him, nor do any of the memoir writers. One might well reflect that had he lived a little later, much would have been made of the fact that this expert on family life came himself from a broken home. For the above quotation see Jean Albert Le Play, *Souvenirs* 1842–1925 (MS). For the family tree see p. 141.

8   L'Abbé A-J-A. Gratry, 1805–72, left the Ecole Polytechnique to enter a monastery; known for his works on science and religion, and later for his strong opposition to papal infallibility (on which he recanted).

C-L-L. Juchault de Lamoricière, 1806–65, the famous general. Michel Chevalier, 1806–79, went to the United States during the July Monarchy, keeping in correspondence with Le Play. He returned to France in 1840 to become Professor of Political Economy at the Collège de France, where he stayed for the rest of his life, apart from a short period in 1848. Chevalier was closely associated with Le Play and took part in many of his projects. Le Play's son married Chevalier's daughter (see family tree).

Le Comte Napoléon Daru, 1807–90, soldier and statesman, held various offices, another opponent of papal infallibility, also a supporter of Le Play's projects later.

Jean Reynaud, 1806–63, mystical philosopher and close friend of Le Play. In 1848 he became Professeur du Droit at the Ecole des Mines, but resigned in 1851 rather than take the oath to Louis Napoleon.

9   Arch. Nat. $F^{14}2731^2$. He added plaintively and no doubt politically that the School had no funds to reward Le Play suitably, whereupon the Minister gave him a collection of books.

10   Preserved in the Library of the Ecole des Mines.

11   Claude Henri de Rouvray comte de Saint-Simon, 1760–1825, was the author of a number of books on social philosophy which were little read at the time but produced a wide following afterwards. He foresaw a rapid industrialisation and advocated that power should be in the hands of the workers and technicians. Among his many unfulfilled projects was an encyclopedia of modern science and technology. This was carried out some years after his death by Jean Reynaud, with Le Play as one of his collaborators, see Bibliography W13.

Charles Fourier, 1772–1837, advocated self-governing cooperative communities; he criticised what he considered the excessive egalitarianism of the Saint-Simonians.

The following letter written to Michel Chevalier would appear to support the claim of the Saint-Simonians that Le Play had been one of them in spite of his later denials: 'I am leaving today [8 April 1832] with Baudin and Malinvaud to make a trip to Le Havre and into Normandy. So I would be very much obliged if you would be so good as to arrange that my daily nourishment, *The Globe* [a Saint-Simonian paper] is forwarded to me at The Havre from to-morrow.

'Do please understand that we will not fail to preach everywhere according

to our faith ... if you need us write, we will give you all the help we can'
(Bibliothèque de l'Arsenal, Fonds-Enfantin, 76001 Correspondence du 'Globe',
Ecole Polytechnique). I am much indebted to Mr B. Radcliffe of the Department of Economic History at Manchester University for drawing my attention
to this letter.

12 For this quotation see W42, foreword. Le Play's accident was described in a
letter of 5 May 1830, from Berthieu (of the Ecole des Mines) to Becquey (the
Minister) preserved, with other documentation used in this chapter, in Arch.
Nat. $F^{14}2731^2$.

13 This is quoted from the English translation of vol. i. Le Play's report, as the
Bibliography shows, forms the major part of vol. iv. During the German
invasion of Russia towards the end of 1941, a newspaper in occupied France
carried the following headline: 'Les 39 milliards de Tonnes d'Anthracite *du
Donbass* furent découvertes par un français. Le Géologue *Le Play* conduisit les
prospections qui permirent l'exploitation intense *Du Bassin Du Donetz*' (*Paris-
Soir* 5 November 1941).

14 Prince Napoleon was a grandson of Napoleon I and hence a cousin of Louis
Napoleon.

15 See Bibliography W11 and W21.

16 This report, often mentioned by contemporaries as of outstanding importance,
seems to have vanished. It was never published, but it would appear that two
copies were made – one for the Ministry of Public Works in Paris, and the
other for Prince Demidov. Extensive searches in Paris (the archives of the
Ministry of Public Works are thin for this period), and enquiries in Switzerland
(where a later report is preserved in the Iron Library at Schaffhausen), Italy
(where Prince Paul of Yugoslavia has inherited the Demidov estate near
Florence), Russia (where M. Kafengauz has been writing on the Demidov
family, but has not come across this particular manuscript) and numerous other
places likely and unlikely, have produced no trace. Some excerpts only from
the report are preserved in some of the case studies; see W42, ii.

17 Porter's letters with copies of Le Play's replies are to be found in the Bibliothèque de l'Institut de France, MS 6063. This correspondence is mentioned in
Les Débuts du Catholicisme sociale en France by Jean-Baptiste Duroselle. I am much
indebted to Monsieur Duroselle for drawing my attention to this correspondence and facilitating my access to it.

18 The date of this letter is illegible, but it answers one from Porter dated 17
April, and is answered by Porter on 25 April.

19 A. L. Dunham in *The Industrial Revolution in France*, New York 1955, pp. 135–6.

20 This session was reported in *Le Moniteur universel* for 24 March 1848. Le Play
later said the report was biased.

21 The original *De Re Metallica*, written by Agricola, was published in 1556; the
Ecole des Mines possesses a first edition. The source for the following sentence
is from Le Play's annual report to the Ministry of Public Works (which he had
to make as a member of the Corps des Mines) dated 20 February 1850. He says
in this that he is spending all his spare time on his proposed book on metallurgy.
In 1852 he was still collecting material for this, some of which he published
in 1853, see W17.

22   *Les Ouvriers des Deux Mondes*; 4 vols were published between 1857 and 1864. See Bibliography, W41.

23   Normally abbreviated to 'La Société d'Economie sociale' (or S.E.S.). In these pages it is often just called 'the Society'. Its name has changed many times, and it is now called La Société d'Economie et de Science sociale. Louis Villermé. 1782–1863, was a doctor and author of a penetrating study of poverty in Paris, The English society mentioned in the next sentence was the National Association for the Promotion of Social Science. Le Play called this 'our daughter society'. It survived about twenty years. An example of how such societies sprang up elsewhere is that years later Le Play's grandson discovered a Le Play circle in China.

24   'Elle était fondue sur une méthode encore trop imparfaite et sur un nombre de faits insuffisants ... les conclusions ... détournèrent le public et Le Play lui-même de l'œuvre purement scientifique et en retardèrent ainsi le développement naturel, alors qu'elle n'était qu'à ses débuts' (E. Demolins, preface to *Frédéric Le Play, sa Méthode et sa Doctrine* by E. Bouchié de Belle, Paris 1906; this booklet is the most interesting brief account of Le Play's sociology). Le Play was impelled to draw some lessons from his studies because of the dangerous times through which France was passing.

25   This was said at a meeting of La Société d'Economie sociale, on 3 June 1868, see *Bulletin* (W69) for that year.

26   C. A. Sainte-Beuve, *Nouveaux Lundis*, 2nd to 5th edns, Paris 1872–81, vol. ix, 161–201.

27   See A. Delor, *La Grève des Ouvriers*, reprint from *La Réforme sociale*, Paris 1888. Le Play's contributions to the development of railways are mentioned in the next chapter.
   More serious comments on his position can be found in Einaudi 1960, pp. 184–5.

28   See *La France,* 14 April 1882.

29   See *Le Petit Journal,* 17 June 1906.

Chapter 2   The engineer

1   See A. Moreau de Jonnès, *Statistiques de l'industrie de France*, Paris 1856.

2   *Annales des Mines*, 2nd sér., v (Paris 1829) 187. See Bibliography for a list of Le Play's entries in the *Annales des Mines*. Hornblende and tourmaline are minerals whose properties were just being explored at the time Le Play was writing.

3   See O. Viennet, *Napoléon et l'industrie française,* Paris 1947.

4   W54, vol. ii, 128–9.

5   See L. Mumford, *Technics and Civilisation,* London 1934.

6   See *De la Conciliation et de l'arbritrage* – Ministère du Commerce, de l'Industrie et des Colonies, Office du Travail, Paris 1839; also G. and H. Bourgin, *Le Régime de l'industrie en France de 1814 à 1830*, 3 vols, Paris 1912–41.

7   *Le Régime de l'Industrie,* ii, 90 ff. The *Conseil* pointed out that it had been found impossible to control the employment of children on these machines in

England! The 'mule' was a machine for spinning cotton invented by Samuel Crompton in the 1770s and becoming common in France about 1820.

8 Bar-le-Duc was the town. The correspondence between the Prefect of the Meuse and the Minister of the Interior is printed in *Le Régime de l'Industrie* (see above note 6), iii, 185 ff.

9 The Lyons riots and the silk industry have been described in numerous books. See, for example, F. Rude, *Le Mouvement ouvrier à Lyon de 1827 à 1832*, Paris 1944. Although there have been more recent works, this is a thorough and readable attempt to unravel the development of the working-class movement in Lyons including the major riots of November 1831. Rude carefully distinguishes the economic and political aspects of the forces involved. He also suggests that, in appealing to the Chartists in England, the workers' leaders for the first time attempted to develop some international organisation.

10 Michel Chevalier, *Des Interêts matériels en France*, Paris 1838.

11 See *Dictionnaire d'économie politique*, ed. Joseph Say, vol. ii, Paris 1892.

12 See A. Perdiquier, *Le livre du compagnonnage*, Paris 1837; P. Moreau, *Réforme des abus du compagnonnage*, Paris 1843; F. Chovin, *Le conseiller des compagnons*, Paris 1860. These three books are by *compagnons* themselves. Levasseur, *L'Histoire des classes ouvrières en France*, Paris 1859, has a section on the subject.

   Le Play's monograph on *compagnonnage* (referred to later) is in *Les Ouvriers européens* (W42), v, ch. 9.

13 For an interesting account of the work of the Martins, father and son, see A. Thuillier, *Emile Martin*, Nevers 1964.

14 See Bibliography W15. The Spanish reference is W19. The Normandy journey W37. A century later, in 1836, a member of Malinvaud's family won the Le Play prize for the best essay on social studies by a student at the Ecole des Mines.

15 For the resulting study see W11.

16 As evidence of this Le Play quoted from Tacitus and Pliny (e.g. Pliny Book xxxiii where subsidence and such phenomena are ascribed to the indignation of holy mother earth, *indignatione sacrae parentis*). At the time of the tour mentioned in the text, Emmanuel Swedenborg (1688–1772) held an appointment in the Swedish Board of Mines. He resigned this post in 1747 to devote himself to the religious activities and writings for which he later became famous.

17 For instance, he scoffed at the idea that the success of the Siberian mineral industry was due to the supply of serf labour. In saying this he did not intend to deny the sufferings of the serfs, but to point out that serfdom was not an economic system of production. Hence Russian competition should not be used as an excuse by Western producers. A well led, educated, free labour force was what industry needed.

18 See W21 and W16. This latter contains a direct reply to the arguments of François.

19 Le Play drafted a whole series of documents on this subject. See W4–9.

20 Henri Joly, *Le Droit naturel et la science sociale*, Paris 1887.

21 Four notebooks of his lectures are preserved at the Ecole des Mines, and two
are in the possession of Mme Le Play. Some passages in the text are translated
directly from these notes.

22 'Dédaignant les livres, documents et rapports Le Play plongea dans le monde
et le regarda vivre', quoted by M. Préaud in a memoir on the future work of
La Société d'Economie et de Science Sociale submitted to the society in 1947
and to be found in its archives. Préaud does not give the source of the
quotation.

23 The reference to the coal price is from W26, iv, 388–9, where it is shown that
the *average* price of 4.10 francs per metric quintal for British coal compares with
the *cheapest* Russian at 4.99. It was more than a century and a half before 'style
of management' was closely studied by social scientists. See, e.g. R. Likert,
New Patterns of Management, New York 1961.

24 This is a quotation from one of his lectures – he refers to a visit he paid to
England during the slump of 1842. He frequently referred to his memories of
this visit in letters later in his life, e.g. a letter to J. R. Porter in April 1848 (Le
Play archives in La Bibliothèque de l'Institut de France), mentioned above in
Chapter 1.

25 See W10.

26 Given, for instance, in his letters to his wife (see W79).

27 See Louis Blanc's own account of this, written in exile in England: *Historical
Revelations: Inscribed to Lord Normanby*, by Louis Blanc, London 1858. Louis
Blanc also wrote *Histoire de la Révolution de 1848*, 2 vols, Paris 1888, *La Révolution
de Février au Luxembourg*, Paris 1849, and *Questions d'aujourd'hui, et de demain*,
Paris 1873–77. References to the Luxembourg Commission can be found in all
the works on the 1848 Revolution, see especially D. C. McKay, *The National
Workshops*, London 1933, and P. de la Gorce, *Histoire de la seconde République*,
vol. i, Paris 1914. For an English translation of the first report of the commis-
sion see W. L. Sargant, *Social Innovators and their Schemes*, London 1858. See also
P. Losteau, *Louis Blanc à la Commission du Luxembourg*, Paris 1908; Edouard
Renard, *La Vie et l'œuvre de Louis Blanc*, Toulouse 1922. Of the three committees
which made up the Luxembourg Commission, only the minutes of the Workers'
Committee seem to have survived. These are to be found in the Archives
Nationales. See Rémi Gossez, *Les Ouviers de Paris 1848–1851, Livre* 1: *L'Organisation*, Paris 1967. Reports of the proceedings of the Commission were
printed in *Le Moniteur Universel* for 1848; see especially the following issues: 2,
13, 19, 20, 24 and 27 March, 7 April.

28 These are not listed in full in *Le Moniteur*, but Renard (see above) gives the
following list of members of the *Comité des Capacités* as it came to be called:

Vidal }
Pecqueur } socialists but anti-Communist

Victor Considérant

Toussel }
Dupoty } journalists and writers
Malarmet }
Pascal }

F. Le Play

Duverget
Dupont-White } lawyers

Jean Reynaud
Cazeau } economists with Saint Simonian views

Wolowsky   *laissez-faire* economist

29 The matter had been brought before the Commission two days earlier and was reported in *Le Moniteur* on 28 March.

30 Louis Blanc, *1848 Historical Revelations*, London 1858.

31 See *Le Moniteur* for 13 May 1848.

32 The names of the members of La Haute Commission des Etudes Scientifiques et Littéraires were listed in *Le Moniteur* for 1 March 1848. The main reference to its work and to the setting up of L'Ecole Administrative are in the following issues: 8, 9, 14, 19, 22 and 24 April. The records of the School are in the Archives Nationales (F^{17} 4142–5).

33 Full details of these and other attempts were given in a document circulated to the Representatives while the Ecole d'Administration was being discussed. This document is preserved in the Archives Nationales (Carton F^{17}4142). The abortive law of 1820 was promoted by Cuvier, himself educated at a School of Administration at Wurtemberg, and the following from a letter of his to Louis XVIII is an interesting example of his 'sales talk': 'In the military profession you progress only in accordance with rules fixed by the king. There would certainly be great benefits to be gained from analogous rules in the Church and the Civil Service. . . . Perhaps it would be possible, and undoubtedly it would be useful, to establish as in Germany a regular system of teaching for the various branches of the Administration, and only to admit as employees those who followed this course of instruction.'

34 'Ces grands metteurs en œuvre d'idées, ces grands practiciens ne font pas leur besogne sans froisser beaucoup d'interêts, sans méconter beaucoup de gens', Henry Fouquier, in *Le Petit 19e Siècle*, 7 April 1882.

35 *Le Moniteur universel,* 8 April 1848.

36 *Le Moniteur,* 24 April 1848.

37 See, for example, *The Economist,* vi (London, 15 April 1848) 242. The full list is given in *Le Moniteur* for 9 April. Porter asked Le Play about these appointments in one of his letters, but Le Play did not reply to this question.

38 'J'ai été appelé a cette chaire sans avoir été consulté, je ne l'ai pas remplie un seul jour, et elle n'existe plus; ma démission serait donc tout à fait superflue' (letter of 4 January 1849 in Archives de l'Ecole Administrative).

39 At this time de Sénarmont, he resigned soon after. All the correspondence referred to in this section is in W30.

40 See W26.

41 For instance he wrote to his wife on 28 May 1853 that he was in Venice because he had to see Demidov before going to Russia, and that he was tired, lonely and discouraged. Two days later he wrote that he was still held up waiting for some

decision from Demidov, adding, 'with anyone else and in any other mental condition, I would enjoy staying in Venice'. There was also the fact that France and Russia were on the verge of war.

Chapter 3   The public figure

1   The assistant director, H. Tresca, wrote to Prince Napoleon on 23 May 1855. His strongly worded note is in Arch. Nat. $F^{12}2892$ among a number of accounts and formal documents, such as redundancy notices. Tresca was vice-principal of the Imperial Conservatory of Arts and Crafts.

2   See, for example, E. Dolléans, *Histoire du Mouvement Ouvrier*, Paris 1936.

3   The financing of these exhibitions is itself a fascinating study. London 1851 was run by a private committee (with the Prince Consort as an active member), was financed by private funds, and made a large profit – out of which grants are still made for educational purposes. Paris 1855 was state subsidised, and even the British contribution was state aided. Paris 1867 was a combination of state and private finance, and made a profit.

4   It was. In 1868 Michel Chevalier produced the following figures for size of Exhibitions (see *Rapports du Jury International*, vol. i, Introduction, pp. ii and iii):

	Exhibitors (thousands)	Visitors (millions)
London 1851	14	6
Paris 1855	24	5
London 1862	29	6
Paris 1867	50	over 10

5   See G. Maw and E. J. Payne. *The French Universal Exhibition of 1867* (London 1866). These writers claim that Le Play copied their idea. Fritz Walch of the Technical University of Karlsruhe tells me that their claim was incorrect and that the idea was original to Le Play. He also tells me that Le Play was partly responsible for the architecture of the Exhibition which was unpopular at the time, but anticipated modern functional ideas. See Fritz Walch, *Die Architektur der Weltausstellung 1867 in Paris*. Technische Universität Karlsruhe, 1966, Doktorarbeit am Lehrstuhl für Kunstaeschichte Professor Dr Klaus Lankheit (unpublished doctoral thesis).

6   See for instance *The Illustrated Catalogue of the Universal Exhibition* (London 1868). See also *The Times* for 1 March 1867, which also refers to the ugliness of the building. See also *The Times* for 3 April 1867. Although opened punctually, the Exhibition was still far from ready.

7   *Notes and Sketches of the Paris Exhibition*, by G. A. Sala (London 1868).

8   The report of this Jury is printed in vol. i of the official report on the Exhibition. See: *Rapports du Jury International* (13 vols, Paris 1868). This report was edited by Michel Chevalier and his introduction should also be consulted.

9   L. Reybaud, 'Economie politique des Ouvriers – Du patronage dans l'Industrie', *Revue des Deux Mondes*, 1 April 1867, p. 737.

10 Summarised in *Bulletin* (W69) for 31 January 1869.

11   See above, Chapter 2 note 11. The speaker was Armand Vicomte de Melun, 1807–77, a statesman and promoter of charitable societies.

12   See above, Chapter 2, note 6. By 1867 the *Conseils de Prud'hommes* had equal numbers of employers and workpeople, but the chairman was appointed by the government and was said to be always an employer.

13   *Report of Artisans selected by a Committee appointed by the Council of the Society of Arts to visit the Paris Universal Exhibition*, London 1867. George Howell's account is in Part I on p. 198.

14   Ibid. Part I, p. 433.

15   For example Schneider and Cheysson.

16   *Rapport sur l'Exposition Universelle de 1867*, Paris 1869 (this is the dating on the titlepage, but some of the appendices were not printed until 1872). Among recommendations in this report is one that immediate legislative provision should be given to the demands of the workers' delegates, namely:

    1. Abolition of *livrets*.
    2. Limitation of work of the women and children.
    3. Promotion of technical education.
    4. Reform of the *Conseils de Prud'hommes*.
    5. Freedom for the trade unions.

17   The word used was 'dévoué'. The documentation of this enquiry, both the questionnaire and Le Play's summary of the results, is among the Le Play archives in the *Bibliothèque de l'Institut de France*.

18   'Réponse distinguée: souvent erronée.' It is possible that the inadequacy of some of the replies may have been due to hostility on the part of the Prefects to this particular enquiry; for they already had to send in detailed reports on the industrial situation to the Ministry of Agriculture, Commerce and Public Works. See, for example, Archives nationales $F^{12}4478$.

19   The following questions form part of a questionnaire used in the Pas de Calais coalfield. The answers were rated as showing conditions that were either 'good', 'indifferent' or 'bad'.

    A. *Conditions*
      1. Physical state of people?
      2. Influence of work on health?
      3. Hygienic arrangements in workshops?
      4. Housing.
      5. Whether owner-occupied?
      6. Any efforts to facilitate house purchase?
      7. Do workers live in lodgings?
     10. Is land work available to workers as well as industrial?
     12. Does the worker live on credit?
     13. What about cooperatives and other means of cheaper living?
     14. What about workers' associations?
     15. Clothing?
     16. Credit facilities?
     17. Thrift?
     18. Social insurance?
        *

B. *Wages*
  2. Is saving possible?
  3. Bonuses?
  4. Goods in kind?
  5. Length of hours?
  6. Age of starting work and retiring?
  7. Profit-sharing?
  8. Supply of labour?
  9. Slumps?
  10. Relations between employers and employed?
  11. Strikes?
  13. Proposals for avoiding conflict?

C. *Moral condition*
  2–6. Education.
  9. Promotion.
  11. Sunday rest.
  13. Attendances on Mondays.

20 The Prince's letter, dated 20 April 1864, is in the *Bibliothèque de l'Institut de France*. Unfortunately, the papers about the scheme that the Prince says he is sending are not there.

21 W54, vol. ii, 233–90.

22 The paper was *La Patrie*. Editorial comment and Le Play's articles appear in the following issues for 1857: 20, 22, 24 April, 3, 5, 7, 9, 12, 14 June. Le Play's monograph on *Le Paysan du Lavedan* (M91) is especially relevant to this discussion.

23 See M99. For his account of this see W45, p. 292, note 2.

24 E. Levasseur, *La Population française*, iii (Paris 1892) 171–7.

25 See Emile Ollivier, *Journal*, entry for 22 May 1858, vol. i, 333, of the edition edited by Theodore Zeldin, Paris 1961.

26 See E. Bonnal, *La Liberté de Tester*, Paris 1866, p. 15. There are references to the debate in *Le Moniteur universel*, issues of 21 January 1864, 6 April 1865, and 13 June 1866. The Emperor's support for the motion is mentioned in Angot de Rotours' account at the Le Play centenary, see Angot de Rotours 1906. Einaudi points out that most of the reforms he advocated have eventually come to pass, see Louise Sommer, ed., *Essays in European Economic Thought*, New York 1960, Chapter 7.

27 See W54, iii, 654–6.

Chapter 4   The social scientist

1 See W78. The subsequent incident is described in Chapter 1, where he also describes the powerful effect of Le Play's personality.

2 See L. R. Villermé, *Tableau de l'Etat physique et morale des Ouvriers* (Paris 1840) see also above Ch. 1, note 23.

3 W78, p. 266.

4   W54, i, 63.

5   See *Principles of Economics*, vol. i, 7th edn, London 1916, p. 116.

6   I am indebted to Magnus Hedberg, author of *The Process of Labor Turnover* (Stockholm 1967), for pointing this out. Mr Hedberg has been able to trace the actual time that Le Play spent in Sweden, where he wrote a case study of a forgeman in Dannemora, from hotel registers. Mr Hedberg has also tried to trace the actual family from the parish records, but no family is there exactly as described by Le Play. Such an accurate check on Le Play's movements is no longer possible for some countries, but it is clear from his itinerary that he did not himself spend long on some of his cases. For a note on Smith of Chesterfield, see below note 14.

7   See W42, 1st edn, pp. 15–46.

8   See W42, i, book i, Ch. 2.

9   W42, ii, 99–141, M143. Le Play is, of course, describing the particular methods of employment which applied to the workers he studied. The varieties of employment in this area in the previous century are discussed fully in R. Portal, *L'Oural au XVIIIᵉ siècle* (Paris 1950). This book also contains diagrams of factories in and near Ekaterineburg (now Sverdlovsk).

10 W42, ii, 179–230, M145.

11 W42, ii, 231–71, M22. This case study was, of course, actually written before the massacres of Bulgarian Christians later in the century; but one year after the greatest of these (in 1876) it was apparently still possible to write of the favourable material situation of Christian workers in Bulgaria. See *Cambridge Modern History*, 1st edn, xii, Cambridge 1910, 383.

12 'draconiennes en apparence, peu efficaces en réalité', (W42, iii, 347). See Bibliography for a list of case studies of English workers. For a general survey of English institutions see W38 – *La Constitution d'Angleterre* – which was an attempt to extend the case study method to a country.

13 'il est résulté des désordres sociaux que l'humanité n'avait jamais connus'. See W42, iii, 350. The following passage in the text is based on this case study, M31.

14 W42, iii, 400, M33. I have been unable to find out anything else about this T. Smith. John Mogey, in his article in *Recueil d'études sociales* (1956) writes of his inability to trace this author whose name appears on this monograph. But there is a possibility that he might be Josiah Timmis Smith (1823–1906), member of a well-known family of Derbyshire ironmasters who worked for a time at Le Creusot. J. T. Smith became in 1859 the first manager of Schneider, Hannay and Company who opened the first ironworks in Barrow-in-Furness in that year. See Philip Robinson, *Supplement to The Smiths of Chesterfield* (Chesterfield 1960). Le Play frequently got initials wrong, and anyway may well have known him as Timmis Smith.

15 He referred specifically to those of 1833, 1842, 1844 and 1847. The firm in the north of England mentioned a few sentences earlier is identified in W54, ii, 146, as the Consett Iron Works employing 15,000 men.

16 So much per thousand 'ems' – the 'em' is a measurement based on the size of the letter 'M' in a certain type. Le Play's formidable contemporary and

opponent, Proudhon, was a printing trade worker, and accounts of the trade can be found in biographies of him.

17 See D. Riesman, *The Lonely Crowd*, New Haven 1950. In some ways Riesman's analysis of tradition-direction and inner-direction is nearer to the thinking of Le Play than some of the latter's own disciples.

Chapter 5   The social thinker

1 Demolins has already been quoted as saying this. See also Philippe Périer, 'Evolution et rénovation de la monographie dans l'Ecole de Le Play', *Etudes sociales*, nouvelle sér. no. 28 (Paris, September 1955), pp. 6–12, and especially p. 8 (this article was a reprint of a speech made by the author at the 16th Congress of the International Institute of Sociology at Beaune in 1954).

   For a discussion of Le Play's ethics relevant to this chapter, see Andrée Michel, 'Les Codes sociaux de la doctrine morale de Frédéric Le Play', in *Cahiers Internationaux de Sociologie*, xxxiv (Paris 1963) 47–68.

2 He said this in the unlikely place of a speech to the *Ligue nationale contre l'Alcoolisme* on 23 March 1909. Incidentally Cheysson describes himself as a disciple of Le Play and goes on to say that one of his main principles in life is optimism about human nature. He obviously did not learn this from Le Play.

   Vico's views are well summarised in W. Stark, *The Fundamental Forms of Social Thought*, London 1962, pp. 219–22. The following sentences refer to this.

3 'Plus je recherche la cause de ces révolutions et des maux qu'elles entraînent, plus je la trouve dans les sophismes qui ont infecté notre nation à la fin du XVIIIᵉ siècle. Le plus dangereux de ces sophismes a été répandu par J.-J. Rousseau.' W54, i, 16, footnote.

4 As in the introduction to vol. vi of *Les Ouvriers européens* (W42). Both Le Play's view of original sin and his theory of the elite are discussed by Einaudi (1960).

5 W54, i, 21.

6 Carle C. Zimmerman, 'Frédéric Le Play as a social change theorist', in *Recueil d'études sociales à la Mémoire de Frédéric Le Play*, Paris 1956, pp. 99–107.

7 *Programme de Gouvernement et d'Organisation sociale*, par un Groupe d'Economistes, Paris 1881.

8 Leopold von Wiese in *Sociology: Its History and Main Problems*, Hanover (U.S.A.) 1928, pp. 16 ff.

9 W42, v, introduction, p. xii.

10 W54, i, 24.

11 Le Play's theory of the family is the one part of his work which has been the subject of a major study in English. See C. C. Zimmerman and M. E. Frampton, *Family and Society*, London 1936; pages 359–595 are a translation in digest of vol. i of *Les Ouvriers européens* by Samuel Dupertuis.

12 A. E. F. Schaeffle, German sociologist and contemporary of Le Play.

13 See F. Butel, *La Vallée d'Ossau*. In the preface to this book Demolins says that it has disproved the concept of the famille souche. See also *Mouvement sociale*, iii (Paris 1894) 65.

14 See Henry Bordeaux, *Paysages Romanesques*, Paris 1906, pp. 333 ff.

15 Op. cit. pp. 57–8. They also list some family studies which show that there are fluctuations in the level of family consumption which cannot just be explained by the business cycle.

16 W54, i, 452.

17 W54, iii, 461. 'Universal franchise' for the *Corps legislatif* was part of the Constitution of Napoleon III. But, we have seen in Chapter 1, this had limited powers and the rest of the apparatus of government was not elective.

18 W54, i, 74, footnote.

19 W54, ii, ch. 47.

20 See R. Frankenberg, *Communities in Britain*, London 1967. See also M. Banton, *Roles*, London 1965, p. 66: 'As societies advance . . . Independent roles become increasingly narrow and specific in character.'

21 The allocation of state contracts was used to promote producers' cooperatives by the Provisional Government of 1848. Later Le Play advocated to the Emperor that contracts should be used as a tool of policy in producing more satisfactory employment practices.

22 W54, ii, 106–131.

23 W54, ii, 126.

24 This view comes out in many places, for example W54, ii, 113–14.

25 A letter from Le Play to an Englishman named Tyler, admitting his ignorance on this subject, is preserved in Keele University Library.

26 See W51, p. 141, footnote.

27 See Jean Gaumont, *Histoire générale de la Coopération en France*, 2 vols, Paris 1926. See also Reports by *Her Majesty's Representatives abroad on the System of Cooperation in Foreign Countries* (Commercial Papers no. 20, 1886).

28 See W76, introduction, p. lvi.

29 The writer was a lawyer named Blome. The letter, dated 26 January 1876, was read to a meeting of the *Société d'Economie sociale*, and is printed in the minutes, see *Bulletin* (W69) v, 200–3.

30 See A. Riche, *Frédéric Le Play*, Paris 1891. In this booklet, which begins with a note from Le Play's widow confirming its accuracy, Riche says that Le Play approached him on 28 November 1879, and said he wanted to become a practising Catholic. Incidentally, with reference to Le Play's pacifism mentioned elsewhere in the text, this booklet tells how he strongly stipulated that he did not wish any military honours at his funeral. His membership of the *Légion d'Honneur* would have entitled him to these.

31 See W42, vi, introduction, p. xii.

32 See L. de Besse, *Le Clergé de France et Frédéric Le Play*, San Remo 1909.

33 See Einaudi 1960; see also de Curzon 1899.

Chapter 6 The followers

1 By J. H. Abraham in *Sociology*, London 1966, p. 24. For Villermé see ch. 1, note 23; for Chevalier and Daru see ch. 1, note 8; Louis Wolowski 1810–76, Polish refugee naturalised French, liberal politician and economist, advocate of land-banks; for Melun see ch. 3, note 11; C. Robert was well known for his advocacy of cooperatives, and de Lesseps as the engineer of the Suez Canal.

2 The minutes of this meeting are printed in *Les Ouvriers des Deux Mondes* (W41), iv, 7 ff. W41 contains the record of some meetings, as also does W70. For the first eight years of the Society, these are the only records that survive. From 1864 onwards complete minutes are printed in the *Bulletin* (W69).

3 This discussion of apprenticeship gives, of course, only the point of view of members of the Le Play School. The *Conseils de prud'hommes* are discussed above in ch. 2, see pp. 35–6.

4 *Bulletin* (W69) for 7 March 1875. The passages mentioned here and elsewhere in the text can be traced in W69 by the dates.

5 Ibid. 30 January 1876.

6 See above, Chapter 3, p. 63–71.

7 On 27 February 1876. Cheysson's writings included papers on industrial relations, housing, social security and industrial accidents and many other subjects.

8 See *Report of Massachusetts railroad commissioners on the Boston and Maine Railroad Strike of February 12th*, 1877.

9 On 1 February 1874 (W69). As explained in note 23 to Chapter 1 *La Société d'Economie sociale* (Social Economy Society) is often called the Society on these pages.

10 On 11 February 1877 (W69).

11 The speaker was Le Pelletier (1864–1939); see *Procès-verbal* (unpublished archives of the *Société d'Economie sociale*) for 30 November 1934. The following year the two societies agreed on a joint publication. They did not actually merge until 1946.

12 See 'La Nomenclature des faits sociaux, d'après Henri de Tourville', a chart facing p. 30 of Robert 1947. This is taken from Roux 1914. The reference later in the text to the controversy over the family types is Périer 1956.

13 See Paul de Rousiers, *La Vie Américaine*, Paris 1892. English translation by A. J. Herbertson, *American Life*, London 1893.

14 See chart mentioned in note 12 above. The French is: 'Patriarchale, Conseil de Communauté, Ouvrier chef de métier, petit patron, patron de fabrique collective, grand patron, Société d'actionnaires.' The translation is not literal, but follows the case studies in *Les Ouvriers des Deux Mondes* which de Tourville was presumably using.

15 Emile Durkheim (1858–1917). See *Les Régles de la méthode sociologique*, 4th edn, 1907, pp. 97–8. For the reference to Simiand below see François Simiand, *L'Evolution sociale et la monnaie*, 2 vols, Paris 1932.

16   See Paul Farmer, 'The social theory of Frédéric Le Play' in *Teachers of History: Essays in Honor of Laurence Bradford Packard*, ed. H. Stuart Hughes, Cornell 1954.

17   See the *Journal of the Royal Statistical Society*, lvi (London 1893) 255 ff. This is the earliest reference by Booth to Le Play that I have been able to find. There has been some suggestion that Le Play influenced Booth, but Professor T. Simey, author of the standard biography of Charles Booth, tells me that there is no evidence that Booth had read Le Play before he wrote his great account of the people of London.

18   The study mentioned is printed in *Parliamentary Papers* C5861, H.M.S.O. 1889, *Labour Statistics: Returns of Expenditure by Working Men.* As a matter of fact this report acknowledges Le Play as the originator of this kind of study, but criticises his use of statistics. One relevant passage (from p. 3) refers to 'Monsieur Le Play and Monsieur Ducpétiaux, the former of whom, about thirty-five years ago, made a study of typical working-class families in differing countries of Europe, without, however, giving his study a properly statistical form, as his work, though minute, related to a very few families only'. The U.S. Department of Labor used techniques learnt from Le Play, see Bibliography, Wright 1906.

19   See W. L. Sargant, *Economy of the Labouring Classes,* London 1857. See also Bibliography entries M30, M31 and W51. Incidentally Sargant says that Le Play asked him not to quote verbatim as an English translation was planned.

20   Patrick Geddes (1854–1932) was a man of many parts like Le Play himself. He went to Paris to study biology. But, says Mairet, 'these months in Paris probably did even more for Geddes as a future sociologist than as a biologist . . . he discovered the social philosopher whose work was so largely to determine his own approach to sociology – Frédéric Le Play' (P. Mairet, *Pioneer of Sociology: the life of Patrick Geddes,* London 1957).

21   Victor Branford (1864–1930) was an indefatigable promoter of sociology as a discipline and a host of social causes as well. Demolins wrote (in a testimonial for a professorship at Manchester): 'Monsieur Victor V. Branford has attended my lectures and has also taken a great interest in social studies pursued according to the method inaugurated by F. Le Play. One of the first in England, he has presented an exposition of our method and its results.' A. J. Herbertson (1865–1915) translated de Rousiers, and his wife wrote a life of Le Play (Herbertson 1950). An obituary of Herbertson in the *Geographical Journal*, xlvi (1915) mentions the influence of the Le Play School.
        The views of Branford, Geddes and their colleagues can be read in the three volumes of reports of the Sociological Society, to which Durkheim also contributed. See *Sociological Papers* 1904 (London 1905), *Sociological Papers* 1905 (London 1906), *Sociological Papers* 1906 (London 1907).
        For accounts of Le Play's English followers see: S. R. Beaver, 'The Le Play Society and fieldwork', *Geography*, xlvii (July 1962) 225–40; and J. Halliday, 'The Sociological movement, the Sociological Society and the genesis of academic sociology in Britain', *The Sociological Review*, xvi, no. 3, 1968.

22   See J. M. Mogey, *Family and Neighbourhood,* Oxford 1956, p. 54.

23   See H. N. Kubali, preface to E. Durkheim, *Professional Ethics* (English transla-
     tion, London 1957); N. S. Kosemihal: 'L'Ecole de Le Play et son influence en
     Turquie', *Recueil d'Etudes sociales à la Mémoire de Frédéric Le Play*, Paris 1956,
     pp. 35–48; M. F. Iribarne: 'La Influencia de Le Play en la Sociologia española
     del siglo XIX', ibid., pp. 29–34.

24   G. C. Homans, *The Human Group*, London 1951, p. 22.

25   Durkheim, ironically enough, has also been credited with playing a part in the
     rise of fascism. See G. E. G. Catlin, Introduction to E. Durkheim, *The Rules of
     the Sociological Method*, English translation, Chicago 1938, p. xxviii.

26   'While Le Play made a contribution to contemporary scientific progress, he
     affirmed that moral progress had not kept pace', Claudio Jannet (1889).

Index

Index

Corps législatif, see Legislative assembly
Coventry, 69
Credit, 4, 173
Crimea, 10–11, 54–5
Crompton, Samuel 1753–1827, 169
Curzon, E. P. de d. 1896, sociologist, 119
Cutlery industry, British, 48, 88, 90–2
 French, 60
Cuvier, J. L. N. F. (Georges) 1769–1832,
 171

Darboy, Georges 1813–70, Archbishop of
 Paris, 63
Daru, le comte Napoléon 1807–90, 6, 120,
 166
Decalogue, 8, 20, 76, 101, 118–19
Demidov, Anatolii 1812–70, 10–13, 16, 54–
 59, 79, 167, 171–2
Demidovich, Nikita *c.* 1665–1745, 11
Democracy, 18
Demolins, Edmond 1852–1907, sociologist,
 vii, viii, 19, 107, 110, 126, 131, 136, 176
Departement, the French equivalent of the
 English county
Derbyshire, 10, 12, 88, 90, 175
De Re Metallica, 16, 167
Descartes, René 1596–1650, philosopher, 77
Determinism, geographical, 133
Devoir Mutel, secret organisation of workers,
 37–8
Diderot, Denis 1713–84, philosopher, 3
Diergart, Von, Prussian silk manufacturer,
 64
Dock workers, 48, 106
Don, river in South Russia, 11, 167
Donets, river in South Russia, 10–11, 43,
 46, 54–5, 167
Dudley, (Worcestershire), 12
Dumas, J. B. A. 1800–84, chemist and
 politician, 122
Dumolart, Bouvier, Prefect of Lyons in
 1834, 37
Durkheim, Emile 1858–1917, sociologist,
 2, 79, 98, 134, 140, 180

Ecole, see also Hautes écoles
 d'Administration, a college for advanced
 studies in administration, 13, 51–4,
 171

 des Arts et Manufactures, a college for
 advanced studies in general and
 technical subjects, 27
 des Mines, a college of advanced technology, 1–3, 6–9, 11, 17, 20, 40, 44–5,
 59, 77, 111, 127, 165–7, 169–70
 des Mineurs à Saint-Etienne, a mining
 college, 27
 des Roches, a boarding secondary school,
 110
 Normale supérieure de l'Enseignement
 technique, a college of advanced
 technology, 27
 Polytechnique, institution of higher
 education in Paris, 3, 5–6, 24, 27, 52,
 165, 167
Economic Club, 135
Economics, 44
 English school, classical, 14, 31, 46, 69,
 109, 113, 115, 123, 130
Economist, The, 135
Education, 45, 54, 67, 83, 88, 91, 100, 110–
 111, 122, 124
 Adult, 35, 111; *see also* Management
 Commission on higher, 51–4, 171
 Ministry of, 52–4
 Primary, 51
 Technical, 2, 27, 69–71, 130, 173
Einaudi, L. 1874–1961, Italian economist,
 119, 174
Elite, *see also* Social authority, 105, 119, 176
Emmerson, Gouverneur 1795–1874,
 physician, translated Le Play's
 Organisation of Work, 135
Empirical studies, Empiricism, ix, 4, 6, 100
Employers, 33–5, 38–9, 46–7, 50, 61, 65–73,
 85, 87, 90, 110–12, 115–16, 123,
 125–6, 173
Employment, exchanges, 71
 of children, 47, 64, 66, 91, 93, 122, 168,
 173
 of women, 47, 64–6, 93, 108, 116, 122,
 130, 173
 security of, 19, 47–8, 87, 90, 92, 102, 115–
 116, 127–8
Engel, Ernst 1821–96, statistician, 137
England, *see* United Kingdom
Equilibrium, social, 104
Eure (French department), 131
Europe, vii, ix, 8, 9, 12–13, 26, 28–9, 41, 46,
 49, 73, 82, 87–8, 104, 114, 136